RADICAL CANDOR

Kim Scott is the founder of Candor Inc. and is a well-known
CEO coach in Silicon Valley. She was a member of the faculty at
Apple University and before that worked at Google, where she led
AdSense, YouTube and DoubleClick teams. Earlier in her career she
was co-founder and CEO of a software start-up, managed a paediatric
clinic in war-torn Kosovo and built a diamond-cutting factory
in Russia. She now runs radicalcandor.com.

RADICAL CANDOR

How to Get What
You Want by
Saying What
You Mean

**FULLY REVISED &
UPDATED EDITION**

KIM SCOTT

PAN BOOKS

First published 2017 by St. Martin's Press, New York

First published in the UK 2017 by Macmillan

This edition published 2019 by Pan Books
an imprint of Pan Macmillan
The Smithson, 6 Briset Street, London, EC1M 5NR
Associated companies throughout the world
www.panmacmillan.com

ISBN 978-1-5290-3834-7

9

A CIP catalogue record for this book is available from the British Library.

Designed by Richard Oriolo
Printed and bound in India by Replika Press Pvt. Ltd.

Visit **www.panmacmillan.com** to read more about all our books
and to buy them. You will also find features, author interviews and
news of any author events, and you can sign up for e-newsletters
so that you're always first to hear about our new releases.

For Andy Scott, the miraculous mixer of romance and stability in my life. For our children, Battle and Margaret, who give us daily surges of crazy joy and sane inspiration. For our parents, who taught us everything. And for our siblings, who helped us find each other.

CONTENTS

PREFACE TO THE REVISED EDITION
Radical Candor on *Radical Candor*

LAST YEAR, I GOT off an overnight flight to find my phone blowing up. Family, friends, and acquaintances wondered if I'd caught the previous night's episode of the HBO show, *Silicon Valley*, the often-hilarious (and sometimes on-point) parody of work where I have made my career. The bad news was that Radical Candor had been parodied as a fig leaf for obnoxious behavior by devious executives. Most of my friends told me not to worry about this—to be parodied on *Silicon Valley* was a good thing. Don't take it to heart.

I wasn't so sure. I had written a book that advised people to listen to criticism, to take it to heart, to learn from it. I knew I should walk the walk here.

So much of what makes the show *Silicon Valley* funny is the way it targets tech's penchant for wrapping up traditional predatory business behavior in idealistic language. Despite my intentions to the contrary, the term "Radical Candor" was, perhaps, being conflated with Manipulative Insincerity and Obnoxious Aggression in the workplace.

In the episode, Ben Burkhardt wants to become the COO for the show's hero, Richard Hendricks. Ben advises Richard to treat an employee cruelly, attributing his advice to a new management philosophy, "Rad Can." Burkhardt represents everything *Silicon Valley* exists to skewer: he's smooth, glib, and utterly hypocritical. He's also a coward; when his boss enters the restaurant where he's meeting Richard, Ben runs to hide—*again* attributing his behavior to Radical Candor.

The show even put out an image of a fake version of my book authored by Ben. (I doctored it to illustrate the dangerous path that the show had captured so well: "The Asshole's Journey: From Obnoxious Aggression to Manipulative Insincerity.")

The *Silicon Valley* episode taught me something important: some people were using Radical Candor as a license to behave like jerks, conflating Obnoxious Aggression and Manipulative Insincerity with Radical

Candor. I had developed a framework to prevent this very confusion, but it hadn't been clear enough.

When I wrote the book, I hoped it would serve as a reminder of what fundamental compassion really means. The misrepresentation of Radical Candor in this episode of *Silicon Valley* made it clear to me that I had more work to do if I was going to achieve that goal.

A few months after the Silicon Valley episode, it was Dilbert's turn to show how obnoxious bosses abuse Radical Candor (see next page). On the one hand, it's hard to take seriously anything by a cartoonist who once wrote in his blog that "women are treated differently by society for exactly the same reason that children and the mentally handicapped are treated differently." On the other hand, the strip does highlight potential confusion between Radical Candor and Obnoxious Aggression:

DILBERT © 2018 Scott Adams. Used by permission of ANDREWS McMEEL SYNDICATION. All rights reserved.

The word "radical" in *Radical Candor* has been a mixed blessing. The juxtaposition of the edgy word "radical," with the conscientious word "candor" got people's attention.

The downside of the term "Radical Candor" is that to many, it sounds like a not-too-distant cousin to the "move fast and break things," disrupt-now-fail-to-hold-yourself-accountable-later ethos of Silicon Valley. Another reason why Radical Candor is so often misunderstood is that it's confused with Ray Dalio's Radical Transparency. While Dalio and I are very much aligned on the importance of challenging directly, there's not much focus on care personally in his "manage as someone operating a machine to achieve a goal" philosophy.* Furthermore, relationships require some privacy, so while I am all for transparency when it comes to business results, I don't believe that Radical Transparency fosters good working relationships, contributes to psychological safety, or results in a productive, happy culture.

To me the word "radical" indicates a management philosophy that is both new and dramatically different from what came before. The idea that bosses should use their power to behave like bullies is old and banal, not new and radical. The key insight behind Radical Candor is that command and control can hinder innovation and harm a team's ability to improve the efficiency of routine work. Bosses and companies get better results when they voluntarily lay down unilateral power and encourage their teams and peers to hold them accountable, when they quit trying to control employees and focus instead on encouraging agency. The idea is that collaboration and innovation flourish when human relationships replace bullying and bureaucracy. By "radical," I mean "essential," in the spirit of the French writer Antoine de Saint-Exupéry's

---

* There are just ten pages on how to "cultivate meaningful work and meaningful relationships" in his book.

The Little Prince: "One sees clearly only with the heart. What is essential is invisible to the eye."

Since the term "Radical Candor" has entered the lexicon, I'm stuck with the task of rebranding the word "radical." You are not. That would be a pain, and I'm trying to make your life easier, not harder. So if you are rolling out Radical Candor, and you think there might be some confusion about what it means, here's a way to help ensure that everyone understands the idea is *not* to act like a jerk: use this new version of the Radical Candor framework (see below). You can cut it right out of this book (see page 297 for a larger version), make photocopies, and put them on your refrigerator, over your desk, or anywhere for a reminder. You can also share copies with your colleagues.

Use THE RADICAL CANDOR *Framework like a compass to guide individual conversations to a better place. Please do NOT use it as a personality test to judge yourself or others. Don't write names in boxes. We all fall into each quadrant multiple times a day.*

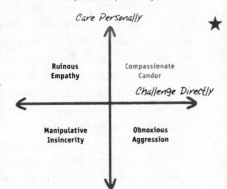

THE RADICAL CANDOR FRAMEWORK:
a compass, not a personality test!

Care Personally

Ruinous Empathy | Compassionate Candor

Challenge Directly

Manipulative Insincerity | Obnoxious Aggression

COMPASSIONATE CANDOR

THE CONTRAST BETWEEN Ruinous Empathy and Compassionate Candor can be confusing and is worth probing. In his book *Against Empathy: The Case for Rational Compassion*, psychologist Paul Bloom explains how empathy can focus our emotions so intensely that we can't reason as clearly as we ought. Empathy also focuses us on the moment, making it harder for us to see the long-term impact of what we are doing. That is what happens in Ruinous Empathy—you're so fixated on not hurting a person's feelings in the moment that you don't tell them something they'd be better off knowing in the long run.

I am not, of course, against empathy—and neither is Paul Bloom. (I have both empathy and compassion for how dangerous two-word titles can be.) Author and Zen Buddhist teacher Joan Halifax explains the relationship between empathy and compassion: "Healthy emotional empathy makes for a more caring world. It can nurture social connection, concern, and insight. But unregulated emotional empathy can be the source of distress and burnout; it can also lead to withdrawal and moral apathy. Empathy is not compassion. Connection, resonance, and concern might not lead to action. But empathy is a component of compassion, and a world without healthy empathy, I believe, is a world devoid of felt connection and puts us all in peril."*

Jeff Weiner, CEO of LinkedIn, is an executive who puts compassion front and center in leadership. "The advice I would give my twenty-two-year-old self is to be compassionate. I wasn't very compassionate when I was your age. As a matter of fact, I wasn't particularly compassionate until the latter stage of my career. . . . When I was thirty years old, I came across a book called *The Art of Happiness*. It's about the teachings of the Dalai Lama . . . [who] explains it this way: picture yourself walking along a mountainous trail. You come across a person being crushed by a boulder on their chest. The empathetic response would be to feel the same sense of crushing suffocation, thus rendering you helpless. The compassionate response would be to recognize that that person is in pain and to do everything within your power to remove the boulder and alleviate their suffering. Put another way, compassion is empathy plus action."** Early in his career, Jeff did in fact have a reputation for being pretty harsh, so he is an example of the transformational possibilities of self-awareness and personal growth.

Compassionate Candor engages the heart (care personally) *and* the mind (challenge directly). Unfortunately, the term "Radical Candor" doesn't communicate that to everyone.

PUT YOUR PHONE AWAY, AND LOOK PEOPLE IN THE EYE

RADICAL CANDOR PUTS building good relationships at the center of a boss's job. In fact, my favorite lines in the whole book are these: "Relationships are core to your job. If you think that you can [fulfill your responsibilities as a manager] *without* strong relationships, you are kidding yourself. I'm not saying that unchecked power, control, or authority can't work. They work

---

* Joan Halifax. *Standing at the Edge*. (New York: Flatiron Books, 2018).
** Adapted from Jeff Weiner's commencement speech at Wharton in 2018.

especially well in a baboon troop or a totalitarian regime. But if you're reading this book, that's not what you're shooting for."

Embarrassingly, I lost sight of this theme after I finished the book. When edits were mostly done but the book had not yet been printed, I found myself with some extra time on my hands. I began thinking about how software might help people put the ideas from the book into practice and had lunch with a venture capitalist to see what he thought of the idea. He offered me ten times as much money as the advance for the book. The book took four years to write. The lunch took just under an hour. My head spun, which didn't improve the clarity of my thinking: *Radical Candor? There's an app for that!* And so Candor, Inc. was born.

Of course, it wasn't *that* ridiculous an idea. Russ Laraway, one of the best leaders I've ever worked with, cofounded Candor, Inc. with me. My board included Shona Brown, the person who, more than any other, operationalized Google's culture. My investors were some of the most successful in Silicon Valley. So it *seemed* like a good idea to a lot of smart people. But it wasn't.

After testing three different variations of our software, we realized that if the goal was to get people to put their phones in their pockets, look each other in the eye, and just *talk*, an app was a value-subtracting round-trip. Matt Dailey, an engineer who worked with us, described an additional problem that software couldn't solve. "Kim, you keep advising people to use what they know about personal relationships at work. The problem is, a lot of people don't know how to have relationships at home, at work, or anywhere." Our app wasn't going to teach them that. The book helped. The talks helped. The workshops helped. The software did not.

We shut down the software company. Russ decided to put the management ideas we care about into practice by going deep at one company: he became the vice president of people at Qualtrics. I decided to go broad. I started another company, Radical Candor LLC, with Jason Rosoff and Amy Sandler. We are focused on the pedagogy (learning how to teach Radical Candor) and the cognitive behavioral techniques—and learning how to help people create a habit of Radical Candor. We may figure out how to use technology to help put these ideas into practice. But for now we are focused on doing in-person work with individual leaders and their teams. We have given talks and held workshops with hundreds of companies and thousands of people around the world, and have learned a lot about how to make these ideas realities. In the afterword, Jason, Amy, and I summarize what we've learned about how to put the ideas in this book into practice.

DIVERSITY AND INCLUSION

DIVERSITY AND INCLUSION may very well be the issue on which we most need, but are least likely to offer or to solicit, Radical Candor. Almost every time we do a talk or a workshop, my colleagues and I get responses like, "How does diversity impact a person's ability to be Radically Candid?" Or, "Radical Candor is more dangerous for women than for men, and even more dangerous for black women than for white women, for gay women than for straight women. Are you sure Radical Candor is safe for people who don't have the kind of privilege that you do?" Or, "I'm a white male. If I'm Radically Candid, everyone assumes I'm an asshole." Many have asked me, "How could you as a woman have written so little about gender in your book?" Once, a tall black man pointed out to me, a short white woman, "The way people experience Radical Candor from you is very different from the way people experience Radical Candor from me. What's safe for you is dangerous for me, and, I imagine, what works for me wouldn't work for you."

He was absolutely correct. Part of the reason I didn't call this book "Compassionate Candor" in the first place is that I'm a woman and I didn't want to seem too "soft." I'm not proud of that, but it's the truth. And so I knew from firsthand experience that my response to him—"Radical Candor gets measured not at the speaker's mouth but at the listener's ear"—barely scratches the surface of the complexity involved in how we offer one another guidance. It can be difficult enough when you're talking about pointing out spinach in the teeth or grammar mistakes. But what if you're pointing out to someone they've been biased? You want to show just how unacceptable what they said was, but you also want to show them some compassion—and you know you risk a powerfully defensive and likely unfair response. You also need to protect yourself.

These questions and conversations prompted my colleagues and me to collaborate with Second City Works, the executive education arm of the comedy club where Tina Fey, Stephen Colbert, and countless others were trained in comedy. We are exploring with Second City Works how people can use improv to practice using Radical Candor to confront bias in the workplace with agency and grace—and the right kind of humor. I'll cover this in more detail in the afterword.

The question of how we can use Radical Candor to build stamina for real conversations about diversity and inclusion is the topic of my next book, which will seek to answer these questions: how can you use Radical Candor to confront unconscious prejudices, beliefs, and gender bullying in the workplace? How can you best respond when you get feedback that you're on the wrong side of these issues? How can you escalate when there's a power imbalance and Radical Candor may not be a safe or sufficient response? And how can you as a leader prevent gender injustice from manifesting in your workplace and ruining your culture?

DON'T LET YOUR CULTURE BECOME TOXIC

SUCCESSFUL START-UPS often begin with a culture where people challenge one another directly and even fiercely, but also show they care personally. That's because they start small, involve people who get to know each other really well, and are fighting for survival. However, as the business grows and new people join the firm, it's impossible to know everyone's name, let alone to have strong relationships with everyone. The kind of super-direct challenges that are easy when people know each other well become difficult. Not wanting to lose the friendly culture of the early days, many hesitate to speak up when they see problems, backing off of Challenge Directly and retreating to Ruinous Empathy. Because Obnoxious Aggression is more effective than Ruinous Empathy, that kind of behavior has an advantage; people who behave badly begin to win, rising in the company. When confronted with a powerful jerk, many people retreat to Manipulative Insincerity, more out of instinctive self-protectiveness than intentional wrongdoing. In this kind of environment, there's an incentive to retreat to Manipulative Insincerity in front of those who are more senior to them, and resort to Obnoxious Aggression with those who are less powerful. The culture becomes toxic—many kissing up and kicking down, few willing to speak truth to power. This kind of behavior won't kill a company right away. Instead, it leads to a slow, painful death of innovation, and lives of quiet desperation.

That's the bad news. The good news is that many companies large and small are now taking active measures to shift to a culture in which caring personally and challenging directly go hand in hand. When people learn to do both simultaneously, bad behavior no longer gives anyone an advantage.

Bad behavior is punished not rewarded, the truth comes out, and the environment is more conducive to both success and happiness.

I HOPE THAT you will join me in making sure that the ideas in this book are not used as an excuse for bad boss behavior. I hope reading *Radical Candor* will help you find a way to be your best, most fully expressed self at work. You can create teams on which people do the best work of their lives and build the best relationships of their careers. You can love your work, and the people you work with.

INTRODUCTION

IKE MOST OF US, I once had a terrible boss—a person who thought that humiliating people was a good way to motivate them. At one point, a colleague mistakenly copied me on an email chain in which my boss had ridiculed me repeatedly to my peers. When I confronted my boss, he told me not to worry my "pretty little head" about it. Really.

Partially as a result of this experience, I started my own company—Juice Software. My goal was to create an environment where people would love their work *and* one another. Friends often laughed when I said that, as if I were talking about a commune instead of a company. But I was serious. I spent a lot more than eight hours a day at my job. If I didn't enjoy my work and my colleagues, the majority of my brief time on this planet would be unhappy.

Unfortunately, while I did succeed in avoiding the mistakes my boss had made—that was easy—I made a very different set of mistakes. In an effort to create a positive, stress-free environment, I sidestepped the difficult but necessary part of being a boss: telling people clearly and directly when their work wasn't good enough. I failed to create a climate in which people who weren't getting the job done were told so in time to fix it.

When I look back on that time, my mind immediately goes to a person I'll call "Bob." Bob was one of those instantly likeable people who make going to work a pleasure. He was a kind, funny, caring, and supportive colleague. What's more, he came to me with a stellar résumé and great references. He seemed to be an A-plus hire, and I was thrilled to have him. There was just one problem: his work was terrible. He lost my confidence shortly after we hired him. He'd been working for *weeks* on a document to explain that Juice allowed people to create Excel spreadsheets that updated automatically. When I reviewed the document he'd been working on so diligently, I was shocked to discover that it was totally incoherent—a kind of word salad. And thinking back to when he handed it over to me, I realized then that Bob *also* knew his work wasn't good enough—the shame in his eye and the apology in his smile when he handed it over to me were unmistakable.

LET'S STOP RIGHT here for a second. If you're a manager, you know already that this was a hinge moment in the relationship between Bob and me, and a significant bellwether of success or failure for my team. Bob's work wasn't even close to good enough. We were a small company, struggling to get on our feet, and we had zero bandwidth to redo his work, or to pick up his slack. I knew this at the time. And yet, when I met with him, I couldn't bring myself to address the problem. I heard myself tell Bob that the work was a good start and that I'd help him finish. He smiled uncertainly and left.

What happened? First, I liked Bob, and I didn't want to come down too hard on him. He had looked so nervous during the meeting when we reviewed his document that I feared he might even cry. Because everyone liked him so much, I also worried that if he did cry, everyone would think I was an abusive bitch. Second, unless his résumé and references were bogus, he'd done great work in the past. Maybe he'd been distracted by something at home or was unused to our way of doing things. Whatever the reason, I convinced myself that he'd surely return to the performance level that had gotten him the job. Third, I could fix the document myself for now, and that would be faster than teaching him how to re-write it.

Let's first deal with how this affected Bob. Remember, he knew his work wasn't good, and so my false praise just messed with his mind. It allowed him to deceive himself into thinking that he could continue along the same course. Which he did. By failing to confront the problem, I'd removed the incentive for him to try harder and lulled him into thinking he'd be fine.

It's brutally hard to tell people when they are screwing up. You don't *want* to hurt anyone's feelings; that's because you're not a sadist. You don't want that person or the rest of the team to think you're a jerk. Plus, you've been told since you learned to talk, "If you don't have anything nice to say, don't say anything at all." Now all of a sudden it's your *job* to say it. You've got to undo a lifetime of training. Management is hard.

To make matters worse, I kept making the same mistake over and over for ten months. As you probably know, for every piece of subpar work you accept, for every missed deadline you let slip, you begin to feel resentment and then anger. You no longer just think the work is bad: you think the person is bad. This makes it harder to have an even-keeled conversation. You start to avoid talking to the person at all.

And of course, the impact of my behavior with Bob didn't stop with him: others on the team wondered why I accepted such poor work. Following my lead, they too tried to cover for him. They would fix mistakes he'd made and do or redo his work, usually when they should have been sleeping. Covering for people is sometimes necessary for a short period of time—say, if somebody is going through a crisis. But when it goes on too long it starts to take a toll. People whose work had been exceptional started to get sloppy. We missed key deadlines. Knowing why Bob's colleagues were late, I didn't give them too hard a time. Then *they* began to wonder if I knew the difference between great and mediocre; perhaps I didn't even take the missed deadlines seriously. As is often the case when people are not sure if the quality of what they are doing is appreciated, the results began to suffer, and so did morale.

As I faced the prospect of losing my team, I realized I couldn't put it off any longer. I invited Bob to have coffee with me. He expected to have a nice chat, but instead, after a few false starts, I fired him. Now we were both huddled miserably over our muffins and lattes. After an excruciating silence,

Bob pushed his chair back, metal screeching on marble, and looked me straight in the eye. "Why didn't you *tell* me?"

As that question was rolling around in my mind with no good answer, he asked me a second question: "Why didn't *anyone* tell me? I thought you all cared about me!"

It was the low point of my career. I had made a series of mistakes, and Bob was taking the fall. Not only was my earlier praise a head-fake—I'd never given Bob any criticism. I'd also never asked him to give *me* feedback, which might have allowed him to talk things through and perhaps find a solution. Worst of all, I'd failed to create a culture in which Bob's peers would naturally warn him when he was going off the rails. The team's cohesion was cracking, and it showed in our results. Lack of praise and criticism had absolutely disastrous effects on the team and on our outcomes.

You can draw a straight line from lack of guidance to a dysfunctional team that gets poor results. It wasn't just too late for Bob. It was too late for the whole company; Juice failed not too long after I fired Bob.

GOOGLE: FREE AT WORK

IT WAS 2004, and I needed a job, so I called a classmate from business school, Sheryl Sandberg. She'd joined Google three years earlier, and I'd recently sat next to her at a mutual friend's wedding. What had struck me was that, though Sheryl clearly cared about the people who worked on her team at Google, I had a feeling she would not make the same mistake I'd made with Bob. Later, I'd learn just how true that was.

After running a gauntlet of twenty-seven interviews, I got an offer to work for Sheryl to lead a team of one hundred people responsible for sales and service of small- and medium-sized groups of AdSense* customers. I didn't even know what AdSense was. What I did know was that Google's culture struck me as the resurrection of my dream about creating an environment where people loved their work and one another, and that Sheryl

---

* **AdSense** is the ad product you use if you want Google to pay you. AdSense puts ads on your Web site or blog. If you have a Web site about, say, camping, you can put an "Ads by Google" box on your site, and Google will fill it with ads about, say, REI tents or North Face sleeping bags. When a user sees or clicks on them, you get paid. The way you put that "Ads by Google" box on your site is by inserting a snippet of code that Google gives you.

struck me as a great boss. As a friend of mine later joked, "In Silicon Valley, you don't fall down; you fall up." (Rest assured, Bob has also landed on his feet.)

SHORTLY AFTER I joined Google, I witnessed an impressive display of productive but extremely direct feedback. I was at a meeting with Larry Page, Google's cofounder, and Matt Cutts, who led the team that fought Webspam.* We were discussing a proposal that Matt and I had. Larry had a different, more subtle plan, which I didn't understand. But it was clear that Matt did understand Larry's plan and didn't like it one bit. Matt—generally a very pleasant, easygoing guy—disagreed, heatedly. When Larry wouldn't back down, Matt started *yelling* at Larry. He said Larry's idea would flood him with "so much crap" he'd never keep up.

I felt unnerved by Matt's reaction. I liked him, and I was afraid he'd get fired for criticizing Larry's position so vehemently. Then I saw the big grin on Larry's face. Not only did he permit Matt's challenging him—he seemed to relish it. I could see from the open, happy way he responded to the argument that he wanted not just Matt but everyone at Google to feel comfortable criticizing authority—especially his. It didn't make any sense to label this conversation "nice" or "mean," "rude" or "polite." It was productive and collaborative. It was free. It was driving to the best answer. How had Larry achieved that?

I decided to try to take a page out of Larry's book. Rather than focus on "giving feedback" to my team, I encouraged them to tell me when *I* was wrong. I did everything I could to encourage people to criticize me, or at least simply to *talk* to me. After a false start (more on that later) the team started to open up. We began to debate openly, and we had more fun together. I was lucky enough to hire some remarkable people, including Russ Laraway, with whom I've cofounded a new company, Candor, Inc., and Jared Smith, cofounder of Qualtrics, whose board I sit on now. I learned just as much from the people who worked for me as from the people whom I worked for about how to be a good boss. We experimented with *not* making any decisions in my staff meeting, instead pushing them out to the people closest

---

* **Webspam**: Sites that game Google's Page Rank system. It's sort of like junk mail or calls from telemarketers that interrupt dinner.

to the facts. We started executing more efficiently. Wanting to make it safe to "speak truth to power" at all levels of the organization, we experimented with "manager fix-it weeks" and carefully designed "manager feedback sessions."

I'll explain all these techniques and more in the second half of this book, but the important thing to know for now is that at Google managers couldn't just rely on "power" or "authority" to get things done. They had to figure out a different, better way.

After six years at Google, I felt confident I'd done just that: I'd learned a better way to be a boss. I didn't repeat my mistake with Bob, but I didn't become an asshole either. The businesses I led had grown revenue by more than ten times, to several billion dollars. A lot of that growth was product-driven, not sales-driven. But we certainly contributed. We were obsessive about efficiency, and we managed to *shrink* headcount in North America even as revenue grew dizzyingly—the definition of scaling Over time, in addition to AdSense, my team included the global YouTube and DoubleClick online sales and operations teams. We started out with one team in North America, and the team's quirky, fun-loving culture was strong enough to be a unifying force between Dublin, São Paulo, Buenos Aires, New York, Mountain View, Sydney, Seoul, Tokyo, Beijing, and Singapore.

Increasingly, though, I found myself caring less and less about the core business metrics (cost per click, revenue, etc.). What really interested me was figuring out how to define and teach others this "better way" to be a boss that I'd developed. It was still more of an instinct than a philosophy, though. I needed time to think, so I could articulate it.

APPLE: "WE HIRE PEOPLE WHO TELL *US* WHAT TO DO, NOT THE OTHER WAY AROUND"

THERE WAS NO job at Google that would allow me to sit back and just *think*, and an operating role doesn't leave much time for quiet contemplation. Fortunately, nine miles to the southwest, Steve Jobs had started Apple University. My business school professor, Richard Tedlow, had just left Harvard to join Job's new factory of good leadership. He described Apple U's mandate like this: "We want to defy the gravitational pull of organizational mediocrity." An important part of achieving that goal was to develop a class: *Man-*

aging at Apple. When I was offered the job to design and teach that class, I jumped at the chance.

Managing at Apple was for first-time managers, but executives found it equally useful for the senior leaders on their teams. Though the class was not required, our biggest problem was keeping up with demand. In the time I worked at Apple, we taught thousands of people, to great reviews. Many more have taken the class since I left.

I learned as much as I taught. A conversation I had with one of Apple's leaders helped me see a critical flaw in my approach to building teams earlier in my career. I'd always focused on the people most likely to be promoted. I assumed that was how it had to be at a growth company. Then a leader at Apple pointed out to me that all teams need *stability* as well as growth to function properly; nothing works well if everyone is gunning for the next promotion. She called the people on her team who got exceptional results but who were on a more gradual growth trajectory "rock stars" because they were like the Rock of Gibraltar on her team. These people loved their work and were world-class at it, but they didn't want her job or to be Steve Jobs. They were happy where they were. The people who were on a steeper growth trajectory—the ones who'd go crazy if they were still doing the same job in a year—she called "superstars." They were the source of growth on any team. She was explicit about needing a balance of both.

This was a revelation. Apple was growing fast, and *bigger* than Google. And yet Apple made room for people with all sorts of different ambitions. You had to be great at what you did and you had to love your work, but you did *not* have to be promotion-obsessed to have a fulfilling career at Apple. At Google, I'd systematically undervalued the so-called rock stars. This mistake had caused a lot of unhappiness for people who contributed significantly. Google's bias for people on a steep growth trajectory was in part a reaction against the norm at traditional companies, which tend to clip the wings of people who want to "change everything." Apple made room for all different types of ambition, and that was part of how it got big while defying "the gravitational pull of organizational mediocrity."

GOOGLE IS FAMOUSLY viewed as a bottom-up company, one that empowers even very young employees to drive decision-making. The managers' role is mostly to stay out of the way, sometimes to help, but never to interfere too much. I expected the opposite at Apple, having bought in to the narrative of the all-controlling Steve Jobs passing down his brilliant vision from on high, brooking no dissent, and driving his team to make it happen. But it wasn't so.

A colleague shared an anecdote about interviewing with Steve that illustrated why this was the case. My colleague asked Jobs several perfectly reasonable questions: "How do you envision building the team? How big will the team be?" Steve's curt response: "Well, if I knew the answer to all those questions, then I wouldn't need you, would I?" Borderline rude, but also empowering. Jobs articulated this approach more gently in an interview with Terry Gross: "At Apple we hire people to tell us what to do, not the other way around." And indeed, this was my experience at the company.

At Apple, as at Google, a boss's ability to achieve results had a lot more to do with listening and seeking to understand than it did with telling people what to do; more to do with debating than directing; more to do with pushing people to decide than with being the decider; more to do with persuading than with giving orders; more to do with learning than with knowing.

YOUR RELATIONSHIPS ARE CORE TO YOUR JOB

THERE'S A WORLD of difference between autonomy and neglect, though . . . I learned what it felt like to get that wrong in my experience with Bob. Here's what I learned about how to get that right.

In *Managing at Apple*, we often played a video of Steve explaining his approach to giving criticism. He captured something very important: "You need to do that in a way that does not call into question your confidence in their abilities but leaves not too much room for interpretation . . . and that's a hard thing to do." He went on to say, "I don't mind being wrong. And I'll admit that I'm wrong a lot. It doesn't really matter to me too much. What matters to me is that we do the right thing."* Amen! Who could argue with that?

But if you rewound that tape just a bit, you'd find the question that had

---

* http://www.magpictures.com/stevejobsthelostinterview/.

prompted Steve's reply. Someone had asked him why he frequently used the phrase "Your work is shit." At face value, these words are, to say the least, unlikely to build trust or make your team feel empowered to take risks. It feels like bullying, and in some cases it might have been. I certainly couldn't recommend that anyone say *that* to people. Initially, I got around this in a flip way. "Remember," I said, "You are not Steve Jobs."

This always got a chuckle, but it actually dodged an important issue. I thought back to that argument between Matt Cutts and Larry Page. For some reason, they could yell at each other and it was OK. Why? I certainly would never say, "Your work is shit," or yell at my colleagues.

Or would I? I recalled a time at Google when we were rolling out AdSense internationally. Jared Smith, who'd worked with me at Juice and was also on my team at Google kept confusing Slovakia and Slovenia and acting as if the distinction didn't matter. After the fifth time he'd confused the two in a thirty-minute meeting, I snapped, "It's *Slovakia*, dumbass!!"

Jared and I had worked together long enough that he (and everyone else in the room) knew how deeply I respected him. He could, and occasionally did, rebuke me in the same affectionately rude way. My sharp correction was simply a short, effective way to get him to focus. He didn't make the mistake again. The only reason it was OK for me to talk to Jared that way was because of the *relationship* we'd formed over the years.

My point is *not* that you need to cuss or shout or be rude to be a great boss. In fact, I wouldn't recommend it, because even if your relationship evolves to the point where you think mutual respect is understood, as boss you sometimes just misread signals. The point is, rather, that if you are someone who is most comfortable communicating in that way, you have to build relationships of trust that can support it, and you have to hire people who can adapt to your style.

SILICON VALLEY WAS an ideal setting in which to explore the relationships between bosses and the people who report directly to them. Twenty years ago, management skills were neither taught nor rewarded in Silicon Valley, but today its companies are *obsessed* with it. This isn't for the reasons you might think—that they are run by new-age gurus ever in search of a theory, or because the people there are fundamentally different from people anywhere else. Nor is it because the companies there have huge budgets for training, or have some fundamental insight into human nature unleashed by access to all that big data.

No, the reason why Silicon Valley turned out to be a good place to study the relationships between bosses and the people who report to them is that the war for "talent" there is *intense*. So many great companies in the Valley are growing and hiring that there's no reason to stay with a company if you are unhappy or think your potential is being wasted. And there's certainly no reason to pay the "asshole tax." If you don't like your boss, you quit, knowing that ten other companies will be lining up to hire you. So the pressure on companies to get these relationships right is enormous.

Even in Silicon Valley, relationships don't scale. Larry Page can't have a real relationship with more than a handful of people any more than you can. But the relationships you have with the handful of people who report directly to you will have an enormous impact on the results your team achieves. If you lead a big organization, you can't have a relationship with everybody. But the relationships you have with your direct reports will impact the relationships they have with their direct reports. The ripple effect will go a long way toward creating—or destroying—a positive culture. Relationships may not scale, but culture does.

Is "relationship" really the right word? Yes. The relationship between Eric Schmidt, Google's CEO from 2001–2011, and Larry Page was one of business history's more interesting dances. And the willingness of Tim Cook, then COO and now CEO of Apple, to give part of his liver to Steve Jobs, and Jobs's refusal to accept the sacrifice, exemplifies a profoundly personal relationship.

What is the proper nature of this relationship? Managerial capitalism is a relatively new phenomenon, so this human bond was not described by ancient philosophers. Even though almost everybody today has a boss at some point, the nature of this connection has gotten short shrift in philosophy, literature, movies, and all the other ways we explore the relationships that govern our lives. I want to fix that, because at the very heart of being a good boss—at Apple, at Google, or anywhere else on earth—is a good relationship.

The term I found that best describes this relationship is Radical Candor.

HOW TO USE THIS BOOK

I 'VE WRITTEN THIS BOOK WITH the end user—you—in mind. What I have learned not only from my own experiences but also from coaching leaders is that, no matter how supportive the environment, bosses often feel *alone*. They feel ashamed that they're not doing a good job, sure that everyone else is doing better, and thus unable or afraid to seek help. But of course no boss is perfect. What drives my mission to share the concepts and methods presented here is is the desire to help you avoid making the mistakes I made. That is why I tell so many personal stories.

Part I is designed to set your mind at ease. Being a good boss is hard for *everyone*, no matter how successful they appear on the outside. You'll find some part of your own experience borne out in the real-life stories described here. I hope you'll also feel the optimism that comes from knowing that 1) you are not alone and 2) a better approach may be less difficult than you fear. Your humanity is an asset to your effectiveness, not a liability.

Part II is the how-to handbook: a step-by-step approach for building Radically Candid relationships with your direct reports, and how Radical Candor can help you fulfill your key responsibility as a boss: to *guide* your *team* to achieve *results*.

As you read on, you might occasionally feel overwhelmed by the number of things I'm suggesting you do as a manager. Take a deep breath. My goal is to save you time, not to litter your calendar with meetings. You do need to spend time with your direct reports to be a great boss, but you don't need to spend ALL your time with them. If you implement every single idea, tool, and technique in this book, the time you dedicate to managing your team will come to approximately ten hours a week, and those ten hours should save you enormous lost time and headaches later. I'll also suggest you block out about fifteen hours a week for you to think and execute independently in your area of expertise. That leaves another fifteen hours in a forty-hour work week. Hopefully you can claim them as your own, though if you're like me you'll have to use most of them to deal with the unpredictable.

While this book was written very much with you, the boss, in mind, I also want to acknowledge your boss, as well as the Human Resources and Learning and Development people who support you. When I led a team of seven hundred people at Google, I saw that managers typically make the same mistakes over and over again. Despite the predictability, successful intervention proved dishearteningly elusive. Some days I felt like I was watching a slow-motion train wreck I'd seen dozens of times before. It was the worst sort of déjà vu. I've recognized the same feeling in the expressions of the HR and L&D people who advised me as I wrote this book. I hope it will help you prevent the endless repetition of predictable mistakes.

Radical Candor is also directly relevant to people struggling with issues of diversity and leadership. Gender, racial, and cultural differences *do* make having Radically Candid relationships harder. It's scary to be Radically Candid with those who look like us. It's scarier when people look different, speak a different language, or practice a different religion. We are all more likely to be "ruinously empathetic" or "obnoxiously aggressive" or "manipulatively insincere" toward people who are different from us. Learning how to push ourselves and others past this discomfort, to relate to our shared humanity, can make a huge difference.

PART I

A NEW MANAGEMENT PHILOSOPHY

BUILD RADICALLY CANDID RELATIONSHIPS

Bringing your whole self to work

IT'S CALLED MANAGEMENT, AND IT'S YOUR JOB

I USUALLY FELT a little surge of pleasure as I stepped off the elevator into the cavernous former warehouse in the East Village we'd rented as the office of Juice Software, the start-up I'd cofounded in 2000. That day, I just felt stressed.

The engineers had worked nights and weekends on an early "beta" version of our product, which would be ready in a week. The sales team had gotten thirty big-name customers lined up for beta testing. If those customers were using our product, we'd be able to raise another round of funding. If not, we'd run out of money in six months.

There was one blocker: me. The night before, one of our angel investors,

Dave Roux, had told me he thought our pricing was all wrong. "Think about the last time you bought a used car—one that cost less than $10,000. Now, think about the guy who sold it to you. That's who your salespeople will be. That's who'll represent you in the market." I knew in my gut Dave was right, but I couldn't go to my sales team or my board and change everything just based on a gut feeling. I needed to sit down and do some analysis—fast. I'd cleared my calendar of meetings for the morning so I could do just that.

I'd gotten only a few steps into the office when a colleague suddenly ran up. He needed to talk right away. He had just learned that he might need a kidney transplant, and he was completely freaked out. After an hour and two cups of tea, he seemed calmer.

I walked toward my desk, past an engineer whose child was in the ICU. *Must check in.* "How'd your son do last night?" I asked. He hadn't improved—and as he told me how the night had gone we both had tears in our eyes. I convinced him to leave the office and go and take care of himself for an hour before returning to the hospital.

I left his desk drained, passing by our quality assurance manager. *His* child had better news: she'd just received the highest score in the entire state on a standardized math test. He wanted to talk about it. I felt emotional whiplash as I jumped from sympathy to celebration.

By the time I got back to my desk, I had no time or emotional reserves to think about pricing. I cared about each of these people, but I also felt worn out—frustrated that I couldn't get any "real" work done. Later that day, I called my CEO coach, Leslie Koch, to complain.

"Is my job to build a great company," I asked, "or am I really just some sort of emotional babysitter?"

Leslie, a fiercely opinionated ex-Microsoft executive, could barely contain herself. "This is not babysitting," she said. "It's called management, and it is your *job*!"

Every time I feel I have something more "important" to do than listen to people, I remember Leslie's words: "It is your *job*!" I've used Leslie's line on dozens of new managers who've come to me after a few weeks in their new role, moaning that they feel like "babysitters" or "shrinks."

We undervalue the "emotional labor" of being the boss. That term is usually reserved for people who work in the service or health industry: psychiatrists, nurses, doctors, waiters, flight attendants. But as I will show in the pages to come, this emotional labor is not just part of the job; it's the key to being a good boss.

HOW TO BE A GOOD BOSS

GIVEN MY LINE of work, I get asked by almost everyone I meet how to be a better boss/manager/leader. I get questions from the people who worked for me, the CEOs I coached, the people who attended a class I taught or a talk I gave. I get questions from people who have submitted their management dilemmas to our Web site (radicalcandor.com). But questions also come from the harried parent sitting next to me at the school play who doesn't know how to tell the babysitter not to feed the kids so much sugar; the contractor who is frustrated when his crew doesn't show up on time; the nurse who's just been promoted to supervisor and is telling me how bewildering it is (as she takes my blood pressure, I feel I should be taking hers); the business executive who's speaking with exaggerated patience into his cell phone as we board a plane, snaps it shut, and asks nobody in particular, "Why did I hire that goddamn moron?"; the friend still haunted by the expression on the face of an employee whom she laid off years ago. Regardless of who asks the questions, they tend to reveal an underlying anxiety: many people feel they aren't as good at management as they are at the "real" part of the job. Often, they fear they are *failing* the people who report to them.

While I hate to see this kind of stress, I find these conversations productive because I know I can help. By the end of these talks, people feel much more confident that they can be a great boss.

There's often a funny preamble to the questions I get, because most people don't like the words for their role: "boss" evokes injustice, "manager" sounds bureaucratic, "leader" sounds self-aggrandizing. I prefer the word "boss" because the distinctions between leadership and management tend to define leaders as BSers who don't actually *do* anything and managers as petty executors. Also, there's a problematic hierarchical difference implied in the two words, as if leaders no longer have to manage when they achieve a certain level of success, and brand-new managers don't have to lead. Richard Tedlow's biography of Andy Grove, Intel's lengendary CEO, asserts that management and leadership are like forehand and backhand. You have to be good at both to win. I hope by the end of this book you'll have a more positive association with all three words: boss, manager, leader.

Having dispensed with semantics, the next question is often very basic: what do bosses/managers/leaders *do*? Go to meetings? Send emails? Tell people what to do? Dream up strategies and expect other people to execute them? It's tempting to suspect them of doing a whole lot of nothing.

Ultimately, though, bosses are responsible for results. They achieve these results not by doing all the work themselves but by guiding the people on their teams. **Bosses guide a team to achieve results.**

The questions I get asked next are clustered around each of these three areas of responsibility that managers do have: guidance, team-building, and results.

First, **guidance**.

Guidance is often called "feedback." People *dread* feedback. They dread getting it, both the praise, which can feel patronizing, and especially the criticism. They dread giving it. What if the person gets defensive? Starts to yell? Threatens to sue? Bursts into tears? What if the person refuses to understand the criticism, or can't figure out what to do to fix the problem? What if there *isn't* any simple way to fix the problem? What should a boss say then? But it's no better when the problem *is* really simple and obvious. Why doesn't the person already know it's a problem? Do I actually have to *say* it? Am I too nice? Am I too mean? All these questions loom so large that people often forget they need to solicit guidance from others, and encourage it between them.

Second, **team-building**.

Building a cohesive team means figuring out the right people for the right roles: hiring, firing, promoting. But once you've got the right people in the right jobs, how do you keep them motivated? Particularly in Silicon Valley, the questions sound like this: why does everyone always want the next job when they haven't even mastered the job they have yet? Why do millennials expect their career to come with instructions like a Lego set? Why do people leave the team as soon as they get up to speed? Why do the wheels keep coming off the bus? Why won't everyone just do their job and let me do mine?

Third, **results**.

Many managers are perpetually frustrated that it seems harder than it should be to get things done. We just doubled the size of the team, but the results are not twice as good. In fact, they are worse. What happened? Sometimes things move too slowly: the people who work for me would debate forever if I let them. Why can't they make a decision? But other times things move too *fast*: we missed our deadline because the team was totally unwilling to do a little planning—they insisted on just firing willy-nilly, no ready, no aim! Why can't they think before they act? Or they seem to be on automatic pilot: they are doing exactly the same thing this quarter that they did last quarter, and they failed last quarter. Why do they expect the results to be different?

Guidance, team, and results: these are the responsibilities of any boss. This is equally true for anyone who manages people—CEOs, middle managers, and first-time leaders. CEOs may have broader problems to deal with, but they still have to work with other human beings, with all the quirks and skills and weaknesses just as apparent and relevant to their success in the C Suite as when they got their very first management role.

It's natural that managers who wonder whether they are doing right by the people who report to them want to ask me about these three topics. I'll address each fully over the course of this book.

RELATIONSHIPS, NOT POWER, DRIVE YOU FORWARD

BUT THE MOST important question, the question that goes to the heart of being a good boss, doesn't usually get asked. An exception was Ryan Smith, the CEO of Qualtrics. I'd just started coaching him, and his first question to me was, "I have just hired several new leaders on my team. How can I build a relationship with each of them quickly, so that I can trust them and they can trust me?"

Very few people focus first on the central difficulty of management that Ryan hit on: establishing a trusting relationship with each person who reports directly to you. If you lead a big organization, you can't have a relationship with everyone; but you *can* really get to know the people who report directly to you. Many things get in the way, though: power dynamics first and foremost, but also fear of conflict, worry about the boundaries of what's appropriate or "professional," fear of losing credibility, time pressure.

Nevertheless, these relationships are core to your job. They determine whether you can fulfill your three responsibilities as a manager: 1) to create a culture of guidance (praise and criticism) that will keep everyone moving in the right direction; 2) to understand what motivates each person on your team well enough to avoid burnout or boredom and keep the team cohesive; and 3) to drive results collaboratively. If you think that you can do these things *without* strong relationships, you are kidding yourself. I'm not saying that unchecked power, control, or authority can't work. They work especially well in a baboon troop or a totalitarian regime. But if you're reading this book, that's not what you're shooting for.

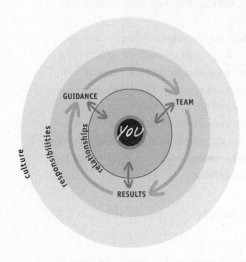

There is a virtuous cycle between your responsibilities and your relationships. You strengthen your relationships by learning the best ways to get, give, and encourage guidance; by putting the right people in the right roles on your team; and by achieving results collectively that you couldn't dream of individually. Of course, there can be a vicious cycle between your responsibilities and your relationships, too. When you fail to give people the guidance they need to succeed in their work, or put people into roles they don't want or aren't well-suited for, or push people to achieve results they feel are unrealistic, you erode trust.

Your relationships and your responsibilities reinforce each other positively or negatively, and this dynamic is what drives you forward as a manager—or leaves you dead in the water. Your relationships with your direct reports affect the relationships they have with their direct reports, and your team's culture. Your ability to build trusting, human connections with the people who report directly to you will determine the quality of everything that follows.

Defining those relationships is vital. They're deeply personal, and they're not like any other relationships in your life. But most of us are at a loss when we set about to build those relationships. Radical Candor, the fundamental concept of this book, can help guide you.

RADICAL CANDOR

DEVELOPING TRUST IS not simply a matter of "do x, y, and z, and you have a good relationship." Like all human bonds, the connections between bosses and the people who report to them are unpredictable and not subject to absolute rules. But I have identified two dimensions that, when paired, will help you move in a positive direction.

The first dimension is about being more than "just professional." It's about giving a damn, sharing more than just your work self, and encouraging everyone who reports to you to do the same. It's not enough to care only about people's ability to perform a job. To have a good relationship, you have to be your whole self and care about each of the people who work for you as a human being. It's not just business; it is personal, and *deeply* personal. I call this dimension "Care Personally."

The second dimension involves telling people when their work isn't good enough—and when it is; when they are not going to get that new role they wanted, or when you're going to hire a new boss "over" them; when the results don't justify further investment in what they're working on. Delivering hard feedback, making hard calls about who does what on a team, and holding a high bar for results—isn't that obviously the job of any manager? But most people struggle with doing these things. Challenging people generally pisses them off, and at first that doesn't seem like a good way to build a relationship or to show that you "care personally." And yet challenging people is often the best way to show them that you care when you're the boss. This dimension I call "Challenge Directly."

"Radical Candor" is what happens when you put "Care Personally" and "Challenge Directly" together. Radical Candor builds trust and opens the door for the kind of communication that helps you achieve the results you're aiming for. And it directly addresses the fears that people express to me when asking questions about the management dilemmas they face. It turns out that when people trust you and believe you care about them, they are much more likely to 1) accept and act on your praise and criticism; 2) tell you what they really think about what *you* are doing well and, more importantly, not doing so well; 3) engage in this same behavior with one another, meaning less pushing the rock up the hill again and again; 4) embrace their role on the team; and 5) focus on *getting results*.

Why "radical"? I chose this word because so many of us are conditioned to avoid saying what we really think. This is partially adaptive social behavior; it helps us avoid conflict or embarrassment. But in a boss, that kind of avoidance is disastrous.

Why "candor"? The key to getting everyone used to being direct when challenging each other (and you!) is emphasizing that it's necessary to communicate clearly enough so that there's no room for interpretation, but also *humbly*. I chose "candor" instead of "honesty" because there's not much humility in believing that you know the truth. Implicit with candor is that you're simply offering your view of what's going on and that you expect people to offer theirs. If it turns out that in fact you're the one who got it wrong, you want to know. At least I *hope* you want to know!

The most surprising thing about Radical Candor may be that its results are often the opposite of what you fear. You fear people will become angry or vindictive; instead they are usually *grateful* for the chance to talk it through. And even when you do get that initial anger, resentment, or sullenness, those emotions prove to be fleeting when the person knows you really care. As the people who report to you become more Radically Candid with each other, you spend less time mediating. When Radical Candor is encouraged and supported by the boss, communication flows, resentments that have festered come to the surface and get resolved, and people begin to love not just their work but *whom* they work with and *where* they work. When people love their job, the whole team is more successful. The resulting happiness is the success beyond success.

CARE PERSONALLY: THE FIRST DIMENSION OF RADICAL CANDOR

MY FIRST LESSON about why it's important to care personally took place in Moscow on July 4, 1992, while I was standing under a tarp in the rain with ten of the world's best diamond cutters, whom I was trying to hire. I was working for a New York diamond company. I'd graduated from college two years earlier with a degree in Russian literature. My education had seemed irrelevant to my current situation. My assignment just required common sense, not a deep understanding of human nature. I had to convince these people to leave the state-owned Russian factory that paid them in rubles, which were almost worthless. I, on the other hand, could pay with U.S.

dollars—a lot of them. And that was how you motivated people, right? You paid them.

Wrong. The diamond cutters wanted a picnic.

And so we stood under the tarp, eating *shashlyk*—grilled chunks of meat—and small, tart apples, passing a bottle of vodka around while the diamond cutters peppered me with questions. Their first assignment would be to cut a 100-carat diamond into a pair of one-of-a-kind earrings. "Who could buy such large jewels?" the diamond cutters wanted to know. I explained they were a gift from a Saudi sheikh to his wife, who was having twins. What did I know about using lasers to cut diamonds? I promised to take them to Israel to see the latest technology, which was still less efficient than the old copper disks they used. They wanted to learn English. I promised to teach them myself. "Would it also be possible to have lunch together every week or so?" Absolutely. As we drained the bottle of vodka, another question came. "If everything went to hell in Russia, would you get us and our families out of here?" I understood this was the only question that really mattered. By the end of our picnic, I finally realized that the most important thing I could do that the state could not do was to simply *give a damn, personally.*

The diamond cutters took the job. Suddenly all those late nights of reading long Russian novels became relevant to the business career I'd stumbled into. I had been deeply ambivalent about becoming a boss because I saw bosses as robotic dream-killers, Dilbert-like soul-crushers. Now I realized the question that led me to study Russian literature—why some people live productively and joyfully while others feel, as Marx put it, alienated from their labor—was central to a boss's job. In fact, part of my job was to figure out how to create more joy and less misery. My humanity was an attribute, not a liability, to being effective.

Two years after this picnic, I'd arranged for these men's first travel outside their homeland; helped them to come to grips with the dissonance they felt between the world they saw and what their Soviet education had led them to expect; improved their English; and hung out with their families. They had cut diamonds for our company that sold in excess of $100 million per year.

IT SEEMS OBVIOUS that good bosses must care personally about the people who report directly to them. Very few people start out their careers thinking,

I don't give a damn about people, so I think I'll be a great boss. And yet, it happens all too often that employees feel they're being treated as pawns on a chessboard, or as inferiors—not just in a corporate hierarchy but on a fundamental human level.

Part of the reason why people fail to "care personally" is the injunction to "keep it professional." That phrase denies something essential. We are all human beings, with human feelings, and, even at work, we need to be seen as such. When that doesn't happen, when we feel we must repress who we really are to earn a living, we become alienated. That makes us hate going to work. To most bosses, being professional means: show up at work on time, do your job, don't show feelings (unless engaged in "motivation" or some such end-driven effort). The result is that *nobody* feels comfortable being who they really are at work.

Fred Kofman, my coach at Google, had a mantra that contradicted the "just professional" approach so destructive to so many managers: "Bring your whole self to work." This saying has become a meme; Google it and you'll get more than eight million results. Sheryl Sandberg referred to it in her 2012 commencement address at Harvard, author Mike Robbins devoted a TEDx talk to it in 2016, and Stewart Butterfield, Slack's CEO, has made it a priority for his company. Bringing your whole self to work is one of those concepts that's hard to define precisely, but you develop a feel for it when you start to open up to it. This often means modeling the behavior yourself by showing some vulnerability to the people who report to you—or just admitting when you're having a bad day—and creating a safe space for others to do the same.

In addition to the obsessive devotion to "professionalism," there's another, less virtuous reason why people fail to "care personally." When they become a boss, some people consciously or unconsciously begin to feel they're better or smarter than the people who work for them. That attitude makes it impossible to be a kick-ass boss; it just makes people want to kick your ass. There are few things more damaging to human relationships than a sense of superiority. That's why I detest the word "superior" as a synonym for "boss." I also avoid the word "employee." I once worked for a man who told me, "In every relationship there is a screwer and a screwee." Needless to say, I didn't work for him for long. Of course, if you are a boss, there *is* some hierarchy involved. There's no use pretending otherwise. Just remember that being a boss is a *job*, not a value judgment.

Caring personally is the antidote to both robotic professionalism and managerial arrogance. Why do I say "caring personally" instead of just "caring"? Because it's not enough to care about the person's work or the person's career. Only when you actually care about the *whole person with your whole self* can you build a relationship.

Caring personally is not about memorizing birthdays and names of family members. Nor is it about sharing the sordid details of one's personal life, or forced chitchat at social events you'd rather not attend. Caring personally is about doing things you already know how to do. It's about acknowledging that we are all people with lives and aspirations that extend beyond those related to our shared work. It's about finding time for real conversations; about getting to know each other at a human level; about learning what's important to people; about sharing with one another what makes us want to get out of bed in the morning and go to work—and what has the opposite effect.

It isn't simply a matter of allowing your approach to your responsibilities to show that you care, however; you must also care deeply about people while being prepared to be hated in return. The movie *Miracle,* which is centered around the head coach of the 1980 U.S. men's Olympic ice hockey team, depicts this really well. Head coach Herb Brooks unifies his team by pushing them so hard that he becomes the common enemy. It's clear watching the movie how much he cares about each player, and it's painful to watch how long it takes the players to see it. Being the boss can feel like a lonely one-way street at times—especially at first. That is OK. If you can absorb the blows, the members of your team are more likely to be good bosses to their employees, when they have them. Once people know what it feels like to *have* a good boss, it's more natural for them to want to *be* a good boss. They may never repay you, but they are likely to pay it forward. The rewards of watching people you care about flourish and then help others flourish are enormous.

CHALLENGE DIRECTLY: THE SECOND DIMENSION OF RADICAL CANDOR

THE PHILOSOPHER JOSHUA Cohen, who taught executives at Twitter and Apple and students at Stanford and MIT, does a great job of explaining why challenging each other is essential not just to doing great work but to building great relationships. He often uses this quote from John Stuart Mill:

> The source of everything respectable in man either as an intellectual or as a moral being [is] that his errors are corrigible. He is capable of rectifying his mistakes, by discussion and experience. Not by experience alone. There must be discussion, to show how experience is to be interpreted.

Challenging others and encouraging them to challenge you helps build trusting relationships because it shows 1) you care enough to point out both the things that aren't going well and those that are and that 2) you are willing to admit when you're wrong and that you are committed to fixing mistakes that you or others have made. But because challenging often involves disagreeing or saying no, this approach embraces conflict rather than avoiding it.

Former Secretary of State Colin Powell once remarked that being responsible sometimes means pissing people off.* You have to accept that sometimes people on your team will be mad at you. In fact, if nobody is ever mad at you, you probably aren't challenging your team enough. The key, as in any relationship, is how you handle the anger. When what you say hurts, acknowledge the other person's pain. Don't pretend it doesn't hurt or say it "shouldn't" hurt—just show that you care. Eliminate the phrase "don't take it personally" from your vocabulary—it's insulting. Instead, offer to help fix the problem. But don't pretend it isn't a problem just to try to make somebody feel better. In the end, caring personally about people even as you challenge them will build the best relationships of your career.

The "challenge directly" part of this program can be particularly difficult, especially at the outset. You may have to criticize somebody's work or change their role while you are still in the process of establishing that trust. I'll dedicate a good deal of time to showing you how to do this throughout the book. But that's not the hardest part. The hardest part of building this trust is inviting people to challenge you, just as directly as you are challenging them. You have to encourage them to challenge you directly enough that *you* may be the one who feels upset or angry. This takes some getting used to—particularly for more "authoritarian" leaders. But if you stick to it, you'll find that you learn a great deal about yourself and how people perceive you.

---

* Harari, Oren. *The Powell Principles: 24 Lessons from Colin Powell, a Legendary Leader.* New York: McGraw-Hill, 2002, p.4.

This knowledge will unfailingly allow you and your team to achieve better results.

MY COFOUNDER RUSS recently hired Elisse Lockhart to lead Candor, Inc.'s content marketing efforts. Russ is pretty opinionated about the way we describe Radical Candor. Elisse was new to the team and so was holding back her opinions. Russ, sensitive to not only this dynamic but also to the fact he was her boss, was careful to make sure that he encouraged Elisse to challenge both of us just as hard as we challenged her.

Building enough trust between people to enable reciprocal challenge irrespective of reporting relationship takes time and attention. I saw a winning moment in building that trust when Russ and Elisse were collaborating on a blog post for our website. Elisse disagreed with some of Russ's suggested wording, and she said so. They went back and forth a few times, and it seemed as if Elisse was going to back down. Sensing this, Russ said, "If we have the data about what works, let's look at the data, but if all we have are opinions, let's use yours," borrowing from Jim Barksdale of Netscape, but offering the opposite prescription. Russ agreed to Elisse's changes, and the data on reception to Elisse's wording proved her right.

Emboldened, the next time she argued her perspective she did so even more forcefully—so much so that she worried maybe she'd stepped over a line with her boss. She hadn't, and to make that clear Russ sent across the "Help me, help you" *Jerry Maguire* clip. In the movie, Jerry and his client Rod get in a big argument, and the punch line features Rod telling Jerry, "See, that's the difference between us—you think we're fightin', and I think we're finally talkin'!"

WHAT RADICAL CANDOR IS NOT

WE TALKED ABOUT the importance of humility. Radical Candor is not a license to be gratuitously harsh or to "front-stab." It's not Radical Candor just because you begin with the words, "Let me be Radically Candid with you." If you follow that phrase with words like, "You are a liar and I don't trust you," or "You're a dipshit," you've just acted like a garden-variety jerk. It's not Radical Candor if you don't show that you care personally.

Radical Candor is also not an invitation to nitpick. Challenging people directly takes real energy—not only from the people you're challenging but from you as well. So do it only for things that really matter. A good rule of thumb for any relationship is to leave three unimportant things unsaid each day.

Radical Candor is not a hierarchical thing. To be Radically Candid, you need to practice it "up," "down," and "sideways." Even if your boss and peers have not bought in to this method, you CAN create a Radically Candid microcosm for yourself and the people on your team. You are entitled to proceed with a little more caution with your boss and your peers. But ultimately, if it's not possible to be Radically Candid with your boss and your peers, I'd recommend finding a different kind of work environment if at all possible.

Radical Candor is not about schmoozing, nor is it about endless extroversion that exhausts the introverts on your team or wears you out if you happen to be the introvert. It's not about getting drunk or driving go-carts or playing laser tag or having endless dinners with colleagues. Those might be good ways to blow off steam, but activities like that take up a lot of time and are not the most efficient way to help you get to know the people you work with, or show them you care personally.

Radical Candor is not unique to the culture in Silicon Valley, nor is it uniquely American. It's human. In fact, it was while working for an Israeli company that I began to develop my thinking about Radical Candor.

RADICAL CANDOR IS UNIVERSALLY HUMAN, BUT INTERPERSONALLY AND CULTURALLY RELATIVE

BOTH DIMENSIONS OF Radical Candor are sensitive to context. They get measured at the listener's ear, not at the speaker's mouth. Radical Candor is not a personality type or a talent or a cultural judgment. Radical Candor works only if the other person understands that your efforts at caring personally and challenging directly are delivered in good faith.

We have to be constantly aware of the fact that what seemed Radically Candid to one person or team may feel too obnoxious (or too touchy-feely) to another. Radical Candor requires even more adjustment when we go from one company to another, and more yet when we go from one country to another. What worked in one culture won't translate directly to another.

* * *

NOW LET'S MOVE on to Radical Candor, Israeli-style. Shortly after I graduated from business school, I took a job with Deltathree, a voice-over IP startup based in Jerusalem. I was raised in the American South, where people will do almost anything to avoid conflict or argument. In Israel, the opposite was true. Conversations seemed to take on a particularly brutal directness. I'll never forget overhearing Noam Bardin, Deltathree's COO, yelling at an engineer, "That design could be fifteen times more efficient. You *know* you could have built it better. Now we're going to have to rip what you did out and start over. We've lost a month, and for what? What were you *thinking*?"

That seemed harsh. Rude, even . . .

I began to understand the Israeli culture better when Jacob Ner-David, one of Deltathree's co-founders invited me over to his home in Jerusalem for Shabbat dinner. His wife, Haviva Ner-David, was studying to be a rabbi, something rare in the Orthodox community. She had come under attack from a number of people in their synagogue. Jacob was enormously supportive of her, and together the two of them explained how they approached traditional doctrine. The way Jacob and his wife questioned ancient interpretations of scripture somehow reminded me of how Noam challenged his engineer. If it was OK to challenge and reinterpret God's doctrine, of course it was not a sign of disrespect to argue vehemently with each other. I'd been raised in a very different culture. Where I grew up it wasn't uncommon to believe that God created the world in precisely seven days and consider any mention of evolution heresy. I wasn't a Creationist any more than Noam was an Orthodox Jew, but somehow the religious cultures of our youth had an impact on our willingness to challenge each other at work. I realized I should take Noam's challenges as a sign of respect rather than rudeness.

I had a very different experience when I managed a team in Tokyo a few years later. The team was enormously frustrated with how the Product team at Google's U.S. headquarters was approaching ads in mobile applications. Yahoo! was growing its business quickly, and there were a number of Japanese competitors not far behind. But the Japanese team was too polite to make the problems clear to the team responsible for product management, so they weren't getting fixed. When I pushed them to challenge the approach to mobile applications at Google headquarters, the team just stared at me as though I were crazy.

Trying to get the team in Tokyo to challenge authority the way Noam Bardin did in Jerusalem wouldn't have worked. The kind of argument that would be taken as a sign of respect in Tel Aviv would have been offensive in Tokyo. Even the term "Radical Candor" would've felt too aggressive. I found my own Southern upbringing helpful in understanding the Japanese perspective: both cultures placed a great emphasis on manners and on not contradicting people in public. So I encouraged that team in Tokyo to be "politely persistent." Being polite was their preferred way of showing they cared personally. Being persistent was the way they were most comfortable challenging Google's product direction.

I was gratified to see the results. The team in Tokyo became not just persistent but relentless in their campaign to be heard. Thanks in part to their polite persistence, a new product, AdSense for Mobile Applications, was born.

Another of my favorite Radical Candor stories is that of Roy Zhou, who worked for Russ and led the AdSense team in China. At first he was extremely deferential to Russ and me, but once we convinced him we really wanted to be challenged, he let it rip. He was a real pleasure to work with—and one of the most Radically Candid managers at Google. A few years ago, he got the opportunity to become president of Yoyi Digital, a five-hundred-person online advertising platform in Beijing. After a few months, he discovered some significant problems with the business. He came clean about them to his board and to all employees. Roy went to extraordinary lengths to show his team that he cared personally and was going to do everything he could to help them be successful. Not only did he make sure they got significant equity, he mortgaged his home before a new round of financing so they could be paid on time. Now Roy is running one of the most successful businesses in China.

I've led teams all over the world. The most surprising thing I've learned is that Brits, despite all their politeness, tend to be even more candid than New Yorkers. This is thanks to an education system that stresses oral argument as much as written. But, I've seen firsthand that it's possible to adapt Radical Candor equally well for Tel Aviv and Tokyo, for Beijing and Berlin.

2

GET, GIVE, AND ENCOURAGE GUIDANCE

Creating a culture of open communication

THE "UM" STORY

SHORTLY AFTER I joined Google, I gave a presentation to Google's CEO and founders on the performance of AdSense. Despite the fact that AdSense was doing great, and even though my boss was sitting next to me in a show of support, I felt nervous. Luckily, we had a good story to tell: the business was growing at an unprecedented rate. As I looked around the room, I caught the eye of CEO Eric Schmidt, whose head had snapped out of his computer when I'd declared how many new customers had signed up in the past month. I'd distracted him from his email—a triumph! "How many did you say?" he asked. I repeated the number, and he almost fell out of his chair.

I couldn't have asked for a better reaction. After I finished, I felt that mix of euphoria and relief that follows a successful presentation. My boss was waiting for me by the door and I half expected a high five. Instead, she asked if I'd walk back to her office with her. I got a sinking feeling in my stomach. Something hadn't gone well. But what?

"You are going to have an amazing career here at Google," Sheryl began. She knew how to get my attention—I had three failed start-ups under my belt and badly needed a win. "And your ability to be intellectually honest about both sides of an argument, not just your own, bought you a lot of credibility in there." She mentioned three or four specific things I'd said to illustrate her point. I'd been worried that I wasn't arguing my points vehemently enough, so this was welcome news to me. "I learned a lot today from the way you handled those questions." This didn't feel like mere flattery—I could tell from the way she stopped and looked me in the eye that she meant it. She wanted me to register that something I'd been worried about being a weakness was actually a strength.

This was interesting, but I wanted to file it away to think about later. That nagging feeling persisted in my stomach. There was an axe waiting to fall here. What I really wanted to know was, what had I done wrong? "But something didn't go well, right?"

Sheryl laughed. "You always want to focus on what you could have done better. Which I understand. I do, too. We learn more from failure than success. But I want you to focus for a minute on what went well, because overall it really *did* go well. This was a success."

I listened as best I could. Finally, she said. "You said 'um' a lot. Were you aware of it?"

"Yeah," I replied. "I know I say that too much." Surely she couldn't be taking this little walk with me just to talk about the "um" thing. Who cared if I said "um" when I had a tiger by the tail?

"Was it because you were nervous? Would you like me to recommend a speech coach for you? Google will pay for it."

"I didn't feel nervous," I said, making a brushing-off gesture with my hand as though I were shooing a bug away. "Just a verbal tic, I guess."

"There's no reason to let a small thing like a verbal tic trip you up."

"I know." I made another shoo-fly gesture with my hand.

Sheryl laughed. "When you do that thing with your hand, I feel like you're ignoring what I'm telling you. I can see I am going to have to be really,

really direct to get through to you. You are one of the smartest people I know, but saying 'um' so much makes you sound stupid."

Now *that* got my attention.

Sheryl repeated her offer to help. "The good news is a speaking coach can really help with the 'um' thing. I know somebody who would be great. You can definitely fix this."

"OPERATIONALIZING" GOOD GUIDANCE

THINK FOR A moment about how Sheryl handled that situation. Even though the overall talk had gone well, she didn't let the positive result get in the way of pointing out something I needed to fix. She did so immediately, so that the problem didn't hurt my reputation at Google. She made sure to point out the positive things I'd accomplished in the presentation, and what's more, she did so thoroughly and sincerely—there was no attempt at "sandwiching" the criticism between bogus positives. Her first approach was gentle but direct. When it became clear that I wasn't hearing her, she became more direct, but even then she was careful not to "personalize," not to make it about some essential trait. She said I "sounded" stupid rather than I *was* stupid. And I wasn't in this alone: she offered tangible help. I didn't feel like an idiot with defects, but a valuable team member she was ready to invest in. But it still stung a little bit.

This conversation was extremely effective on two counts. First, it made me want to solve my "um" problem immediately; after only three sessions with a speech coach, I had made noticeable improvement. Second, it made me appreciate Sheryl and inspired me to give better guidance to *my* team. The way she gave praise and criticism got me thinking about how to teach other people how to adopt this style of management.

All this from a two-minute encounter.

WOW. HOW MANY times have you tried to give feedback that totally falls flat? How can you, like Sheryl, give guidance in a way that confronts a specific situation *and* creates ripple effects that change how everyone communicates?

I have spent the decade since that encounter coaching the next generation of Silicon Valley leaders to change their approach to guidance—both praise and criticism. It's surprisingly simple. Anyone can learn it. There are two dimensions to good guidance: care personally and challenge directly.

As discussed in chapter one, when you do both at the same time, it's Radical Candor. It's also useful to be clear about what happens when you fail in one dimension (Ruinous Empathy), the other (Obnoxious Aggression), or both (Manipulative Insincerity). Being clear about what happens when you fail to care personally or challenge directly will help you avoid backsliding into old habits too common to all of us.

Many of the people I coach have found this framework helpful in being more conscious of what kind of guidance they are getting, giving, and encouraging. Another essential thing I stress with my clients: it's vital to remember that very important lesson from the "um" story—don't personalize. The names of each quadrant refer to *guidance*, not to *personality traits*. They are a way to gauge praise and criticism, and to help people remember to do a better job offering both. They are *not* to be used to label people. Labeling hinders improvement. Ultimately, everyone spends some time in each of the quadrants. We are all imperfect. I've never met anyone who is *always* Radically Candid. To repeat, this is not a "personality test."

Let's walk through the quadrants.

RADICAL CANDOR

GUIDANCE DOESN'T JUST come at work. Every so often, a stranger offers some Radical Candor, and it can change your life if you're listening. This happened to me shortly after I adopted a golden retriever puppy named Belvedere. I *adored* Belvedere and spoiled her utterly. As a result, she was completely out of control. One evening we were out for a walk, and Belvy began to tug at her leash as we waited at a crosswalk, even though cars were speeding by only a few feet in front of us. "Come on sweetie, sit," I implored. "The light will be green in a second." Despite my reassurances, she yanked even harder on the leash and tried to lunge into the street.

A stranger also waiting to cross looked over at me and said, "I can see you really love your dog." In the two seconds it took him to say those words, he established that he cared, that he wasn't judging me. Next, he gave me a really direct challenge. "But that dog will die if you don't teach her to sit!" Direct, almost breathtakingly so. Then, without asking for permission, the man bent down to Belvy, pointed his finger at the sidewalk, and said with a loud, firm voice, "SIT!"

She sat. I gaped in amazement.

He smiled and explained, "It's not mean. It's clear!" The light changed and he strode off, leaving me with words to live by.

Think for a second about how this might have gone down. The man could have easily said something judgmental ("you have no right to own a dog if you don't know how to take care of one!") and thus left me defensive and unwilling to take his simple but essential advice. Instead, he acknowledged my love for the dog, and explained why his recommendation was the right way to go (not mean, clear!). There was a decent chance I would tell him to go to hell and mind his own business, but he didn't let that stop him. He was, in his own way, a leader—and I suspect that he's a good boss in his day job. Granted, I didn't form a relationship with him. But if I'd worked with him instead of just bumping into him on the street, this little interaction would have been the seed from which a relationship could grow.

I hope I've never spoken to a person like a dog, but I'll never forget the stranger's words. "It's not mean, it's clear!" has become a management mantra, helping me to avoid repeating the mistake I described in the Introduction, which was not telling Bob when his work wasn't good enough. My efforts to be nice ended with my having to fire him. Not so nice after all. That brief incident at the crosswalk taught me that I don't have to spend a lot of time getting to know a person or building trust *before* offering Radically Candid guidance. In fact, a great way to get to know somebody and to build trust is to offer Radically Candid praise and criticism.

Radically Candid praise
"I admire that about you"

Recently my cofounder Russ and I were filming a video tip for giving Radically Candid praise. Russ was talking about why giving really specific praise is important, and he gave an example from coaching Little League. "I really admire that you are a Little League coach," I said, offhandedly. I had been meaning to tell him this for a while, and it just popped into my head in the moment. He said, "Thank you." Usually, that would've been that. But I realized later that my compliment had not been specific—I hadn't told Russ *why* I admired that he was a coach. I mentioned the irony to Russ. He replied, "Well, the real problem is that I don't think you meant it—you hate sports." Now, I realized, it was even worse than I'd thought. It wasn't just that I'd been vague and unhelpful. He knew I cared about him, but he thought my praise was insincere.

There we were, giving people advice on giving good praise, and here I was, totally screwing it up! And it should have been easy, I was talking to Russ, my cofounder and a person I'd known for years. Giving meaningful praise is hard. That's why it's so important to gauge your guidance—to find out how it lands for people. Now that I knew how Russ felt, I tried again.

"The other day I gave you a hard time about leaving early for practice, and I then felt bad about it," I began. "Because in fact I really admire that you are a Little League coach. You do as good a job integrating your work and your life as anyone I know. I always wonder if I'm spending enough time with my kids, and the example you set by coaching helps me do better. Also, the things you've learned from the Positive Coaching Alliance have been enormously helpful in our work."

This time, the comment was contextualized, far more personal, and specific. And, this time, Russ said, "Now *that* was Radically Candid praise!"

Radically Candid criticism
To keep winning, criticize the wins

Andre Iguodala, the swingman for the Golden State Warriors, explained why being willing to challenge the people you work with is so important to success. The secret to winning, he said, is to point out to great players what they could have done better, even when they have just won a game. *Especially* when they have just won a game. The problem with living at the top of a hill is that you always have to walk uphill just to get back home. Of course, Andre's teammates weren't always happy to hear his Radically Candid criticism. They sometimes accused him of Obnoxious Aggression. But, as we will see in the next section, Obnoxious Aggression looks and feels very different.

OBNOXIOUS AGGRESSION

WHEN YOU CRITICIZE someone without taking even two seconds to show you care, your guidance feels obnoxiously aggressive to the recipient. I regret to say that if you can't be Radically Candid, being obnoxiously aggressive is the second best thing you can do. At least then people know what you think and where they stand, so your team can achieve results. This explains the advantage that assholes seem to have in the world.

Let me be clear. I refuse to work with people who can't be bothered to show basic human decency. I want you to keep your humanity intact. If more people can be Radically Candid, there will be less reason to tolerate Obnoxious Aggression.

But here's a paradox of being a good boss. Most people *prefer* the challenging "jerk" to the boss whose "niceness" gets in the way of candor. I once read an article that claimed most

people would rather work for a "competent asshole" than a "nice incompetent." This article was a useful expression of the Catch-22 that worried me about being a boss. Of course I didn't want to be incompetent. Nor did I want to be an asshole.

Fortunately, the "asshole or incompetent" thing is a false dichotomy: you don't have to choose between those two extremes. Time and again, I have seen that it was kinder in the long run to be direct, even if articulating my criticism caused some momentary upset. ("It's not mean, it's clear!") Furthermore, it's the fear of being labeled a jerk that pushes many people toward Manipulative Insincerity or Ruinous Empathy—both of which are actually worse for their colleagues than Obnoxious Aggression, as we'll see in later sections.

Still, Obnoxious Aggression is debilitating, particularly at the extreme. When bosses belittle employees, embarrass them publicly, or freeze them out, their behavior falls into this quadrant. This Obnoxious Aggression sometimes gets great results short-term but leaves a trail of dead bodies in its wake in the long run. Think about the Anna Wintour–inspired character played by Meryl Streep in *The Devil Wears Prada*. Or Bobby Knight, the Indiana basketball coach who had a winning record but was reported to have thrown chairs and choked a player and was ultimately fired. When bosses criticize others to humiliate them rather than to help them improve, or permit personalized attacks among team members, or discourage praise as "babysitting people's egos," their behavior feels obnoxiously aggressive to the people around him.

The worst kind of Obnoxious Aggression happens when one person really understands another's vulnerabilities and then targets them, either for sport or to assert dominance. I once had a boss who really knew how to push my buttons—he possessed what I thought of as "cruel empathy." Almost nothing will erode trust more quickly than using one's insights into what makes another person tick to hurt them.

It happens all too often that bosses view employees as lesser beings who can be degraded without conscience; that employees view their bosses as tyrants to be toppled; and that peers view one another as enemy combatants. When this is the toxic culture of guidance, criticism is a weapon rather than a tool for improvement; it makes the giver feel powerful and the receiver feel awful. Even praise can feel more like a backhanded compliment than a celebration of work well done. "Well, you got it right *this* time."

Obnoxiously aggressive criticism
Front-stabbing

Let's take the example of criticism offered by a former colleague whom I'll refer to as "Ned." Ned organized a party for his global team and asked people to come in their national costumes. The culture of the company was whimsical, and everybody came dressed in goofy outfits. Ned, who was new to the company, came in an expensive tux. I guess he felt silly being so absurdly overdressed for his own party, and to cope with his own insecurities he went into belittling mode. He strode up to a friend of mine, one of his new direct reports, who had dressed as a leprechaun for the party. In front of a large crowd, Ned bellowed at my friend, "I said to dress in your national costume, not to dress like a fool!"

It's tempting to dismiss Ned as a jerk, but this is exactly the kind of attribution error that Radical Candor teaches us to avoid. Blaming people's internal essence rather than their external behavior leaves no room for change. And why had Ned never changed? Because nobody ever bothered to challenge his behavior, and so he never had to learn. His obnoxiousness just escalated.

I'm not proud to admit that I was a silent party to this. I was standing right there when Ned told my friend that he looked like a fool, and I didn't say anything. Nor did I say anything later to Ned in private. Why? Because I had already dismissed Ned as an asshole, and therefore deemed him not worth talking to. So I was making the fundamental attribution error, and my behavior was "manipulatively insincere." I'm still ashamed of that. If ever anyone needed a dose of Radical Candor, it was Ned.

Remember, Obnoxious Aggression is a *behavior*, not a personality trait. Nobody is a bona fide asshole all the time. Not even Ned. And *all* of us are obnoxiously aggressive some of the time. This includes me, unfortunately. I will assert that I am not usually a jerk, but here's a time when I behaved like one:

A couple of months after joining Google, I had a disagreement with Larry Page about his approach to a policy. In a fit of frustration, I sent an email to about thirty people, including Larry, which said, "Larry claims he wants to organize the world's information, but his policy is creating 'clutter sites,' muddling the world's information." I went on to imply that he was recommending the policy because he was focused on increasing Google's revenue rather than doing the right thing for users.

If Larry had worked for me instead of the other way around, I would never have sent such an arrogant, accusatory email. I would have asked him privately why he was proposing a policy that seemed to be in violation of Google's mission. If I agreed with his rationale, that would have been that. If I disagreed, I would have explained—again, privately—that he seemed inconsistent and tried to understand his rationale. I didn't do any of that with Larry, though. If I had, of course, I would have learned that he was not just fifteen, but more like 115 steps ahead of me. I simply didn't understand how things worked yet.

Why did I behave this way? Partly because I believe there's a special place in hell for those who "kick down and kiss up." At least I wasn't making *that* mistake. And yet my mistake was simply the other side of the same coin. I wasn't really thinking of Larry as a human being. I saw him as a kind of demigod whom I could attack with impunity. Fundamental human decency is something every person owes every other, regardless of position. And it wasn't as though Larry was shut down to criticism, as I had seen in his conversation with Matt Cutts. He'd given me no reason to be so strident.

The incident with Larry is a good example of how criticism can be obnoxiously aggressive if you don't care personally. I probably thought I was being Radically Candid—"speaking truth to power"—but I wasn't. It was a clear-cut case of "front-stabbing." Better than backstabbing, but still really bad.

The first problem with my email was that it wasn't humble. I had just joined the company, and I didn't understand much about how Google's systems worked. Nor had I bothered to find out why Larry might be taking the stance he was taking. Instead, I just made a bunch of assumptions and concluded—wrongly, as it turned out—that Larry was more concerned with making money than he was with Google's mission. Furthermore, my suggestions were not at all helpful because I didn't fully understand the underlying issue that Larry was trying to address. My other miscalculation was criticizing Larry in a public forum, rather than in private, which would have been the respectful thing to do. And worst of all, I personalized. I should have been talking about the AdSense policy, but instead I attacked Larry's character, implicitly accusing him of being greedy and hypocritical. As I would see over and over in the next six years at Google, Larry was certainly neither of those things. He was fair and consistent. But the point here is that I shouldn't have been talking about Larry's character, either positively or negatively. I was personalizing.

Obnoxiously aggressive praise
Belittling compliments

Praise can be obnoxiously aggressive, too. Consider this email that a boss at a legendary Silicon Valley company sent out to his team of about six hundred people, seventy of whom had just gotten bonuses. I've removed the names to avoid embarrassing these people further:

From: **JohnDoe** <JohnDoe@corpx.com>
Date: April 27 at 11:53 AM
Subject: Bonus Winners!
To: giantteam@corpx.com

Dear Giant Team,
In Q3 there was a number of you that really excelled and went above and beyond the rest of us to deliver significant impact to Corpx. These team members and their accomplishments have been recognized with the Q3 spot bonus attributed by the Management Team. I want to take this opportunity to share who these extraordinary people are and provide you an overview of their accomplishments in the list below.

--John
John Doe
Vice President, Giant Team
Worldwide

- **Person 33:** level 5 seller, he drove the highest QTD revenue of any display seller: $7.5M in Q3. His comp at $70k base and OTE of $116k is 50% below market; retention risk.

- **Person 39:** she has done all of the dirty work in getting XYZ off the ground with endless spreadsheets, updates, legal calls, and has done a great job (well above her level 3 status).

- **Person 72:** exceptional effort in the past 4+ months. Additional responsibility covering John Doe.

Imagine how Person 33 felt when he saw that his private compensation information had been sent out to six hundred people. I doubt it made him feel better to learn that he was being paid half of what he should have been and that his boss thought he was probably looking for other jobs!

Just think how motivating it must have been for Person 39 to learn that she did all the "dirty work." I doubt it was any consolation to learn she was "well above her level 3 status." At least there was some comedy in the fact that Person 72 had to be given a bonus for "covering John." In other words, John Doe was such a jerk that the company had to pay people a bonus if they worked closely with him.

Even if you give John Doe the benefit of the doubt and assume he was simply lazy and/or tin-eared rather than intentionally hurtful, it's indubitable that he was not demonstrating that he cared personally about his people.

He had obviously gathered this information by asking all the managers who worked for him to send him a justification for the bonus. But he cared so little about the people he was praising that he didn't even bother to read the justifications. He just copied and pasted them into a new email and fired it off. It's not easy to pay people a compliment backed up by a big bonus and make them feel worse rather than better, but John Doe's email pulled that off.

MANIPULATIVE INSINCERITY

MANIPULATIVELY INSINCERE GUIDANCE happens when you don't care enough about a person to challenge directly. People give praise and criticism that is manipulatively insincere when they are too focused on being liked or think they can gain some sort of political advantage by being fake—or when they are just too tired to care or argue any more. Guidance that is manipulatively insincere rarely reflects what the speaker actually thinks; rather, it's an attempt to push the other person's emotional buttons in return for some personal gain. "He'll be happy if I tell him I liked his stupid presentation, and that will make my life easier than explaining why it sucked. In the long run, though, I really need to find someone to replace him."

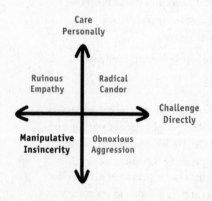

Apple's Chief Design Officer Jony Ive told a story about a time when he pulled his punches when criticizing his team's work. When Steve Jobs asked Jony why he hadn't been more clear about what was wrong, Jony replied, "Because I care about the team." To which Steve replied, "No, Jony, you're just really vain. You just want people to like you." Recounting the story, Jony said, "I was terribly cross because I knew he was right."

That's why Colin Powell said leadership is sometimes about being willing to piss people off. When you are overly worried about how people will perceive you, you're less willing to say what needs to be said. Like Jony, you may feel it's because you care about the team, but really, in those all-too-human moments you may care too much about how they feel about you—in other words, about yourself. I've been there, too. We all have.

Give a damn about the people you challenge. Worrying about whether or not they give a damn about *you*, however, is not "caring personally" about them, and it's likely to push you in the wrong direction on the "challenge directly" axis. That's not going to help your team achieve great results, or take a step in the direction of their dreams. Let go of vanity and care personally. But if you don't care, don't waste your time and everyone else's by trying to fake it.

Unfortunately, conventional wisdom and a lot of management advice pushes bosses to challenge less, rather than encouraging them to care more. Generally, the resulting praise and criticism feels to employees like flattery or backstabbing. Needless to say, this doesn't build trust between boss and direct report.

Manipulatively insincere praise
The false apology

Let's go back to my obnoxiously aggressive email to Larry Page. After it went out, a couple of people called me up and asked me why the hell I'd sent it. I realized I'd been unbelievably rude, and I felt ashamed—and a little scared. What had I been *thinking*?

I *still* didn't understand why my assessment of Larry's new policy was wrong, but now I was more concerned with keeping my job. So the next time I saw Larry, I stopped him and said, "I'm sorry about that email, Larry. I know you are right." Now, there would have been nothing wrong with apologizing for the tone I'd taken, but instead, without explanation, I abruptly reversed my intellectual position. My insincerity was obvious, and it was exactly the wrong move. Larry had a finely tuned BS meter, and I'm not a very good liar. He said nothing, but his look of disdain spoke volumes. As Larry walked away, a colleague standing nearby smiled in sympathetic solidarity and muttered to me, "He likes it better when you disagree with him."

When you behave badly and get called out for it, an all-too-natural response is to become less genuine and more political—to move from Obnoxious Aggression to a worse place, Manipulative Insincerity. It would've been better to have said nothing than to move in the wrong direction on the "challenge directly" axis. Better yet to have moved up on the care personally axis—to have taken the trouble to understand Larry's thinking and then come up with a solution that addressed his concerns and mine. In that context, admitting that I had behaved badly would probably have been better received.

RUINOUS EMPATHY

THERE'S A RUSSIAN anecdote about a guy who has to amputate his dog's tail but loves him so much that he cuts it off an inch each day, rather than all at once. His desire to spare the dog pain and suffering only leads to more pain and suffering. Don't allow yourself to become that kind of boss!

This is an extreme example of what I call Ruinous Empathy. Ruinous Empathy is responsible for the vast majority of management mistakes I've seen in my career. Most people want to avoid creating tension or discomfort at work. They are like the well-meaning parent who cannot bear to discipline their kids. They are like me with my dog Belvy.

Bosses rarely *intend* to ruin an employee's chance of success or to handicap the entire team by letting poor performance slide. And yet that is often the net result of Ruinous Empathy. Similarly, praise that's ruinously empathetic is not effective because its primary goal is to make the person feel better rather than to point out really great work and push for more of it. These were the painful mistakes I made in the story from the Introduction with Bob, whom I didn't criticize and then had to fire.

Ruinous Empathy can also prevent a boss from asking for criticism. Typically, when a boss asks an employee for criticism, the employee feels awkward at best, afraid at worst. Instead of pushing through the discomfort to get an employee to challenge them, bosses who are being ruinously empathetic may be so eager to ease the awkwardness that they simply let the matter drop.

When bosses are too invested in everyone getting along, they also fail to encourage the people on their team to criticize one another for fear of sowing discord. They create the kind of work environment where "being nice" is prioritized at the expense of critiquing, and therefore, improving actual performance.

Bosses often make the mistake of thinking that if they hang out in the Ruinous Empathy quadrant they can build a relationship with their direct reports and *then* move over to Radical Candor. They're pleasant to work with, but as time goes by their employees start to realize that the only guidance they've received is "good job" and other vaguely positive comments. They know they've done some things wrong, but they're not sure what, exactly. Their direct reports never know where they stand, and they aren't being given an opportunity to learn or grow; they often stall or get fired. Not such a great way to build a relationship. On the flip side, when Ruinous Empathy prevents bosses from *soliciting* criticism, they have no idea anything is wrong until a person quits. Needless to say, this strategy does not build trust on either side.

Ruinously empathetic praise
"Just trying to say something nice"

A friend of mine told a cautionary tale about "just trying to say something nice" as a leader. Wandering around at 2 A.M. the night before a launch, he bumped into an engineer, "Anatoly," and asked him about a particular feature. Anatoly answered his question, and told him about several important aspects of the feature. A couple of days later, when celebrating the launch, my friend congratulated Anatoly on his excellent work on the feature in front of the whole company.

Problem was, Anatoly was only one of a handful of strong engineers on the project. All the other engineers who had worked on it now thought that Anatoly had claimed credit for the feature himself. Embarrassed, Anatoly sent out an email to the whole company, listing all the people who had worked on the project with him.

My friend realized he had been ruinously empathetic. He was just trying to make Anatoly happy by praising him, but he'd accidentally thrown him under the bus. My friend's suggestion to managers who worked at his company: when giving praise, investigate until you really understand who did what and why it was so great. Be as specific and thorough with praise as with criticism. Go deep into the details.

MOVING TOWARD RADICAL CANDOR

OFTEN WHEN I talk to people about developing a culture of Radical Candor, they agree with the idea but feel nervous about putting it into practice. My advice is to start by explaining the idea and then asking people to be Radically Candid with *you*. Start by *getting* feedback, in other words, not by dishing it out. Then when you do start giving it, start with praise, not criticism. When you move on to criticism, make sure you understand where the perilous border between Radical Candor and Obnoxious Aggression is.

Start by asking for criticism, not by giving it
Don't dish it out before you show you can take it

There are several reasons why it makes sense to begin building a culture of Radical Candor by asking people to criticize you. First, it's the best way to show that you are aware that you are often wrong, and that you want to hear about it when you are; you want to be challenged. Second, you'll learn a lot—few people scrutinize you as closely as do those who report to you. Maybe it will prevent you from sending out ill-conceived emails like the one I sent to Larry. Third, the more firsthand experience you have with how it feels to receive criticism, the better idea you'll have of how your own guidance lands for others. Fourth, asking for criticism is a great way to build trust and strengthen your relationships.

Bosses get Radically Candid guidance from their teams not merely by being open to criticism but by *actively soliciting* it. If a person is bold enough to criticize you, do *not* critique their criticism. If you see somebody criticizing a peer inappropriately, say something. But if somebody criticizes *you* inappropriately, your job is to listen with the intent to understand and then to reward the candor. Just as important as soliciting criticism is encouraging it between your team members. (You can find specific tools and techniques for soliciting and encouraging guidance from your employees in Part II, Chapter Six.)

When I worked at Google, it was often the people on the team in Dublin who'd come out with the most memorable criticism for me. These zingers were enormously helpful, once I got over the momentary sting. David Johnson once said to me after I'd sent out a particularly ill-advised email, "Kim, you're awfully fast to hit Send!" To this day, I still hear the warning voice of David before I hit Send. And even though I haven't seen him in years, he continues to save me almost weekly from sending a note I'll regret.

Another time I delayed the start of a meeting with the team in Dublin because I didn't want to cut short my morning hour with my newborn twins. I thought everyone would understand, but a young father on the call fired back, "Ya know, Kim, we have children, too!" I'd unthinkingly pushed the meeting into their dinner hour. I was deeply ashamed but, once I'd gotten over feeling defensive, also grateful to him for pointing it out.

The key to soliciting criticism from the Dublin team was not to react defensively. The difficulty in soliciting criticism from the team I worked with in Japan, however, was enduring the silence. I'll never forget my first meeting with the AdSense team in Tokyo. My plan was to hold regular meetings with them to ask for suggestions, concerns, improvements. My previous experience in such meetings in other countries had been that if I asked a question like, "What could I do or stop doing that would make your lives better?" and then counted to six in my head, somebody would say *something*. I counted to ten. Crickets. I asked a different way. Still, crickets. Finally, I told them a story about Toyota that I'd learned in business school. Wanting to combat the cultural taboos against criticizing management, Toyota's leaders painted a big red square on the assembly line floor. New employees had to stand in it at the end of their first week, and they were not allowed to leave until they had criticized at least three things on the line. The continual improvement this practice spawned was part of Toyota's success. I asked my team what they thought: did we need a red box? They laughed, and, fearing I might just paint a red box somewhere, somebody opened up just a tiny bit. It wasn't much, frankly—a complaint about the tea in the office—but I rewarded the candor handsomely. I thanked the person publicly, I sent a handwritten note, I approved funds to make sure there was better tea, and I made sure everyone knew that there was better tea now because somebody had complained about it in the meeting. Later, more substantive issues got raised.

Balance praise and criticism
Worry more about praise, less about criticism—but above all be sincere

We learn more from our mistakes than our successes, more from criticism than from praise. Why, then, is it important to give *more* praise than criticism? Several reasons. First, it guides people in the right direction. It's just as important to let people know what to do more of as what to do less of. Second, it encourages people to keep improving. In other words, the best praise does a lot more than just make people feel good. It can actually challenge them directly.

Some professionals say you need to have a praise-to-criticism ratio of 3:1, 5:1, or even 7:1. Others advocate the "feedback sandwich"—opening and closing with praise, sticking some criticism in between. I think venture capitalist Ben Horowitz got it right when he called this approach the "shit sandwich." Horowitz suggests that such a technique might work with less-experienced people, but I've found the average child sees through it just as clearly as an executive does.

In other words, the notion of a "right" ratio between praise and criticism is dangerous, because it can lead you to say things that are unnatural, insincere, or just plain ridiculous. If you think that you *must* come up with, say, two good things for every bad thing you tell somebody, you'll find yourself saying things like, "Wow, the font you chose for that presentation really blew me away. But the content bordered on the obvious. . . . Still, it really impresses me how neat your desk always is." Patronizing or insincere praise like that will erode trust and hurt your relationships just as much as overly harsh criticism.

In the case of criticism, most people are nervous about hurting someone's feelings, so they often say nothing. In the case of praise, some people are eager to please those around them, so they always say something—sometimes inane things. Other people just aren't in the habit of giving praise. *If I'm not firing you, it means you're doing fine.* That's not good enough. Andy Grove told me he realized it was time to get better at praising people when somebody put a laminated plaque reading SAY SOMETHING NICE! in his cubicle.

When I am criticizing, I try to be less nervous, and focus on "just saying it." If I think too much about how to say it I'm likely to wimp out and say nothing. And when I am praising, I try to be at least *aware* of how praise can go wrong, and put more energy into thinking about how to say it. Karen Sipprell, a colleague at Apple, asked two questions that were instructive: "How long do you spend making sure you have all the facts right before you criticize somebody? How long do you spend making sure you have all the facts right before you *praise* somebody?" Ideally you'd spend just as long getting the facts right for praise as for criticism.

Understand the perilous border between Obnoxious Aggression and Radical Candor
"Your work is shit"

Radically Candid criticism is an important part of the culture at both Google and Apple, but it takes very different forms at the two companies. Google emphasizes caring personally more than challenging directly, so I'd describe criticism there as Radical Candor with a twist of Ruinous Empathy. Apple does the opposite, so I'd describe its culture of criticism as Radical Candor with a twist of Obnoxious Aggression.

In the Introduction, I described briefly a documentary in which tech journalist Bob Cringely interviews Steve Jobs and asks what he means when he tells people "your work is shit."* It's worth reading the transcript to explore the perilous border between Obnoxious Aggression and Radical Candor.

> CRINGELY: What does it mean when you tell someone their work is shit?
>
> JOBS: It usually means their work is shit. Sometimes it means, "I think your work is shit. And I—I'm wrong."

Saying "your work is shit" is generally not OK. It's deep in the "Obnoxious Aggression" quadrant. But later in the interview with Cringely, Jobs clarified his thoughts about what he said.

> JOBS: The most important thing I think you can do for somebody who's really good and who's really being counted on is to point out to them when they're not—when their work isn't good enough. And to do it very clearly and to articulate why . . . and to get them back on track.

Notice that Jobs catches himself. He's careful not to personalize the criticism—not to say "when they're not good enough." Instead, he says "when their *work* isn't good enough." It's an important distinction. Jobs is struggling with a common problem that arises when criticizing another person: the fundamental attribution error, which highlights the role of personal traits rather than external causes. It's easier to find fault in that person than to look for the fault within the context of what that person is doing. It's easier to say, "You're sloppy" than to say, "You've been working nights and weekends, and it's starting to take a toll on your ability to catch mistakes in your logic." But it's also far less helpful.

Saying "your work is shit" is way better than saying "you are shit," but it's still totally obnoxious. What Jobs says next is key, though: for criticism

---

* You can see the outtakes of the interview for the PBS documentary *Triumph of the Nerds*, in *The Lost Interview*.

to be effective, it's crucial "to do it very *clearly* and to articulate *why* . . . and to get them *back on track*." [My italics.] In other words, "your work is shit," even stated less aggressively, is not enough. The boss needs to explain *why*; that is, be invested in helping the person improve. Toward the end of the interview, Jobs offers some explanation of why he chose the words he did.

> **JOBS:** You need to do that in a way that does not call into question your confidence in their abilities but *leaves not too much room for interpretation* . . . and that's a hard thing to do. [My italics.]

"Your work is shit" certainly doesn't leave any room for interpretation, but I expect for most people it might also call into question confidence in their ability. Far be it for me to justify this word choice, but there are a couple of reasons why it might not be as bad as it sounds to say such a thing. First, the nature of the relationship is key. In the Introduction, I told a story about a time I called a guy on my team a dumbass. I'm not advocating you do the same. I'm just saying that because of the relationship we had, I knew that he knew I admired him tremendously and that I only used those words to get his attention. Second, it might be the case, particularly when you're dealing with highly accomplished people, that you have to go to some extremes to break through their tendency to filter out critical messages.

Jobs *does* articulate why guidance often involves walking a knife's edge. I have always found it enormously difficult to reassure people that I have confidence in their abilities while simultaneously making it clear that I think the work is not good enough. Being extremely clear about the quality of the work can sometimes feel like you're just being mean.

How do you criticize without discouraging the person? First, as I described in Chapter One, focus on your relationship. Also, as I described in the previous two sections: ask for criticism before giving it, and offer more praise than criticism. Be humble, helpful, offer guidance in person and immediately, praise in public, criticize in private, and don't personalize. Make it clear that the problem is not due to some unfixable personality flaw. Share stories when you've been criticized for something similar. (For more tips, see Chapter Six, which details giving impromptu guidance.)

A leader I worked with at Apple described how he would help new employees learn to take criticism in stride. He'd been at Apple for many years and had a godlike reputation. After their first design review, he'd show new employees two binders he kept in his office. One had ten sheets of paper in it. The other had more than a thousand. "This is my 'yes' file," he explained, pointing to the slim binder. "The design ideas that got approved." Then, he'd pick up the fat binder and drop it for effect. "And this is my 'no' file. Don't let the criticism discourage you."

Everyone must find their own way to criticize people without discouraging them. Steve Jobs's guidance style is certainly not for everyone, but it's worth understanding where he was coming from.

> **JOBS:** I don't mind being wrong. And I'll admit that I'm wrong a lot. It doesn't really matter to me too much. What matters to me is that we do the right thing.

In my experience, people who are more concerned with getting to the right answer than with being right make the best bosses. That's because they keep learning and improving, and they push the people who work for them to do the same. A boss's Radically Candid guidance helps the people working for them do the best work of their lives.

Think of a simple example
"Your fly is down"

As the "your work is shit" example shows, it can be harder than you might think to decide if you are being Radically Candid or not. One way to solve a hard problem is to think of a simpler but similar one, recall how you solved it, and then apply that technique to the harder problem. You can use the same approach with emotional situations. When you're faced with telling a person something that will be extremely hard to hear, pretend you're just saying, "Your fly is down," or "You have spinach in your teeth." These less-fraught scenarios can help you approach bigger problems more straightforwardly.

To see how to apply the Radical Candor framework to giving guidance, imagine a simple scenario: a colleague, Alex, has walked out of the restroom, fly down, shirttail sticking out the front. What do you say?

Let's say you decide to overcome the awkwardness and speak up. You know Alex will be embarrassed when you point out the zipper, but if you

say nothing, ten more people will probably see Alex looking ridiculous. So you pull Alex aside and quietly say, "Hey, Alex, your fly is down. I always appreciate when people point it out to me when I've done the same thing. I hope you don't mind my mentioning it." Your behavior is in the Radical Candor quadrant—both caring personally and challenging directly.

If on the other hand you point out Alex's fly loudly in front of other people, trying to be funny by intentionally humiliating Alex, your behavior is in the Obnoxious Aggression quadrant. However, that's not the worst possible scenario from Alex's perspective, since you gave her the chance to fix the problem.

If you know Alex is shy and will be embarrassed, maybe you decide to say nothing and hope Alex notices the fly without your saying anything. This behavior puts you in the Ruinous Empathy quadrant. In this scenario, ten more people see Alex's fly down with the ridiculous white shirt sticking out of the front, and by the time Alex notices, it's obvious her fly has been down for a really long time. Now Alex is even *more* embarrassed than if you'd said something immediately—and probably wonders why you didn't have the courtesy to mention it.

Finally, imagine you decide not to say anything because you're thinking about your own feelings and reputation. You're silent not because you're concerned for Alex, but because you want to spare *yourself.* You care deeply about being liked, and you're worried Alex won't like you if you say something. You're also worried if people overhear you saying something to Alex, they will judge you. So you walk on by and say nothing. If you're really shameless, you might whisper to the next person who comes along to go check out Alex's fly. Congratulations—your behavior is in the worst quadrant: Manipulative Insincerity!

It's tempting to think that Radical Candor should be reserved only for people you know well, like your friends and family. Tempting to think that if you hung out in Ruinous Empathy or Manipulative Insincerity while you got to know Alex, then one fine day it would be easy to say, "Hey, Alex, my friend, your fly is down." But the need for honest communication doesn't always wait until you've built a close personal relationship, and even a near-stranger's silence invites more awkwardness and mistrust than saying, "Hey, your fly is down," would have. Next time Alex sees you, there's going to be some awkwardness at the memory. Why didn't you say anything? The seeds of mistrust are sown in your reticence. That's why Kim Vorrath, a leader on the iOS team at Apple that built the software for the iPhone, gave this simple advice about criticism: "Just say it!"

This framework is easy enough to keep in mind in the heat of the moment, and it can help you see when you're moving in the wrong direction. Then next time you spot a metaphorical fly down and are tempted not to say anything, imagine where that puts you on the framework: Ruinous Empathy or Manipulative Insincerity? The little jolt might just move you toward Radical Candor.

When confronted with somebody who is really upset, really angry, or shutting down, most people retreat to Ruinous Empathy. A few hold their ground but defend themselves against this onslaught of emotion by ceasing to care, and therefore become obnoxiously aggressive. Even really well-intentioned people are sometimes tempted both to give ground and to quit caring, retreating to Manipulative Insincerity.

If you imagine what you're about to say and see that it's going to land in one of these bad quadrants, it will almost certainly move you toward Radical Candor. You already know how to be Radically Candid because you know how to care personally and to challenge directly.

From the moment you learned to speak, you started to challenge those around you. Then you were told some version of "If you don't have anything nice to say, don't say anything at all." Well, now it's your job to say it. And if you are a boss or a person in a position of some authority, it's not just your job. It's your moral obligation. *Just say it!*

You were also born with a capacity to connect, to care personally. Somehow the training you got to "be professional" made you repress that. Well, stop repressing your innate ability to care personally. *Give a damn!*

3

UNDERSTAND WHAT MOTIVATES EACH PERSON ON YOUR TEAM

Helping people take a step in the direction of their dreams

RETHINKING AMBITION

LET'S RETURN TO the "care personally" dimension of Radical Candor. In order to build a great team, you need to understand how each person's job fits into their life goals. You need to get to know each person who reports directly to you, to have real, human relationships—relationships that change as people change. When putting the right people in the right roles on your team, you'll also have to challenge people even more directly than you did with guidance—and in a way that will impact not just their feelings but also their income, their career growth, and their ability to get what they want out of life. Building a team is *hard*.

A leader at Apple had a good way to think about different types of ambition that people on her team had so that she could be thoughtful about what roles to put people in. To keep a team cohesive, you need both rock stars and superstars, she explained. Rock stars are solid as a rock. Think the Rock of Gibraltar, not Bruce Springsteen. The rock stars love their work. They have found their groove. They don't want the next job if it will take them away from their craft. Not all artists want to own a gallery; in fact, most don't. If you honor and reward the rock stars, they'll become the people you most rely on. If you promote them into roles they don't want or aren't suited for, however, you'll lose them—or, even worse, wind up firing them. Superstars, on the other hand, need to be challenged and given new opportunities to grow constantly.

In order to distinguish between the two, you must let go of your judgments and your own ambitions, forget for a while what you need from people, and focus on getting to know each person as a human being. For many bosses, this means rethinking ambition.

If I say a person is "ambitious," do you have a positive or a negative reaction? Do you assume the person is hell-bent on personal gain and slightly sinister, willing to trample others to achieve personal goals? Or do you assume that the person is responsible and gets things done, a force for positive change in the larger group?

If I say a person is "stable," what is your "blink" reaction? That the person is a snooze whom you'd rather not sit next to at a dinner party? Or do you get a sense of relief and comfort and think that this is the sort of person you'd like to have more of in your life? If I say a person is "content," what is your reaction? Do you admire that person? Would you like to be more that way yourself? Or do you assume this is someone who is going nowhere?

Now, let go of all these reactions and judgments. Look at the following two columns of words and think about *positive* examples of people you've worked with who would fall into each column. Think about teams you've worked on that have needed some of each and what the right ratio would be. Then think about times in your life when you've been in each of the columns and why. Ideally, the choice would have been yours and not your boss's.

STEEP GROWTH TRAJECTORY	GRADUAL GROWTH TRAJECTORY
Change agent	Force for stability
Ambitious at work	Ambitious outside of work or simply content in life
Want new opportunities	Happy in the current role
"Superstar"	"Rock Star"

Shortly after I joined Google, Larry Page told me about a time when he'd had a boss who was suspicious of ambition. While on a summer internship, Larry had been given an assignment that would have taken him a couple of days if he'd been given the freedom to do it his way. He explained the advantages of his approach to the boss, but the boss would have none of it: he insisted that Larry do it "the way they'd always done it." Instead of two days, Larry was forced to spend all summer working on the project. The wasted time and effort were pure torture for him. As most of us have, Larry discovered that a boss who held him back could make life miserable. "Three months of my life wasted and gone forever. I never want anyone at Google to have a boss like that. *Ever*," Larry told me once, and I saw he meant it by the way he led at Google. Larry went to great lengths to make sure bosses couldn't squash their employees' ideas and ambitions. I loved that about Google.

Now here's a story about a boss on a steep growth trajectory—me—who insisted that everybody share my ambitions, and how my experiences at Apple set me straight.

Unfortunately, for too long I believed that pushing everybody to grow super-fast was simply "best practice" for building a high-performing team. I was always looking for the best, the brightest, the brashest, and the most ambitious. For the first twenty years of my career, it never occurred to me that some people did not *want* the next, bigger job. When I designed *Managing at Apple*, an early iteration of the class encouraged managers to focus the lion's share of attention and resources on the most ambitious people on their teams, often to the detriment of people doing equally good work and happy to keep doing it—the backbone of a strong team. And, ironically, the kind of person I had become at that stage in my career.

Scott Forstall, who built the iOS team and worked directly for Steve Jobs, helped me understand that this approach was profoundly out of step with Apple's ethos—and, moreover, that it didn't create the optimal team.

We were discussing the performance-potential matrix that so many companies use for succession planning or "talent management." McKinsey & Company originally developed it to help General Electric decide which businesses to invest in, and HR departments at thousands of organizations have adapted it for talent management.* This matrix asks managers to assess both the performance and the potential of all employees and then put them into one of nine boxes—"high performance/high potential" being the best and "low performance/low potential" being the worst.

"'Potential' doesn't seem like the right word," I said. "I don't think there is any such thing as a low-potential human being." There was an idealistic side to my hard-charging approach to team-building.

"Words matter," Scott said. "Let's wrestle with it."

We debated it for some time. One problem with the "potential" category was that it didn't seem to allow for a positive evaluation of people who were great at what they did and wanted to keep doing it. Scott needed to keep people like that happy and productive, and he expected all the managers in his organization to do the same.

Scott proposed using the word "growth" instead of "potential," to help managers think about what opportunities to give to which people on their teams. Changing one word made a world of difference. Instead of asking an implicitly judgmental question like, "Is this a person with high or low potential?" we encouraged managers to ask themselves questions like, "What growth trajectory does each person on my team *want* to be on right now?" or "Have I given everybody opportunities that are in line with what they really want?" or "What growth trajectory do my direct reports believe they are on? Do I agree? And if I don't, why don't I?" Sometimes people really want to grow and are capable of contributing more than they have been allowed to; at other times, they simply want more money or recognition but don't really want to change the way they work or contribute any more than they do already. As the boss, you're the one who's going to have to know your direct reports well enough to make these distinctions and then have some Radically Candid conversations when you see things differently.

This set of questions around growth trajectory can help you discover what motivates each person much better than a set of questions around

---

* http://tomtunguz.com/nine-box-matrix-hr/.

"potential" or "talent" could. And the insights it produces will help you avoid burning out the rock stars and boring the superstars. These questions will help remind you that trajectories change and that you shouldn't put permanent labels on people. They will help you build stable teams that achieve astounding results.

Scott was right. Words matter.

GROWTH MANAGEMENT

It's getting better all the time

SHIFTING FROM A traditional "talent management" mind-set to one of "growth management" will help you make sure everyone on your team is moving in the direction of their dreams, ensuring that your team collectively improves over time. Creativity flourishes, efficiency improves, people enjoy working together.

You can use this "growth management" framework to clarify your thinking about how to manage the two different types of high performers—those on a steep growth trajectory and those on a more gradual growth trajectory—differently. It will remind you to help people conduct their careers in the way *they* desire, not in the way *you* think they should want to. You can also use it to remember to push *everyone* on a team toward excellent performance,

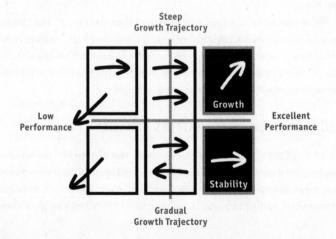

as well as to figure out whom to hire, whom to fire, and when a person's poor performance might just be the boss's (your) fault.

The most important thing you can do for your team collectively is to understand what growth trajectory each person wants to be on at a given time and whether that matches the needs and opportunities of the team. To do that, you are going to have to get to know each of your direct reports at a personal level. It's also going to require you to have some of the hardest conversations you'll ever have. Sometimes, you'll even have to fire people.

The axes of this framework are past performance and future growth trajectories. The assessment of past performance on the horizontal axis of this framework does go from "bad" to "good," but *not* the vertical axis. It's just as good to be in the bottom-right quadrant as in the upper-right. Rock stars are just as important to a team's performance as superstars. Stability is just as important as growth. The right mix of each will change over time, but you'll always need some of each.

When assessing a person's past performance, it's useful to consider both their results and more intangible things like "teamwork." The expected results for a given quarter or year are ideally set by the employee; they should be as objective and as measurable as possible. The intangibles are usually impossible to measure but not too hard to describe, and so expectations should be clear here as well. Performance is not a permanent label. No person is always an "excellent performer." They just performed excellently last quarter.

The past is much easier to understand than the future. The future is best described by each person's current "growth trajectory." Before considering how to manage each type of employee to ensure your team is cohesive, it's worth taking a little more time to understand exactly what I mean by "growth trajectory," and why it matters so much.

UNDERSTANDING WHAT MATTERS AND WHY

TO BE SUCCESSFUL at growth management, you need to find out what motivates each person on your team. You also need to learn what each person's long-term ambitions are, and understand how their current circumstances fit into their motivations and their life goals. Only when you get to know your direct reports well enough to know why they care about their work, what they hope to get out of their careers, and where they are in the present moment in time can you put the right people in the right roles and assign the right projects to the right people. (For a specific technique, see "Career Conversations," Chapter Seven.)

"Steep growth" is generally characterized by rapid change—learning new skills or deepening existing ones quickly. It's *not* about becoming a manager—plenty of individual contributors remain on a steep growth trajectory their entire careers, and plenty of managers are on a gradual growth trajectory. Nor should steep growth be thought of as narrowly as "promotion." It's about having an increased impact over time.

Gradual growth is characterized by stability. People on a gradual growth trajectory, who perform well, have generally mastered their work and are making incremental rather than sudden, dramatic improvements. Some roles may be better suited to a rock star because they require steadiness, accumulated knowledge, and an attention to detail that someone in a superstar phase might not have the focus or patience for.

People in a superstar phase are bad at rock star roles, and people in a rock star phase will hate a superstar role. The team of diamond cutters I managed in Russia—the guys I wrote about in chapter one who taught me to "care personally"—were master craftsmen, as skilled as anyone in the world. They were rock stars; they had no desire for my boss's job. My boss, Maurice Tempelsman, on the other hand, told a story about himself when he was a younger, extremely ambitious, restless man. As he was building his company, he decided to try his hand at diamond cutting. One day he got on the phone, started negotiating a big deal, got distracted, and ground a million-dollar diamond away to dust. True story. That's why you don't want a person on a steep-growth trajectory in a gradual-growth-trajectory job.

Most people shift between a steep growth trajectory and a gradual growth trajectory in different phases of their lives and careers, so it's important not to put a permanent label on people. For example, there were two aspiring Olympic athletes on my team at Google. Both women did great work, but right out of college, when they were at their athletic prime, they poured as much energy into training as into work. They were on a gradual growth trajectory at work, a steep growth trajectory in sports. Five years later, both pivoted, pouring all that drive and energy into their careers rather than into sports. Their career trajectories rocketed.

Of course, most of us aren't aspiring Olympic athletes. I certainly am not. There are lots of reasons why people shift between a gradual and a steep growth trajectory, and circumstances that spur one person to do one thing spur another person to do the opposite. Take having a child. Sometimes the financial burden of parenthood spurs ambition; sometimes the desire to get home in time to play with young children spurs a desire for more predictability. Sometimes an ill relative requires a person to get on a more gradual growth trajectory but, when the illness passes, ambition kicks back in. Generally, an ambition or a commitment outside of work enhances a person's value to the team—that means you get, say, a great artist as your graphic designer, as long as you don't insist that the artist get on the fast track at work.

THE PROBLEM WITH "PASSION"

IT'S A BASIC axiom that people do better work when they find that work meaningful. I don't disagree with this basic premise. However, bosses who take this to mean that it is their job to provide purpose tend to overstep. Insisting that people have passion for their job can place unnecessary pressure on both boss and employee. I struggled with this at Google, where we were hiring people right out of college to do dull customer-support work. I tried convincing them that we were "funding creativity a nickel at a time." One young woman who'd studied philosophy in college, called BS immediately. "Look, the job is a little boring," she said. "Let's just admit that. It's OK. Plutarch laid bricks. Spinoza ground lenses. Tedium is part of life." I loved her approach to finding meaning, but it was unique to her. A slogan like "Spinoza ground lenses" would not have been inspiring for the broader team.

In a burst of Radical Candor, *Financial Times* writer Lucy Kellaway explained why she chose to work for the companies she did: "I went for JPMorgan and later for the *FT* because they were the only companies offering me a job. It seemed a great reason to pick them then. It is still a great reason today."*

---

* http://www.ft.com/cms/s/0/0ccb0658-596a-11e6-9f70-badea1b336d4.html?siteedition=intl#axzz4Gx OrK1Bg.

There's nothing wrong with working hard to earn a paycheck that supports the life you want to lead. That has plenty of meaning. A wise man once told me, "Only about five percent of people have a real vocation in life, and they confuse the hell out of the rest of us." Trying to describe a job in lofty, save-the-world terms is often going to make you look like the ridiculous Hooli CEO Gavin Belson from the show *Silicon Valley*. Which brings us back to the main point of this chapter: your job is not to provide purpose but instead to get to know each of your direct reports well enough to understand how each one derives meaning from their work.

A story about Christopher Wren, the architect responsible for rebuilding St. Paul's Cathedral after the Great Fire of London, explains what I mean. Wren was walking the length of the partially rebuilt cathedral when he asked three bricklayers what they were doing. The first bricklayer responded, "I'm working." The second said, "I'm building a wall." The third paused, looked up, and then said, "I'm building a cathedral to the Almighty."

Many people use this story to celebrate the person who has a sense of vision and can imagine his individual efforts as part of a grand collective enterprise. In current-day Silicon Valley, inspirational slogans run more along the lines of "putting a ding in the universe," as Steve Jobs put it. But motivations are highly personal. Although I admire Jobs, it seems to me that the universe, or at least our world, is plenty dinged up already. So, I don't find his call to put a "ding in the universe" inspirational, though others do. Sure, it's a boss's job to put the team's work in context, and if you share why the work gives *you* meaning, that can help others find their own inspiration. But remember, it's not all about you.

For me, the most instructive part of Wren's story is that he didn't come up with a sense of purpose himself and pound it into everyone's head. Each bricklayer cared about something different, even though all three were working on the same thing. Wren's role was to listen, to recognize the significance of what he heard, and to create working conditions that allowed everybody to find meaning in their own way.

EXCELLENT PERFORMANCE

Keep your top performers top of mind

BEFORE DELVING INTO the differences between how to manage rock stars or superstars, it's useful to focus on what *both* need from you. Your role is to

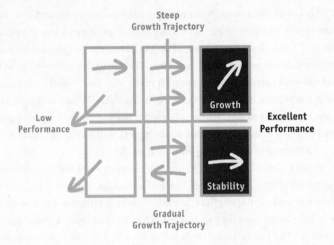

focus on them and to make sure they are getting everything they need to continue doing great work.

Be a partner, not an absentee manager or a micromanager

One of the most common mistakes bosses make is to ignore the people who are doing the best work because "they don't need me" or "I don't want to micromanage." Ignoring somebody is a terrible way to build a relationship.

Some management bloviators will advise you simply to hire the right people and then leave them alone. Dick Costolo, Twitter's CEO from 2010–2015, explained succinctly how crazy this advice is. "That's like saying, to have a good marriage, marry the right person and then avoid spending any time with them. Ridiculous, right?" he exclaimed. "Imagine if I went home and told my wife, 'I don't want to micromanage you, so I'm not going to spend any time with you or the kids this year.'"

The "choose and ignore" strategy is just as crazy for management as it is for marriage. If you don't take the time to get to know the people who get the best results, you can't understand how they want and *need* to be growing in their jobs at that particular moment in their lives. You'll assign the wrong tasks to the wrong people. You'll promote the wrong people. Also, if you ignore your top performers, you won't give them the guidance they need. Every minute you spend with somebody who does great work pays off in the team's results much more than time spent with somebody who's failing. Ignore these people and you won't, in short, be *managing*.

You don't want to be an absentee manager any more than you want to be a micromanager. Instead, you want to be a partner—that is, you must take the time to help the people doing the best work overcome obstacles and make their good work even better. This is time-consuming because it requires that you know enough about the details of the person's work to understand the nuances. It often requires you to *help do* the work, rather than just advising. It requires that you ask a lot of questions and challenge people—that you roll up your own sleeves.

Managers often devote more time to those who are struggling than to those who are succeeding. But that's not fair to those who are succeeding—nor is it good for the team as a whole. Moving from great to stunningly great is more inspiring for everyone than moving from bad to mediocre. And seeing what truly exceptional performance looks like will help those who are failing to see more clearly what's expected of them.

EXCELLENT PERFORMANCE/GRADUAL GROWTH TRAJECTORY

Recognize, reward, but don't promote

FOR MOST OF my career, I was all about finding and rewarding people who were breaking the sound barrier of achievement. Then one day, in 2008, I realized *I* was the one now on a gradual growth trajectory at work. A Twitter board member came to ask me if I wanted to interview to be the company's new CEO. That was the kind of role I would have given my left arm to have had a couple of years earlier. But at that moment in my life, I was interested in a very different kind of growth. I was forty years old, pregnant with twins, and it was a high-risk pregnancy. When I consulted my doctor about this stressful new opportunity, she advised me, "Just ask yourself which is more important: this job or the hearts and lungs of your children?"

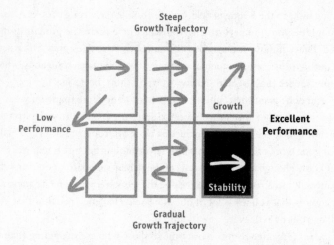

Enough said. What mattered most to me at that moment was not growth at Twitter or my career growth at Google, but the tiny creatures growing inside of me. And with its delicious healthy food at every turn and the maternal massage therapist one floor up from my office and a lap pool for the swims my doctor recommended, Google was still the *perfect* place for a high-risk pregnancy. I didn't need to quit, but I did I need to stay on a more gradual growth trajectory at work. I was able to continue to lead the AdSense, DoubleClick, and YouTube teams, but I was not able to push for the next job. And so I stayed where I was, carried the twins to term, and gave birth to two healthy babies. For the rest of my life, I'll be grateful to Google for affording me that opportunity.

I am not saying that other pregnant women can't be fully committed CEOs—many have proven it's possible. I'm just saying I couldn't. It wasn't till the twins turned seven that I felt I had the capacity to get back on a steep growth trajectory and start a company. I am also not saying that parents (men have children, too) of toddlers can't found a company or be on a super-steep growth trajectory. I'm not even saying I couldn't. I'm just saying that I didn't want to. I am also not saying that having children is the most common reason for people to get on a more gradual growth trajectory. Your people might not look at all like me: they might look more like Einstein in the patent office or T. S. Eliot in the bank.

What I am saying is we *all* have periods in our lives when our professional growth speeds up or slows down. Recreation is essential for creation. Just as there is nothing inherently ignoble about ambition, there is no shame in being in the same job for many years. We all need a bit of both growth and stability in our lives and on our teams. Unfortunately, even though I was living that reality, I still didn't fully respect it. Instead of expanding my viewpoint after having my children, I began looking down on myself the way I had looked down on others earlier in my career. "That which does not grow, rots," said Catherine the Great. Rather than recognizing the whole person—*my* whole person, who was growing and changing every day, along with my twins—I was deeply afraid I'd begun to rot.

In other words, I still believed that pushing everybody to grow was best practice for building a team. As I described above, when I left Google and went to Apple, both the company in general and Scott Forstall in particular helped clarify my thinking. But I *still* didn't fully accept it in my heart of hearts. It was on a day I stayed home from work with my toddler son that I finally learned the lesson deep in my gut. He had a 104-degree fever and was too listless to do anything other than watch *The Lorax*, the film adaptation of the Dr. Seuss book. The Lorax's advice to the Onceler in the "biggering" song finally brought the lesson home:

I'm figuring on biggering!
But that biggering's just triggering more biggering!

As my son's fever broke, I realized that not only was my blind obsession with growth misaligned with my personal humanity, it wasn't even the best way to build a great team. When I looked back over my career, I thought with shame about the considerable number of people I'd undervalued or dismissed. This moment radically altered my personal approach to the rest of my career.

In an almost poetic twist of fate, it was Dick Costolo, the CEO who took Twitter public, who gave me the opportunity that allowed me to write this book and spend more time with my toddlers. He asked me to help him design a class, *Managing at Twitter*. I was happy to do so, and after we'd worked together on it, he asked me if I wanted to interview for a big operating role on his team. As I went through the interview process, it became clear to both of us that I didn't have the energy at that time in my life for the role. He asked me if I'd be interested in becoming his coach instead: a cushy one-hour-every-other-week gig. Dick's ability to help identify the perfect role for me at that time in my life has made an enormous difference in my career. It not only allowed me to be on a gradual growth trajectory at work when I wanted to write and be with my kids, it also set me up perfectly for when I was ready to shift gears again.

What's the best way to manage rock stars, the people whom you can count on to deliver great results year after year? You need to recognize them to keep them happy. For too many bosses, "recognition" means "promotion." But in most cases, this is a big mistake. Promotion often puts these people in roles they are not as well-suited for or don't want. The key is to recognize their contribution in other ways. It may be a bonus or a raise. Or, if they like public speaking, get them to present at your all-hands meetings or other big events. If they like teaching, get them to help new people learn their roles faster. Or if they are shy, make sure that you and others on the team thank them privately for the work they do. Consider, carefully, tenure awards. If your organization gives performance ratings and/or bonuses, make sure they are fair to the rock stars.

Fair performance ratings

In some companies, rock stars don't get the performance review they deserve because all the top ratings are reserved for people who are in line to get promoted. A lot of companies ration the number of top ratings. Avoiding "grade inflation" is a good idea. However, an unintended consequence is often that rock stars get lower ratings than they should. In fact, *all* of your top performers should get top ratings. When performance ratings have an impact on compensation, this is especially important.

If one person is doing much better work than others on the team, it seems obvious they should get a better rating and a higher bonus. But when ratings are primarily used to justify future promotions, rather than to recognize past performance, this doesn't happen.

Recognition

In addition to top ratings, a great way to recognize people in a rock star phase is to designate them as "gurus," or "go-to" experts. Often this means putting them in charge of teaching newer team members, if they show the aptitude for it. Bosses can be reluctant to use a top performer this way, wanting them to do the job rather than to teach others. However, this attitude prevents an organization from getting as much leverage out of experts as they otherwise would.

In World War II, the U.S. Air Force took their very best pilots from the front lines and sent them home to train new pilots. Over time this strategy dramatically improved the quality and effectiveness of the U.S. Air Force. The Germans lost their air superiority because they flew all their aces until they were shot down; none of them trained new recruits. By 1944 new German pilots had clocked only about half of the three hundred hours an Allied pilot would have flown in training.

Too many companies hire people for training whom they would never hire to do the actual job. Or, worse, rather than fire people who are not performing well in a particular role, they send them off to teach others how to do it. This sounds absurd, but I've seen that very thing happen at some great companies. This kind of blind-leading-the-blind practice gives training a bad name. Generally, people who are great at a job enjoy teaching it to others; giving them this role can not only improve the performance of the whole team but also give the rock stars a different sort of recognition.

Of course, some people hate teaching and are terrible at it: this role should be an honor, not a requirement. And there are times when being *the* go-to expert might drive a person off the team because the person hates being interrupted with questions all day long. So be sensitive to that. But if a person enjoys teaching and answering questions, by all means encourage and reward them for doing it.

Of all the companies I know well, Apple did the best job of creating a great environment for people in a rock star phase. The company's organizational design optimized for deep functional expertise. There were no "general managers." There was no iPhone division. Instead, there were operating system engineers, camera experts, audiophiles, and glass gurus who came together around the iPhone. There were always people around who knew some functional aspect of the product more deeply than anyone else, and they were revered for it.

I was struck by the deference given to people who had been in a particular role for years at Apple. At Google and many other Silicon Valley companies, being in the same role for too long was a badge of shame. Some companies even have a so-called "up or out" policy and *fire* these people. Steve

Jobs, on the other hand, paid close attention to retention and talked warmly about people who'd been with Apple for a long time.

This focus on tenure at Apple was confusing to me at first, because I tended to think of tenure rewards as something that happened at traditional companies or in academia, not at fast-growing tech companies. I realized, though, that honoring tenure was an important alternative to promotions for people who'd been doing the same job for years. Apple gave framed awards to people at the five-, ten-, fifteen-, and twenty-year marks. Then Jony Ive, Apple's chief design officer, designed a leaded glass plaque, vapor-honed for an especially beautiful finish, with Apple's logo etched into it. Everyone who'd been at the company for more than ten years got one. Plenty of bloggers have mocked this award, but there are several things that made it work at Apple. It was reflective of the company's design aesthetic, so it wasn't just a random gold watch. Leaders at the company invested personally in it. These awards were presented by leaders who knew the work of the recipient well. And the award was presented at a team meeting or other venue that would give the person public recognition. For most people who received it, the award had meaning and personal significance.

Respect

Before T. S. Eliot was able to make a living as a publisher, he was a clerk at Lloyd's Bank. Eliot's boss once said, patronizingly, that if Eliot played his cards right, he might even be lucky enough to become a branch manager. Of course, Eliot was focused on writing poetry that would eventually win him a Nobel Prize, not on becoming a branch manager. He needed a steady income and a steady job so that he could go home in the evenings and write. If Eliot's boss had wanted to retain him, he should have figured out how to let him leave an hour earlier each day, not encouraged him to put in the extra effort that a promotion would likely entail.

Life is so much better when people are great at their work and love it. The idea of climbing a corporate ladder is not inspiring to plenty of people. And yet those on a gradual growth trajectory are often referred to pejoratively as "B-players," or as having "capped out."

To manage these people well, it's obviously important to reject these derogatory characterizations. Those who find work they can continue to love for five or ten or thirty years, even if it doesn't lead to some sort of advancement, are damn lucky. And their teams and their bosses are lucky to have them. Kick-ass bosses never judge people doing great work as having "capped out." Instead, they treat them with the honor that they are due and retain the individuals who will keep their team stable, cohesive, and productive.

The dangers of promotion obsession

Let's look at what happens when bosses promote when they shouldn't. One result is described hilariously in Laurence J. Peter's book *The Peter Principle*. The Peter Principle results in people getting promoted beyond their level of competence—an unhappy situation for everyone, especially the person who's been promoted.

Another version of the bad promotion occurs when people are competent for the next job but have no desire to do it at that moment in their lives. I once had a colleague who'd planned carefully so that when he had his first baby he was in a job that he'd mastered and thus could get home to be with his newborn. His boss, however, had different plans for him: a promotion. When informed of his promotion, the man declined it. When told it wasn't optional, he quit. What a waste.

Don't do this to your rock stars!

PART OF BUILDING a cohesive team is to create a culture that recognizes and rewards the rock stars. I'm afraid for most of my career I treated them like second-class citizens. I'm grateful that my experiences at Apple set me straight.

EXCELLENT PERFORMANCE/ STEEP GROWTH TRAJECTORY

Keep superstars challenged

WHEN I THINK of people who are in superstar mode, I think of Catharine Burhenne and David Sanderson.

I first met Catharine when she interviewed for a job babysitting our twin infants. The twins were immediately comfortable with Catharine, and I hired her on the spot. However, what she really wanted was not a babysitting gig, but a job at Google. I loved having Catharine taking care of our children, but I knew my job was to encourage her to pursue her dreams, not to try to keep her in her current role. I helped her get an interview, and she

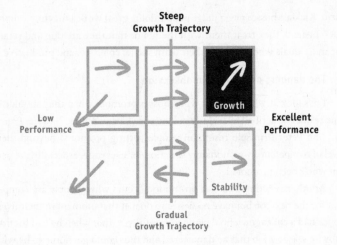

**Steep
Growth Trajectory**

Low
Performance

Growth

Excellent
Performance

Stability

Gradual
Growth Trajectory

got a job there; then Facebook hired her away from Google, and then Twitter hired her away from Facebook.

When I first met David, he, too, was babysitting my twins. He was spending the summer in Silicon Valley to be with Catharine, whom he was dating, and trying to figure out what to do with his life. When I asked him what he loved to do, he talked about music. I learned from Catharine—he was too modest to tell me—that he didn't just love music, he was the top-rated pianist in Canada in his age bracket. I asked him if he wanted to be a professional musician, and he said no, because the financial sacrifices he'd have to make were just too great. I wished I could tell him to follow his passion, but I was sympathetic—I love writing novels but would never try to support my family that way.

Meanwhile our sprinkler system was going haywire. I certainly had no expectation that David would fix the irrigation pipes as well as take care of the children; I myself often could not find time to take a shower when I was watching them on the weekends. But David went to the hardware store after work one night and figured out how to fix the whole thing the next day while the twins were napping. I was beginning to get the picture: David noticed when things were broken and rolled up his sleeves to fix them, even if they weren't in his job description. I asked him what job he'd had that he enjoyed.

He'd loved all his jobs. When he worked at a shop in Vancouver, he not only became the top salesperson but he improved the shop's inventory system, decreasing wait time; improved customer satisfaction; and increased sales for all the salespeople, not just himself. Clearly David would always push for excellence in his work, no matter what job he had. He would not just do more than was required; he'd do things you didn't even think were possible. He exemplified the advice from Ecclesiastes: "Whatsoever thy hand findeth to do, do it with thy might."

I also knew that as much as I loved having David around, it was my job to help him keep growing. I made introductions for him, edited his résumé, and did a practice interview with him. He got himself a job at Facebook and, to no one's surprise, set the company record for the most promotions the fastest.

Catharine and David went on to live the Silicon Valley dream. They've started a company, ReelGood, that makes it much faster and easier to figure out what movie or TV show to watch.

Here's some advice about what to do when you are lucky enough to have people like Catharine and David on your team:

Keep them challenged (and figure out who'll replace them when they move on)

The best way to keep superstars happy is to challenge them and make sure they are constantly learning. Give them new opportunities, even when it is sometimes more work than seems feasible for one person to do. Figure out what the next job for them will be. Build an intellectual partnership with them. Find them mentors from outside your team or organization—people who have even more to offer than you do. But make sure you don't get too dependent on them; ask them to teach others on the team to do their job, because they won't stay in their existing role for long. I often thought of these people as shooting stars—my team and I were lucky to have them in our orbit for a little while, but trying to hold them there was futile.

Don't squash them or block them

It's vital not to "squash" these people. Recognize that you'll probably be working for them one day, and celebrate that fact. When I first hired Jared Smith to be a product manager at Juice, I quickly realized that I'd be lucky if he one day returned the favor. Sure enough, a decade later he hired me as an executive coach and board member at Qualtrics, the company he cofounded with his brother. I'm working not just for Jared but for his whole family.

Of all the companies I've worked for, Google did the best job of putting safeguards in place so that managers couldn't curb the ambitions of their direct reports. This was directly tied to the company's efforts to limit the power of managers to quash rather than accelerate the careers of people on a steep growth trajectory. For example, consider the promotion process that Shona Brown, SVP of Business Operations, designed at Google. Bosses at Google can't simply promote people on their teams at their own discretion. In engineering, managers can encourage or discourage a person from pursuing another job, and they can lobby for the person or not, but people nominate *themselves* for promotion, and a committee makes the decision. Once a "promotion packet" consisting of a list of accomplishments and recommendations has been assembled, a committee reads it and decides if the promotion should go through. The manager is not on that committee. The manager can appeal a decision, but the manager is not the decider. This prevents managers from curbing the ambition of their direct reports or from offering promotions to reward personal loyalty rather than great work.

Google also makes it pretty easy for people to seek new opportunities by transferring from one team to another team. No boss can "block" such a transfer. I once took a person onto my team who had convinced me that he was great but that his boss had it out for him—despite the fact that he had received terrible ratings. Nobody tried to stop this from happening. And that was a good thing because on our team, this person thrived. Allowing transfers is important because it prevents bosses from blackballing employees who want to move on, and allows for the fact that sometimes two people just don't work that well together.

Google didn't get everything right, though. There was a crazy-strict rule in Product Management that you had to have a computer science degree to join the team. Many people wanted to transfer to Product because they had ideas they wanted to pursue, but they were prevented because they didn't have the right degree. One was Biz Stone who, stymied by the rule, left Google to cofound Twitter. Another was Ben Silbermann, who, similarly blocked, left Google to found Pinterest. Kevin Systrom also left Google to cofound Instagram when he couldn't join the PM team because of his college degree.

Not every superstar wants to manage

Lack of interest in managing is not the same thing as being on a gradual growth trajectory, just as interest in managing is not the same thing as being on a steep growth trajectory. Management and growth should not be conflated.

Imagine if Albert Einstein had been told, just as he was developing his theory of relativity, that he needed to stop spending so much time alone with his work and instead take on management responsibilities for a team of people. The result would have been a frustrated Einstein, a demoralized and poorly managed team, and a great loss to humanity's understanding of the universe.

Yet a version of this happens all the time. The careers of many great engineers and salespeople have foundered when they are promoted to manager. Why does this happen? Because there's no other role to promote them to that acknowledges the kind of growth trajectory they want to be on.

This points to another problem with the language used in the traditional performance-potential matrix. Often the matrix is not just analyzing "potential" but "leadership potential." The unintended consequence of this is that whole armies of people systematically cap the careers of others who are on a steep growth trajectory but who don't want to become managers. This in turn systematically caps the rewards that can be given to people who are more interested in deepening their expertise and advancing human knowledge rather than being a boss. Don't get me wrong—I believe great management is important. But it's certainly not the only path to major impact.

Google's engineering teams solved this problem by creating an "individual contributor" career path that is more prestigious than the manager path and sidesteps management entirely. This has been great for the growth of these engineers; it's also good for the people whom they would otherwise have been managing. When people become bosses just to "get ahead" rather than because they want to do what bosses do, they perform, at best, a perfunctory job and often become bosses from hell.

When management is the only path to higher compensation, the quality of management suffers, and the lives of the people who work for these reluctant managers become miserable.

MANAGING THE MIDDLE

Raise the bar—there's no such thing as a B-player

AS I SAID above, I do not believe there is any such thing as a "B-player" or a mediocre human being. Everyone can be excellent at *something*. That's very different from saying anyone can be good at anything—definitely not true. And this brings me to the people who just aren't that good at a job, or are treading water.

Sadly, lots of people never find work they are truly excellent at because they stay in the wrong job so long that any change would require a step or two backward. They may have come to depend on the prestige and money of the current position, and feel pressure from family to keep it. Bosses keep this kind of employee on for several reasons: they're not sure they can find someone better; it takes time and effort to train new people; and they like the person and feel it would be unfair to encourage them to find a job they are better suited for.

This lack of courage and energy leads to a tremendous loss of human potential—to lives of quiet desperation. Assuming that people who are not thriving are therefore "mediocre" and can't do any better is both unjust and unkind. Allowing them to continue down that path may be the worst case of Ruinous Empathy that managers regularly display and a great source of

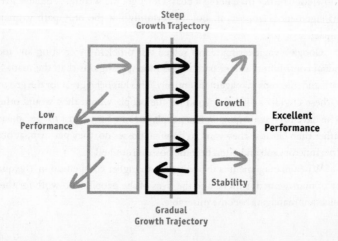

wasted possibility. Of course, treating these people fairly requires that you know them well enough to understand why they aren't thriving; if they are simply going through a rough period, it's better to give them the time and space to recover than to push for more than they have to give just then.

One of the least popular things I did with my teams at Google was to insist that people who had not done exceptional work for more than two years be given an opportunity to work on a project that would let them shine. If their work still continued to be mediocre, we began encouraging these people to look for jobs elsewhere.

This policy was hard to enforce and created a lot of stress. It was the managers who minded it the most, because it forced them to have a lot of challenging conversations and to push those who reported to them really hard. Of course, it was also difficult for people who'd been doing OK for a couple of years to get pushed out of their comfort zone. But I don't believe that it created as much misery for them as being labeled permanently "mediocre" would have.

I did it because I believed that everyone can be exceptional somewhere and that it was my job to help them find that role. I also believed that we should strive to have 100 percent of the team doing exceptional work. If somebody hadn't proven in the course of two years that they could do exceptional work, they almost certainly would never get there. It was time to help them find a job where they could shine and time for us to start looking to replace them with somebody who could shine on our team. For some people, that meant leaving Google to do something more in line with their dreams—like becoming a teacher or landscape architect, or opening a tea shop. In other cases, people went on to do similar work but at smaller companies where they could be more of a jack-of-all-trades. Sometimes, people just needed to be thrown out of the nest to spread their wings. In all cases, the people wound up much happier, even though making a change was hard.

In many ways, your job as the boss is to set and uphold a quality bar. That can feel harsh in the short term, but in the long run the only thing that is meaner is lowering the bar. Don't get sucked into Ruinous Empathy when managing people who are doing OK but not great! Everybody can excel somewhere. And to build a great team that achieves exceptional results, everybody needs to be doing great work. Accepting mediocrity isn't good for anybody.

POOR PERFORMANCE/
NEGATIVE GROWTH TRAJECTORY

Part ways

WHEN SOMEBODY IS performing poorly and, having received clear communication about the nature of the problem, is showing no signs of improvement, you must fire that person. How you do it goes a long way to defining your long-term success as a boss, because it sends a clear signal to everyone on your team whether or not you truly care about people for more than what they can do for you on the job.

It goes without saying that getting fired is one of the most soul-challenging things that can happen to a person. Its effects are bad enough for the people themselves, and they ripple out to their families in the form of financial difficulties, loss of medical benefits, marriage troubles, and, worst of all, the strain of seeing someone you love suffer.

The knowledge that you are about to inflict some measure of suffering on someone you may care a lot about obviously makes actually doing it very hard. I once talked to a crazy-successful New Yorker who seemed far more brash than compassionate about firing people. He told me that on mornings when he was going to fire somebody, he always woke up in a cold sweat. I

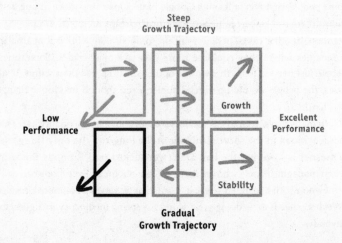

hadn't known that anything could make him sweat! If *he* felt bad, no wonder I did, and no wonder you do, too. So we avoid it at all costs—again, with negative consequences for everyone. So you need to approach firing thoughtfully and deliberately.

How do you know when it's time to fire somebody?

Let's say that someone on your team, "Peggy," is terrible at her job, not getting any better, or even getting worse. Is it time to fire her? There's no absolute answer to that question, but here are three questions to consider: have you given her Radically Candid guidance, do you understand the impact of Peggy's performance on her colleagues, and have you sought advice from others?

Have you given Radically Candid guidance? Have you demonstrated to Peggy that you care personally about her work and her life, and have you been crystal clear when you have challenged her to improve? Has your praise been substantive and specific about what she has done right, rather than simply a salve to her ego? Have you been humble as well as direct in your criticism, offering to help her find solutions rather than attacking her as a person? And have you done these things on multiple occasions over the course of time? If the answer is yes and you have not seen improvement, or have seen only flickers of improvement, it's time. Remember—the definition of insanity is continuing to do the same thing and expecting different results.

How is this person's poor performance affecting the rest of the team? Peggy's shortcomings aren't only your problem. As a manager, it's your job to make sure you understand everyone else's perspective, as well, and how her poor performance affects other members of the team. Generally, by the time one of your direct report's poor performance has come to your attention, it's been driving their peers nuts for a long time.

Have you sought out a second opinion, spoken to someone whom you trust and with whom you can talk the problem through? Sometimes you may think you've been clear when you haven't been. Getting an outside perspective can help you make sure you're being fair. Also, if you don't have experience firing somebody, talk to somebody who does. In today's world, most companies have strict guidelines that must be followed when someone is being fired, and there are lots of legal "gotcha"s that can consume tons of time down the road if you're not careful.

Common lies managers tell themselves to avoid firing somebody who needs to be fired

Managers almost always wait too long to fire people. Being too cautious may be preferable to being too hasty, but I'd say that most managers wait *far* too long to do it because they have fooled themselves into believing that it's unnecessary. Below are four common "lies" managers tell themselves to avoid firing somebody:

1. *It will get better.* But of course it won't get better all by itself. So stop and ask yourself: *how*, exactly, will it get better? What are you going to do differently? What will the person in question do differently? How might circumstances change? Even if things have gotten a little better, have they improved enough? If you don't have a pretty precise answer to those questions, it probably won't get better.

2. *Somebody is better than nobody.* Another common reason why bosses are reluctant to fire a poor performer is that they don't want a "hole" on the team. If you fire "Jeffrey," who will do the work he was doing? How long will it take you to find a replacement? The fact is that poor performers often create as much extra work for others as they accomplish themselves, because they leave parts of their job undone or do other parts sloppily or behave unprofessionally in ways that others must compensate for. Steve Jobs put it succinctly, if harshly, when he said, "It's better to have a hole than an asshole."

3. *A transfer is the answer.* Because firing people is so very hard, it's often tempting to instead pass them off to an unsuspecting colleague at your company, even if they don't have skills your colleague needs or are a poor cultural fit. It feels "nicer" than firing them. This is obviously not so nice for the unsuspecting colleague and is generally a mistake for the person you're trying to be "nice" to as well.

4. *It's bad for morale.* It's also tempting to tell yourself that you're not firing somebody because doing so would discourage the team. But keeping someone on who can't do the job is far worse for morale—yours, the person who's doing a crummy job, and everyone

else who's doing a great job. Again, this comes down to having built a good relationship with the person you're firing, and the rest of the team. It comes back to having demonstrated that you care personally.

Be Radically Candid with the person you're firing

The way you fire people really matters, and to do this hard job well, it's important not to distance yourself from the person you're about to fire. If you try to avoid feeling the pain that is inherent in the situation, especially for the person you're firing, you'll make a hash of it. To be in the right frame of mind, remember the following:

1. *Recall a job you were terrible at and think how glad you feel that you're no longer in it.* One summer in high school I got a job as a bank teller. I don't do math well in my head, and so I often counted out the wrong change. Since customers generally caught errors in the bank's favor but weren't always honest when they came out ahead, I gave away a lot of the bank's money. My boss did not fire me. Instead, she said, "You can do this! If you just *try*, if you just *focus*, you can balance *every day*!" Now what had just been a math problem felt like a character flaw. But the harder I tried, the worse I became. Still my boss continued to cheer me on. I was miserable. I should have quit and gotten a job mowing grass. If my boss had simply fired me by saying, "You are clearly not interested in this work. Why don't you find a different job this summer?" she'd have done me a big favor—and saved the bank a lot of money. Instead, I suffered and muddled through until the summer's end. But what if it had been a permanent job and I had stayed on indefinitely?

   When you fire someone, you create the possibility for the person to excel and find happiness performing meaningful work elsewhere. Part of getting a good job is leaving a bad one, or one that's bad for you. As my grandmother once said to me, "There's a lid for every pot." Just because the person is not good at the job they do for you doesn't mean there isn't another job out there they could be great at. I know that this can sound very Pollyanna-ish, so before our meeting, I try to imagine specifically what that job might be. I also try to reframe the problem, for both me and the person I'm firing: it's not the person who sucks, it's the job that sucks—at least for this person. What job would be great for that person? Can I help by making an introduction?

2. *Retaining people who are doing bad work penalizes the people doing excellent work*. Failing to deal with a performance issue is not fair to the rest of the team. Work undone generally winds up getting picked up by the top performers, overburdening them. In practice, morale has always *improved* once I've removed a poor performer, whereas I've sometimes lost the people I most wanted to keep by hanging on to a low performer for too long. Retaining a bad boss is especially damaging, because bad bosses have such a negative impact on the people who report to them. This is the opposite of managerial leverage.

    As I'm writing these words, a senior leader I know is putting off firing a bad manager who substitutes yelling for a knowledge of the facts. One person working under that manager is developing hives; another has not slept well in months. And still the process drags on. The manager in question suspects that it is only a matter of time until they get fired, so the whole situation is like a strange game of cat and mouse. Nothing about the situation is "nice" to anyone involved!

LOW PERFORMANCE/STEEP GROWTH TRAJECTORY

Manager, look at yourself in the mirror!

ONE OF THE most perplexing management dilemmas is when a person who ought to be taking on more and more and getting better every day is instead screwing up or just doing a lousy job. I've seen this happen for five different reasons that are worth parsing.

Wrong role

Sometimes you will put a great person into the wrong job. That is why I call this the "look at yourself in the mirror" quadrant—if you put somebody in the wrong role, their poor performance is actually your fault. When this is the case, you want to put the person in a better role.

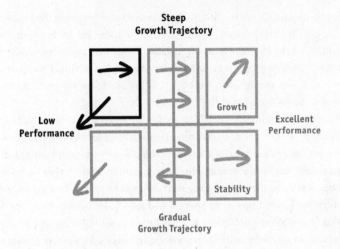

Steep
Growth Trajectory

Growth

Low
Performance

Excellent
Performance

Stability

Gradual
Growth Trajectory

For example, I once put "Mareva," who was one of the best leaders I've ever worked with, on the hardest challenge we faced as a team. The decision seemed obvious: you match up the people doing the best work with your hardest problems and the problems get solved. Right? Not so in this case. Mareva was a great leader of people, and she shone when she was managing a large team. Her new job, though, was to manage a tiny team. The potential was huge but the reality was small. Time passed, but the team wasn't getting any closer to realizing the potential business opportunity. The team seemed demoralized, and Mareva seemed, well, bored. Disengaged. I asked her if she was having issues in her personal life. She said no. I pushed her to try harder. Nothing changed, so I gave her the lowest rating she'd ever gotten and then a lower one the next quarter. I talked with Mareva in detail about why things weren't going well; she didn't disagree with me, but she had no good explanation. I grew increasingly frustrated and began to worry about her career prospects.

But then it dawned on me; the problem I'd asked her to solve was an analytical one. The sort of person best suited to solve this problem would be spending 75 percent of their time alone in an office crunching numbers. But Mareva's real gift was that she was a kick-ass boss. I had her stuck in her office with spreadsheets, where she wasn't really exercising her talent, instead of with people. When I shared my revelation with her, the relief on her face was enormous. Of course, Mareva had known in her gut what the problem was, but she hadn't wanted to offer excuses or blame me for her poor performance. Happily, there was a big, meaty management challenge involving several hundred people on another team that needed solving. I put Mareva on it and, sure enough, she was back to being one of the top performers—not just on my team but at the company.

Another example. "Clay" led a team in a particular country, call it "Atlantis," where he was an enormously effective leader and had also grown revenue faster than anyone else. He wanted a growth opportunity, and I positioned him to take over another, bigger team in Atlantis. However, Clay really wanted to move on to a regional role, and he approached me about it when one opened up on my team. I had significant doubts about the fit because this job required great political finesse, a skill Clay had not demonstrated—to his credit as far as I was concerned—but which was necessary to perform successfully in this particular role. I shared my concerns frankly with him, but he persisted until I gave in. Almost as soon as he had assumed his new role, however, he grabbed a political hot potato and got burned.

It's not always clear when you are giving people an opportunity to grow and when you are sending them into the lion's den, but in this case I made a bad call. I put Clay in the wrong role. Unfortunately, I left the company and Clay was eventually fired. I didn't have the opportunity to look myself in the mirror, and Clay took the fall for my mistake, which I've always felt terrible about. (Fortunately, he's gone on to become an enormously successful entrepreneur in Atlantis.)

New to role; too much too fast

Obviously when you hire someone who has never done a job before and they have to learn it from scratch, they sometimes take longer than expected to progress. If the person gives you reason to believe they can be great in the role, if they show signs of "spiking," it's worth investing more. But sometimes it isn't that obvious.

In these cases, it can help to ask yourself these questions: are expectations clear enough? Is the training good enough? If the problem is that *you* have not explained the role or the expectations clearly enough, you should invest more time to do so if you think the person can become a kick-ass employee.

Another mistake that bosses sometimes make is to dump too much on a person all at once, setting them up to fail. Sometimes managers simply have unreasonable expectations about what one human being can do. Other times, managers map their own capacity onto the people who work for them. They forget that a person with ten years less experience than they have simply doesn't know certain things.

Personal problems

Sometimes people who have been on a tear in their careers suddenly stop performing well because they are having a personal issue. If the problem is a temporary one, it's best simply to give such people the time they need to get back on track.

I had a family crisis while I was working for Sheryl Sandberg. I will always be grateful for her response: "Get on a plane, go home, take all the time you need, and don't worry about anything at Google. Don't count this as your vacation time—just take the time. We have you covered." Her words left me feeling luckier than ever to be part of her team—and doubly motivated when I returned.

Poor fit

Sometimes a person *seems* to be in the perfect role, given their experience and expertise, but just can't get traction at a particular company or on a team because there is a misalignment between the culture of the group and the individual's personality. When a highly successful person takes a job with a new company and the "fit" isn't right, it can be painful for everyone. If neither the culture nor the individual can change, it's best to part ways. You generally can't fix a cultural-fit issue.

For example, I knew a person whose "launch and iterate" approach made him enormously successful at Google. Google's culture was all about experimentation. When he got to Apple, which had a culture of perfecting and polishing ideas before launching them, he tried the same thing, and it killed his credibility. There was nothing wrong with the person or with Apple—it was just a bad fit.

NO PERMANENT MARKERS

People change, and you have to change with them

IT'S HARD NOT to lock in your perceptions of people. "Jane is a rock star. Once a rock star, always a rock star." "Sean is my Rock of Gibraltar. I'd be lost without him in his role." My biggest concern with the terms "rock star" and "superstar" is that you'll use them as permanent labels for people. Please do not! It's tempting to see certain people as fit only for a certain role or having a certain set of skills/weaknesses that will never change. The truth is, people really do change. Somebody who's been on a gradual growth trajectory may suddenly become restless and yearn for a new challenge at work. Or, a person who's been on a steep growth trajectory for years may be craving a period of stability. This is another reason why you *have to manage*. Being a great boss involves constantly adjusting to the new reality of the day or week or year as it unfolds. But you can't adjust if you haven't been paying attention or if you don't know the person well enough to notice that something significant has shifted.

It's not only important to remember that nobody is always on a steep or growth trajectory; people's performance changes over time, too. Be careful not to label people as "high performers." Everybody has an off quarter occasionally. To combat permanent labels, Qualtrics cofounder (and my colleague from Juice and Google) Jared Smith came up with the performance ratings "off quarter," "solid quarter," and "exceptional quarter."

Such adjustments are particularly hard when it comes time to move people who have been making your life easier into new roles that will make your life harder—at least in the short term. You have relied on "Jean" to get a particular job done well for years. Now Jean wants a new job. Or, "Pat" has been picking up new challenges for years, and now Pat is ready to quit changing roles so often; you have to hand those off to somebody without the same track record of success that Pat has. It's stressful for you!

Over the course of our careers, most of us go through waves. Sometimes we are in learning mode or transition mode. Sometimes our priorities change: a spouse takes a new job and we need to be home more, or we want to devote time to a passion outside work. It is important for the team member and the boss to be clear about what is driving the degree of trajectory at each juncture, so that both the team member and the company can benefit.

So use this simple framework, but don't abuse it. Make sure that you are seeing each person on your team with fresh eyes every day. People evolve, and so your relationships must evolve with them. Care personally; don't put people in boxes and leave them there.

4

DRIVE RESULTS COLLABORATIVELY

Telling people what to do doesn't work

TELLING PEOPLE WHAT TO DO DIDN'T WORK AT GOOGLE

AT FIRST BLUSH, it seems like achieving results is more a matter of challenging directly than caring personally. But the ultimate goal of Radical Candor is to achieve collaboratively what you could never achieve individually, and to do that, you need to care about the people you're working with.

Steve Squyres, who led the Mars Exploration Rover Mission, described perfectly the thrill of collaboration: "Over four thousand people have worked on this mission. There's no one person who can really get their arms around the whole thing and say, 'I understand everything about this vehicle.' It burst the bounds of our brains." I was sitting next to Larry Page when I watched the documentary, and he turned to me and said, "Wow, that really makes you feel like you can *achieve* something doesn't it?" On the one hand I agreed, whole-heartedly. On the other hand, it seemed nuts that the guy who cofounded Google needed to watch a documentary to make him feel like he could achieve something.

If you want your team to achieve something bigger than you could achieve alone, if you want to "burst the bounds of your brain," you have to care about the people you are working with. You'll get more done if you take the time to incorporate their thinking into yours, and yours into theirs.

Don't let your focus on results get in the way of caring about the people you work with. I made that mistake when I first got to Google. I was laser-focused on getting stuff done, and fast. That slowed me down in the end.

The AdSense team I was leading was responsible for sales and support of small and medium AdSense customers. We had five main jobs: to approve new customers, bring them on board, offer account management, provide customer support, and enforce policy. There were about one hundred people doing this work, and when I arrived on the scene things had been growing crazy-fast, so it was something of a free-for-all; everybody did a little bit of everything. When the team was behind on approvals and somebody happened to notice, they'd send a blast email out to all one hundred people, saying, "Please stop what you're doing and work on approvals." If nobody noticed, we just got further behind. Google was data-obsessed, so everything was tracked. But when the numbers went in the wrong direction there was a collective sense of guilt, rather than a clear plan to fix the problem, since nobody was accountable for any one thing. We weren't executing well, and everyone was stressed.

One of my mentors once told me, "There's a fine line between success and failure." Now I saw what he meant. By any normal measure, our growth was great, but it quickly became clear it could be a lot better if we operated less like a soccer team of seven-year-olds: all of us chasing the ball, none of us in position. For example, after asking a bunch of questions, I realized we weren't doing any real account management (i.e., we weren't working with our biggest customers to help them improve in ways that would make them, and Google, more money.) When I asked why, the answer was "That wouldn't be Googley! We treat all our customers exactly the same, no matter how big or small they are." My suggestion that we prioritize was met with looks that made it clear my very morality was suspect.

The reporting structure was faulty as well, which was why there was no real accountability. When a new person got hired, they were assigned randomly to the manager who had the fewest direct reports. But there was no particular relationship between the work they were doing and who their boss was. And, per Google's culture, they didn't really see why they needed to *have* bosses, other than to give the bosses "leadership experience" so they could get into business school. Having a boss on paper was a necessary evil people had to put up with so that they, too, could become bosses and get into business school.

What a mess! How could such a nonsensical situation arise at such a successful company? A friend of mine didn't at first believe this story. At *The New Yorker,* she said, the fact-checkers would never report to the head of the copyediting department, because only the head of the fact-checking department would really understand their work. What was going on at Google? Actually, I've seen even crazier stuff happen at other Silicon Valley "unicorns."* When a company led by extremely bright but inexperienced people takes off, anything can happen. But I relished the mess, since it was why I'd been hired. At thirty-seven, I was older than my boss, and more than a decade older than the average Googler. I was "adult supervision."

And I knew exactly what to do. Rather than having a team of one hundred in which everybody did a little bit of everything, with a random management structure, I created five smaller teams. I made each of the managers working for me accountable for just *one* thing: approvals or on-boarding or account management or customer support or policy. Then, I reshuffled everyone's direct reports so that the more sales-y people would work as one team, reporting to the manager responsible for account management; the more structured people would work on one team, reporting to the manager responsible for policy; and so forth. Now, people's bosses would understand their work, and could both help their direct reports, and be held accountable.

An entirely reasonable change, don't you agree? The result: three of my five direct reports complained to my boss, Sheryl Sandberg, that they couldn't stand working for me—I was too autocratic, I left too many people out of important decisions. One even described feeling "sad and bad and left out." All three left to join other Google teams, as they were free to do, without

---

* The term venture capitalist Aileen Lee coined to describe a start-up that quickly achieves a $1 billion valuation.

my permission. Where had I gone wrong? What needed to happen had seemed so obvious. I went to Sheryl for advice.

She agreed with the way I'd restructured the work, but not with the way I'd gone about it. "Kim, you're moving too fast. It's like you're spinning a long rope," Sheryl said, miming an imaginary rope spinning in a big circle over her head. "It doesn't seem like the rope is going that fast to you because you're in the center holding it, just flicking your wrists. But if you're at the end of the rope, you're hanging on for dear life. It's scary. You can't do that to people and expect them to stick around."

Telling people what to do didn't work. At a time when we were obviously in need of big changes, it had seemed like it was the fastest way forward, but it wasn't. First, because I didn't involve my team in decision-making; I just made the decisions myself. Second, because even after making them I didn't take the time to explain why or to persuade the team I'd made good decisions. So, instead of executing on decisions they didn't agree with or even understand, my team dissolved, and I wasn't going to improve our results until I rebuilt it.

The great thing about working at Google was that the company gave me a chance to fix my mistake. My boss explained exactly what I'd done wrong—and then let me hire people to replace those I'd lost. I was able to bring several people who'd worked for me at Juice to Google. It was a painful but instructive lesson: to drive results at Google, I had to learn to be more collaborative.

Decisions really didn't get made by authority at Google—not even by the founders. At one point, Google's engineers decided to redesign the AdWords* front end to make it easier for advertisers to choose different kinds of ad formats. Since most of Google's revenue came from AdWords, it was important to get this right. In one meeting, I watched Google cofounder Sergey Brin try to persuade a team of engineers to try his solution to the challenge of presenting to advertisers all the choices they had—different kinds of ad formats, different ways to make sure their ads showed up when and where they wanted, etc.—in the simplest possible way. The team proposed a different solution from Sergey's. He suggested that they put a couple

---

* **AdWords** is Google's ad product. If you want to advertise your tents, you bid on keywords like "tent" and if you win the auction, your ads will run on Google's search pages when people type in the word "tent." Your ads might also run on other people's Web sites if they are about tents. When users click on your ad, you pay Google.

of people working on his approach and let the rest of the team pursue their favored solution. The team refused.

Sergey, in a rare burst of frustration, banged the table and said, "If this were an ordinary company, you'd *all* be doing it my way. I just want a couple of people to try my idea!" He was clearly exasperated, but his grin showed that he was also proud of having built a team that would stand up to him. In the end, the team convinced him that theirs was the better way.

Of course, not all companies *insist* on collaboration or let anyone change teams when they are unhappy with their boss. But I've found, again and again, that even if you work at a place that allows you to act in a more authoritarian way, you'll get better results if you lay your power down and work more collaboratively.

TELLING PEOPLE WHAT TO DO DIDN'T WORK FOR STEVE JOBS EITHER

"FUCKING STEVE *ALWAYS* gets it right," barked Andy Grove, Intel's legendary CEO, over a cup of Jamoca Almond Fudge at Baskin-Robbins in Los Altos. I was asking his advice on whether I should join Apple.

I laughed, thinking he was making a joke, but Andy shook his head at me vehemently. "No. You didn't understand me. Steve really *always* gets it right. I mean it, precisely, like an engineer. I am not joking, and I am not exaggerating."

I knew Andy was telling me something important, and a part of me hoped it was true. One of the things that was appealing about going to Apple after Google's creative chaos was seeing what it would be like to work at a company where more assertive management, even telling people what to do, actually worked. I assumed that was how things got done at Apple— that Steve Jobs, visionary, told people what to do. But I still assumed Andy was exaggerating. *Always* right?

"Nobody's *always* right," I said.

"I didn't say Steve *is* always right. I said he always *gets* it right. Like anyone, he is wrong sometimes, but he insists, and not gently either, that people tell him when he's wrong, so he always gets it right in the end."

Andy's words tapped into a complex and somewhat paradoxical set of beliefs and ideals I had about how great bosses get a team to execute well. On the one hand, I loved Google's approach and subscribed to the Antoine de Saint-Exupéry school of management: "If you want to build a ship, don't drum up people to collect wood and don't assign them tasks and work, but rather teach them to long for the endless immensity of the sea." On the other hand, as my anecdote about the beginning of my time with AdSense reveals, I also occasionally longed either to *have* or to *be* an uncontested leader.

After I took the job at Apple, I learned that Andy's description had been accurate. Steve often demonstrated that he was willing—eager, even—to change his mind when he was proven wrong. But this rarely played out in a gracious "You were right, the mistake was mine" manner. People were often infuriated by the way that Steve changed his mind.

One colleague told me about a time he'd argued with Steve but eventually backed down, even though he wasn't convinced by Steve's reasoning. When events subsequently proved my colleague right, Steve marched into his office and started yelling. "But this was your idea," said my colleague. "Yes, and it was your job to convince me I was wrong," Steve replied, "and you failed!" From then on, my colleague argued longer and more loudly, and he kept arguing until either he convinced Steve he was right or Steve convinced him he was wrong. Thus, Steve got it right by being willing to be wrong and by insisting that the people around him challenge him. There is no doubt that his style didn't work for everyone. He hired people who were not afraid to argue with him, and then he pushed that fearlessness further.

Another colleague told me about an argument she'd had with Steve. She eventually persuaded him he was wrong, but then he so thoroughly adopted her position that it was as if it had been his all along. She speculated that Steve was so focused on getting to the right answer that he genuinely didn't care who'd said what. Obviously, this approach could be frustrating—people want credit for their ideas. But the relentless focus on challenging himself and those around him to "get it" right rather than to "be" right was part of what drove Apple's breathtaking ability to execute so well.

THE ART OF GETTING STUFF DONE WITHOUT TELLING PEOPLE WHAT TO DO

CERTAINLY PART OF why Steve "always got it right" was that he was a genius. You can't operationalize or imitate genius. But genius was only part of the story; there are plenty of geniuses with brilliant ideas who can't turn them into anything tangible. More important than genius was the way Steve led people at Apple to execute so flawlessly *without* telling them what to do. This is something you *can* operationalize and imitate. To do it, though, you'll have to push yourself and your team further out on the "challenge directly" axis than will probably be immediately comfortable.

In fact, both Google and Apple achieved spectacular results without a purely autocratic style. This leads to important questions: how did everyone in the company decide what to do? How did strategy and goals get set? How did the cultures at these two companies, so strong and so different, develop? How did tens of thousands of people come to understand the mission? It played out very differently at both companies—more orderly at Apple, more chaotic at Google—but at a high level, the process was the same.

The process, which I call the "Get Stuff Done" (GSD) wheel, is relatively straightforward. But the key, often ignored by people who think of themselves as "Get Stuff Done" people, is to avoid the impulse to dive right in, as I did in the example that begins this chapter. Instead, you have to first lay the groundwork for collaboration.

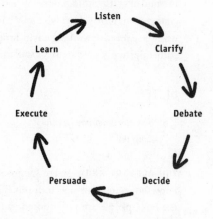

When run effectively, the GSD wheel will enable your team to achieve more collectively than anyone could ever dream of achieving individually—to burst the bounds of your brain. First, you have to *listen* to the ideas that people on your team have and create a culture in which they listen to each other. Next, you have create space in which ideas can be sharpened and *clarified*, to make sure these ideas don't get crushed before everyone fully understands their potential usefulness. But just because an idea is easy to understand doesn't mean it's a good one. Next, you have to *debate* ideas and test them more rigorously. Then you need to *decide*—quickly, but not too quickly. Since not everyone will have been involved in the listen-clarify-debate-decide part of the cycle for every idea, the next step is to bring the broader team along. You have to *persuade* those who weren't involved in a decision that it was a good one, so that everyone can execute it effectively. Then, having *executed*, you have to *learn* from the results, whether or not you did the right thing, and start the whole process over again.

That's a lot of steps. Remember, they are designed to be cycled through quickly. Not skipping a step and not getting stuck on one are equally important. If you skip a step, you'll waste time in the end. If you allow any part of the process to drag out, working on your team will feel like paying a collaboration tax, not making a collaboration investment.

You may very well be in a situation where your boss is skipping steps and just telling you what to do. Does that mean you have to do the same with your team? No, of course not! You can put these ideas into practice with the people who report to you even if your boss doesn't subscribe to this method of getting things done. When your boss sees the results, things may change. But, if they don't, you may have to change jobs. When more people insist on a positive working environment, not only will results for your company improve, your happiness will as well.

LISTEN

"Give the quiet ones a voice."
—JONY IVE

YOU ALREADY KNOW you're supposed to listen, and you probably already know how (and how not) to listen. The problem is that when you become the boss, people are predisposed to tell you that you must totally change your style of listening, and you can't do that.

The good news is you can stick to your own style and still make sure that everyone on your team gets heard and is thus able to contribute.

Jony Ive, Apple's chief design officer, once said at an Apple University class that a manager's most important role is to "give the quiet ones a voice." I love this. Google CEO Eric Schmidt took the opposite approach, urging people to "Be loud!" I love

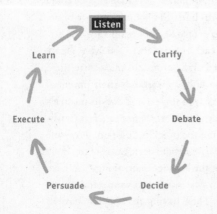

this, too. The two leaders took different approaches to ensure that everyone was heard. This is your goal as well, but there is more than one way to achieve it. You have to find a way to listen that fits your personal style, and then create a culture in which everyone listens to each other, so that all the burden of listening doesn't fall on you.

Quiet listening

Tim Cook, Apple's CEO, is the master of silence. Before I interviewed at Apple, a friend warned me that Tim tended to allow long silences and that I shouldn't let it unnerve me or feel the need to fill them. Despite this warning, in our first interview I reacted to a long period of silence by anxiously talking nonstop, and in the process inadvertently told him far more about a mistake I'd made than I had intended. Just when I realized, panic-stricken, that I was about to reveal something that might well cost me the job, the room began to shake.

"Earthquake?" I asked, with what I suspect was undisguised relief.

Tim nodded, looking up at the movement of the walls. "Pretty good-sized one too, I'd say."

Seizing the chance to listen rather than talk, I asked about the building's design, which the engineer in Tim couldn't resist describing to me. Because the building was on top of rollers, the earthquake's movement felt more pronounced; scarier but safer. Tim smiled at the contradiction.

Following in Tim's footsteps, one of my students in the *Managing at Apple* class said that he tried to make sure to spend at least ten minutes in every one-on-one meeting listening silently, without reacting in any way. He would keep his facial expression and body language totally neutral.

"What did you learn in that ten minutes that you didn't learn the other fifty?" I asked.

"I heard the things I didn't want to hear," my student said, validating Tim's technique. "If I gave any reaction at all, people would often tell me what they thought I wanted to hear. I found that they were much more likely to say what they really thought—even if it wasn't what I was hoping to hear—when I was careful not to show what I thought."

There are real advantages to quiet listening, but it also has a downside. When you're the boss and people don't know what you think, they waste a lot of time trying to guess. Some will even use your name in vain—"Well, what the boss wants to do is X"—and then go on to describe what *they* want to do instead. And since nobody can be sure what you really think, they can sometimes get away with it. In addition, plenty of people are made very uncomfortable by silence, as the examples above demonstrate. It can feel like playing a high-risk poker game instead of having a Radically Candid conversation. Some people feel a quiet listener is not listening at all but instead setting a trap: waiting for others to say the wrong thing so they can pounce.

If you're a quiet listener, then, you need to take steps to reassure those made uncomfortable by your style. Don't be pointlessly inscrutable. To get others to say what they think, you need to say what you think sometimes, too. If you want to be challenged, you need to be willing to challenge. The manager in my class was expressionless for only ten minutes of his 1:1s, not the full hour. If he'd been utterly expressionless the whole time, it would have been hard for people to trust him or to relate to him. Tim Cook wasn't always silent either, of course. But because he was generally so quiet, people leaned forward to listen to what he said. And when he spoke, albeit very quietly, his thinking was always crystal clear.

Quiet listening clearly works for many managers, but I cannot pull it off. Luckily, there is another model.

Loud listening

If quiet listening involves being silent to give people room to talk, loud listening is about saying things intended to get a reaction out of them. This was the way Steve Jobs listened. He would put a strong point of view on the table and insist on a response. Why do I call this listening, instead of talking, or even yelling? Because Steve didn't just challenge others; he insisted that they challenge him back.

Obviously this approach works only when people feel confident enough to rise to the challenge. Just as some people are spooked by quiet listening, other people are offended by loud listening. If you are a loud listener, how do you deal with people who are either constitutionally unable to stand up to an aggressive boss or whose position is too marginal to allow them to feel secure, even if the larger culture welcomes this behavior? How do you listen to a person who has just started at the company and doesn't feel established enough to take a high-profile stand? That person might know a good reason why you are wrong. And yet they won't speak up.

If you have a loud listening style, you need to go to some lengths to build the confidence of those whom you're making uncomfortable. And as people witness one another challenging the boss, they will grow to feel it's safe to do so as well. Jony Ive said that Steve would often come to him and say, "Jony, here's a dopey idea. . . ." He wasn't quiet about his idea, but he was inviting Jony to challenge it by calling it dopey.

Randy Nelson, the dean of Pixar University and a faculty member at Apple University, captured this when he said of Steve Jobs, "He's a lion. If he roars at you, you'd better roar back just as loudly—but only if you really are a lion, too. Otherwise he'll eat you for lunch."

Steve didn't surround himself with people who'd tell him when he was wrong by making everybody feel comfortable. The people who worked closely with him knew they had better speak up when they saw a problem or a flaw in his logic, or face his wrath later. This didn't mean they had to be loud themselves. Steve worked really well with both Tim Cook and Jony Ive and both of them were quiet listeners. But they did have to be strong and super-confident.

You don't have to adopt Steve's style to be a loud listener. Paul Saffo, an engineering professor at Stanford, describes a technique he calls "strong opinions, weakly held." Saffo has made the point that expressing strong, some might say outrageous, positions with others is a good way to get to a better answer, or at least to have a more interesting conversation. I love this approach. I've always found that saying what I think really clearly and then going to great lengths to encourage disagreement is a good way to listen. I tend to state my positions strongly, so I have had to learn to follow up with, "Please poke holes in this idea—I know it may be terrible. So tell me all the reasons we should not do that." Once I put a YOU WERE RIGHT, I WAS WRONG trophy on somebody's desk after her position on something proved to be correct and mine dead wrong.

Loud listening—stating a point of view strongly—offers a quick way to expose opposing points of view or flaws in reasoning. It also prevents people from wasting a lot of time trying to figure out what the boss thinks. Assuming that you are surrounded with people who don't hesitate to challenge what you say, stating it clearly can be the fastest way to get to the best answer.

Perhaps most important is to stick to the style that feels most natural to you. Many leadership books push for quiet listening. But if you're a loud listener, it's really hard to follow that advice. Attempting to behave in ways that feel deeply unnatural can make your team feel less comfortable with you rather than more so. Instead, try to strengthen your awareness of how your style makes your colleagues feel and work on improving that dynamic. Figure out how to listen to give the quiet ones a voice without weirding out their louder colleagues. You don't want a tyranny of the most verbose on your team; you want to get to the best answer together.

Create a culture of listening

It's hard enough to get *yourself* to listen to your team members and let them know you are listening; getting them to listen to one another is even harder. The keys are 1) have a simple system for employees to use to generate ideas and voice complaints, 2) make sure that at least some of the issues raised are quickly addressed, and 3) regularly offer explanations as to why the other issues aren't being addressed. This system should not merely empower anyone to point out things that could be better but also enable others to help fix those things or make changes. You have to agree to let them ask you for *some* help, and to champion the system enthusiastically. Define clear boundaries of how much time you can spend—and then make sure that time is highly impactful.

At Google, people constantly came to me with good ideas—more than I could handle, in fact—and it became overwhelming. So I organized an "ideas team" to consider them. For context, I circulated an article from *Harvard Business Review* (HBR) that explained how a culture that captures thousands of "small" innovations can create benefits for customers that are impossible for competitors to imitate. One big idea is pretty easy to copy, but thousands of tweaks are impossible to see from the outside, let alone imitate.*

Next, I talked through some key principles that ought to guide the ideas team, first among them empowerment. The ideas team had to commit to listening to *any* idea that *anyone* brought to them, to explain clearly why they rejected the ideas they rejected, and to help people implement ideas that the ideas team deemed worthwhile. If somebody's idea seemed especially promising, they could even negotiate with the person's manager to give them some time off from their "day job" to work on implementing it. They were encouraged to assign me up to three action items a week.

After this innovation, instead of feeling stressed whenever I would hear a cool idea in a meeting or receive an inspired email, I could react enthusiastically and delegate it to the ideas team. Soon, lots of people were submit-

---

* https://hbr.org/2008/02/getting-the-best-employee-idea

ting ideas they had for improving the product, growing the business, and making our processes more efficient. We created an ideas tool (basically just a wiki) that allowed people to submit an idea, have it reviewed by the team, and voted up or down. That was a form of listening, and people whose ideas got voted up definitely felt heard by their colleagues. People whose ideas were not voted up knew that their ideas had been explicitly rejected: a much clearer signal than radio silence from overburdened management. However, a vote is not always the best way to identify the best ideas, or to make sure people are listening to each other. Therefore, I asked the ideas team to read *all* the ideas and talk to all the people who submitted them—to *listen*. After that development, the team used a combination of votes and judgment to select the best ideas.

More important, the ideas team helped people get the selected ideas implemented. Occasionally this was about getting time for people to work on them, or getting some input from me, but often all it took was just the validation and encouragement that came from listening and responding. "Yes, that's a cool idea! Do it!"

Sarah Teng, a recent college graduate on the AdSense team, came up with the idea of using programmable keyboards to create shortcuts for phrases or paragraphs they used over and over when communicating with customers. It seemed like a good idea, so the ideas team asked me to approve the budget to buy programmable keypads. I did as they asked, and this simple idea increased the global team's efficiency by 133 percent. This meant that everyone on the team had to spend far less time typing the same damn words over and over and had more time to come up with other good ideas—a virtuous cycle. Bam!

When Sarah presented her project to the team, I didn't just thank her; I also showed a graph of how this idea would improve our efficiency over time. But efficiency is not what people cared most about, so I also stressed to the team how her innovation would make people's jobs more fun and help them grow in their careers, since they'd get to spend less time doing grunt work and more time doing work they found interesting. I explained that Sarah would have an opportunity to share her idea with leaders from another, much larger team, for an even larger impact. And I sent around *again* the HBR article showing how competitive advantage tends to come not from one great idea but the combination of hundreds of smaller ones.

Why did I add all that context? First, to demonstrate just how great the impact of her idea was. The use of programmable keypads by itself was hardly revolutionary, but when people saw the cumulative effect of that idea and others like it over time, Sarah's innovation felt a lot bigger. Second, it inspired people who had other ideas like this to be vocal about them. Third, and most importantly, it encouraged people to *listen* to each other's ideas, to take them seriously, and to help one another implement them without waiting for management's blessing. It's so easy to lose "small" ideas in big organizations, and if you do you kill incremental innovation.

Hundreds of really smart people had been working in Online Sales and Operations for years. It was hard for me to believe that nobody else had ever had the programmable keypad idea before, but if they had, management hadn't listened. If you can build a culture where people listen to one another, they will start to fix things you as the boss never even knew were broken.

Most meaningful to me was that morale on the team soared. At one point the "Googlegeist" survey on employee morale showed that the team of people who were answering customer support emails for AdSense felt much better about the role that innovation played in their work than the engineers working on Search did—despite the fact that those engineers were probably some of the most creative engineers in the world.

Sometimes creating a culture of listening is simply a matter of managing meetings the right way. When just a couple of people were doing all the talking at a meeting, I'd stop and go around the table to ensure that everyone got heard. Other times, I would stand up in the next meeting and walk around, physically blocking a person who was talking too much. Sometimes I'd have a quick conversation with people before a meeting, asking some to pipe up and others to pipe down. In other words, part of my job was to constantly figure out new ways to "give the quiet ones a voice."

Adapt to a culture of listening

My friend Astrid Tuminez has a great story about how important it is to adapt to a culture of listening in a new situation. She grew up in a tiny fishing village in the slums of the Philippines but went on to have a career that spanned Moscow (where I worked with her), New York, and Singapore. While working at the U.S. Institute of Peace, she was invited to work on the peace process with the Moro Islamic Liberation Front in the southern Philippines. When she first arrived, she acted like a New Yorker—very business-like, making back-to-back appointments.

Then a member of the Philippine negotiating team told her that some-one from the Muslim/Moro group had sent a note to Manila saying, "Who is this woman and what planet is she from?" The person who gave Astrid feedback was particularly invested in Astrid's success because they had con-nected over the fact that they were from the same province.

To the Muslims, Astrid had come across as unfeeling, inhospitable, and foreign (even though she was Filipino and could speak Filipino). Thinking it over, she realized that she'd made some significant mistakes—such as hosting meetings with people without offering them real food, which was so impor-tant in the culture. She spent the next few months listening, and making only "loose" appointments. She attended public events and made the rounds without scheduling people back-to-back. And she made sure she had a lot of food available when she hosted meetings.

By taking time to get to know people and by just listening she was able to build trust and show she cared deeply about the peace process. Eventu-ally the Moros became very willing to speak to her and to take her places where other outsiders couldn't or wouldn't go. It made all the difference in her ability to be effective in the complex and nuanced negotiations her job required.

CLARIFY

> "It is only by selection, by elimination, and by emphasis that we get at the real meaning of things."
> —GEORGIA O'KEEFFE

ONCE YOU'VE CREATED a culture of listening, the next step is to push your-self and your direct reports to understand and convey thoughts and ideas more clearly. Trying to solve a problem that hasn't been clearly defined is not likely to result in a good solution; debating a half-baked idea is likely to kill it. As the boss, you are the editor, not the author.

Speaking at an Apple memorial service for Steve Jobs, Jony Ive noted that Steve Jobs had understood how important it was to nurture and clarify new ideas. "He treated the process of creativity with a rare and a wonderful reverence," Jony said. "He understood that while ideas ultimately can be so powerful, they begin as fragile, barely formed thoughts, so easily missed, so easily compromised, so easily just squished."

New ideas don't have to be grandiose plans for the next iPad. Your team may be saying something like, "I'm frustrated by this process," or "I'm not feeling as energized by my work as I was," or "I think our sales pitch could be stronger," or "I'd do better work if there were more natural light in the office," or "What if we just stopped doing *X*?" or "I'd like to start working on *Y*."

Of course, it's tempting to shut down in the face of these sorts of statements—"I don't have time to deal with this right now!" But taking the moments to help clarify the ideas will save you time in the long run. Take the time to help your direct reports explain what they mean, so that they can do something about fixing the problem or pursuing the opportunity rather than just complaining about it.

It's important to push the people on your team to clarify their thinking and ideas so that you don't "squish" their best thinking or ignore problems that are bothering them. It's not just important to understand new *ideas* clearly; it's equally important, and often more difficult, to understand the *people* to whom your team will have to explain the ideas clearly.

Be clear in your own mind
Create a safe space to nurture new ideas

Part of your job as the boss is to help people think through their ideas before submitting them to the rough-and-tumble of debate. Russ Laraway explained that I was doing this all wrong when I told my team at Google not to bring me problems; instead, I told them, bring me three solutions and a recommendation. "But then you're not helping people innovate," Russ explained. "You're asking them to make decisions before they've had time to think things through. When do they get to just talk, brainstorm with you?" I realized Russ was right; I was abdicating an important part of my job by insisting on the "three solutions and a recommendation" approach.

Susan Wojcicki, who is now CEO of YouTube, was great at helping her team nurture new ideas before they got bruised in debates. Early in Google's history, people brought new ideas *directly* to Google's Executive Management Group (EMG). That group included the founders, the CEO, and a number of executives. Debate in those meetings could be brutal, and they started to feel like the place where new ideas went to die. Susan, recognizing the stress this caused for her team and the danger it posed for innovation at Google, stepped up and created a pre-EMG meeting where new ideas could be developed. Here people could help one another sharpen new ideas, or define problems more clearly.

There's a lot of research demonstrating that when companies help people develop new ideas by creating the space and time to clarify their thinking, innovation flourishes.* Throughout Silicon Valley, different companies have experimented with different ways to give people that kind of freedom. Google famously has 20-percent time, where anybody can theoretically work on any idea they want to with 20 percent of their regular full-time hours. Not too many take 20-percent time, so this policy belongs more to the fantasy Google than the real Google. But fantasy informs reality—and it's also true that a number of important products, including Gmail, did start as 20-percent-time projects.

Scott Forstall, who built the iOS team at Apple, experimented with a different approach, called Blue Sky. People came up with a project they wanted to work on and could apply to Blue Sky. If approved, they got two weeks off from their day job to further develop the idea. Similarly, Twitter, Dropbox, and many start-ups have regular Hack Weeks throughout the year during which people can spend time pursuing new ideas.

Brainstorming sessions are often used to surface and clarify new ideas. These sessions are not just random conversations where nobody is allowed to say anything negative, though. There are plenty of bad ideas, and they need to be recognized as such. Poking holes in new ideas doesn't necessarily kill them—it can push people to clarify their thinking. There are also great ideas that look bad at first blush. A good brainstorming session distinguishes between the two without killing too many good ideas or wasting too much

---

* http://www.wsj.com/articles/SB115015518018078348

time on the bad ones. Pixar has a technique called "plussing." Rather than saying, "No, that is a bad idea," people must offer a solution to the problem they are pointing out.

Less dramatic than these kinds of formalized meetings and programs are your weekly 1:1s. (See Chapter Eight for specific suggestions on making 1:1s more productive.) These meetings should be a safe place for your direct reports to come and talk to you about new ideas. In this context, you shouldn't judge the ideas but rather help your direct reports clarify their thinking. This is a form of "plussing." You can point out problems but with the aim of figuring a way around those problems, not killing ideas.

Be clear to others
Make thoughts/ideas drop-dead easy for others to comprehend

When I was at business school, one of my professors told a story about a meeting between President Franklin Delano Roosevelt and the economist John Maynard Keynes. FDR was enormously busy, but he spent well over an hour with this academic. If FDR had understood Keynesian economics, some think the Great Depression might have ended sooner and enormous suffering could have been prevented. But at the end of the meeting, the president was not persuaded.

My professor asked the question, "Whose fault was it? FDR's for not understanding, or Keynes's for not explaining it well?" This was one of those moments in my education that changed my life. I'd always shifted the burden of responsibility for understanding to the listener, not to the explainer. But now I saw that if Keynes's genius was locked inside his head, it may as well not have existed. It was his responsibility to make the ideas that seemed so obvious to him equally obvious to FDR. He failed. Far too often we assume that if somebody doesn't understand what we're telling them, it's because they are "stupid" or "closed minded." That is very rarely the case. While we know our subject matter, we may fail to know the person to whom we are explaining the subject, and therefore may fail to get our idea across.

You'll be heard more accurately if you take the time to understand the people you are talking to. What do they know, what don't they know? What details do you need to include to make it easy for them to understand—and, more importantly, what details can you leave out?

When you are listening to people on your team, take on the responsibility to understand—to actually listen—rather than putting the burden to communicate onto them. But when you are helping them prepare to explain their ideas to others—whether they are peers or cross-functional colleagues or executives—it's your job to push your direct reports, and yourself, to do a better job than Keynes did. You need to push them to communicate with such precision and clarity that it's impossible not to grasp their argument.

Georgia O'Keeffe said, "It is only by selection, by elimination, and by emphasis that we get at the real meaning of things." Choosing what to select, what to eliminate, and what to emphasize depends not only on the idea but on the audience. If you are sending an email about a challenge at work to your grandmother, you may want to emphasize how it impacts your love life and perhaps choose to pass over revenue implications entirely. If you are writing to your boss about the same subject, it will probably be the reverse. The essence of making an idea clear requires a deep understanding not only of the *idea* but also of the *person* to whom one is explaining the idea.

The next time you spend two hours helping somebody edit an email until it's just two sentences, don't feel you are wasting your time. You are getting to the essence of the idea, which allows the recipient to absorb it quickly and easily. And you are teaching an invaluable skill.

DEBATE

The rock tumbler

ONCE YOU'VE SPENT all that time clarifying an idea—getting it really clear in your own mind and making it easy for others to understand—it's tempting to feel like you're done. Not so fast! The point of spending all that time in clarification mode was just to get the idea ready for a debate. If you skip the debate phase, you'll make worse decisions, you'll be unable to persuade everyone who needs to execute, and you'll ultimately slow down or grind to a halt. Once again, you don't have to be in every debate—in fact, you shouldn't be. But you've got to make sure that they happen, and that there is a culture of debate on your team.

When Steve Jobs was a kid, his neighbor showed him a rock tumbler—a can that spun on a motor. The neighbor asked Steve to gather up some ordinary rocks from the yard. He took the stones, threw them into the can, added some grit, turned on the motor, and, over the racket, asked Steve to come back two days later. When Steve returned to the noisy clatter of the garage, the neighbor turned off the contraption and Steve was astounded to see how the ordinary rocks had become beautiful polished stones. Steve would later say that when a team debated, both the ideas and the people came out more beautiful—results well worth all the friction and noise.*

Your job as a boss is to turn on that "rock tumbler." Too many bosses think their role is to turn it *off*—to avoid all the friction by simply making a decision and sparing the team the pain of debate. It's not. Debate takes time and requires emotional energy. But lack of debate saps a team of more time and emotional energy in the long run.

Of course, it's also possible to leave the rock tumbler on too long, leaving nothing in the can but some dust. Here are some ideas that can help you keep debate going without grinding everyone down too much.

Keep the conversation focused on ideas not egos

Make sure that individual egos and self-interest don't get in the way of an objective quest for the best answer.† Nothing is a bigger time-sucker or blocker to getting it right than ego. On a broad level, this means intervening when you start to sense that people are thinking, "I'm going to win this argument," or "my idea versus your idea," or "my recommendation versus your recommendation," or "my team feels . . ." Redirect them to focus on the facts; don't allow people to attribute ownership to ideas, and don't get hijacked by how others who aren't in the room might (or might not) feel. Remind people what the goal is: to get to the best answer, as a team. You're creating a collaboration of great minds, not monitoring a high school debate competition or running a presidential election. If you have to, set ground rules at the beginning of the meeting, or—if your team would find it amusing and useful rather than ridiculous—put a prop like an "ego coat check" outside the door.

---

* from *The Lost Interview*.
† At first I wrote "the truth" instead of "the best answer." "The truth" implies permanence, a notion that can be dangerous to "learning" and, as described in the previous section, can promote arrogance, which is disastrous for Radical Candor.

Another way to help people search for the best answer instead of seeking ego validation is to make them switch roles. If a person has been arguing for A, ask them to start arguing for B. If a debate is likely to go on for some time, warn people in advance that you're going to ask them to switch roles. When people know that they will be asked to argue another person's point, they will naturally listen more attentively.

Create an obligation to dissent

I once interned at McKinsey for a summer, and what impressed me most about the company was its ability to spur productive debate. How'd they do it? McKinsey had very consciously created an "obligation to dissent." If everyone around the table agreed, that was a red flag. Somebody *had* to take up the dissenting voice. McKinsey alums often brought this with them into the companies they later worked for. One ex-McKinsey executive at Apple struggled to foster a culture of debate on a team he inherited in Japan. He had a bunch of gavels made up with "duty to dissent" written in Japanese on them. If there wasn't a robust enough argument in a meeting, he'd slide the gavel across the table to someone, as a sign to take up the opposite point of view. This simple prop was surprisingly effective.

Pause for emotion/exhaustion

There are times when people are just too tired, burnt out, or emotionally charged up to engage in productive debate. It's crucial to be aware of these moments, because they rarely lead to good outcomes. Your job is to intervene and call a time-out. If you don't, people will make a decision so that they can go home; or worse, a huge fight stemming from raw emotions will break out. If you've gotten to know each person on your team well enough, you'll be sufficiently aware of everyone's emotions and energies so that you'll know when it's necessary to step in and defer the debate till people are in a better frame of mind.

Use humor and have fun

The spirit with which a debate is launched often determines the tenor of what follows. I have found that people on a team I lead key off my mood to an almost alarming extent; when I find a way to have fun with a debate, others often follow suit. In some cases, it might be simple humor or opening the meeting with a good self-effacing story. What you say is less important than the tone it conveys, and the mood it sets for what follows.

Finally, it's important to be aware that not everyone enjoys debate. Some people find the very act of debate aggressive and/or threatening. I recall a time when we were developing a class at Apple on communication, and I described my ideas on creating positive space for debate. Suddenly a colleague next to me smiled and burst out, "Oh! You have been debating me all this time just to make the class better. I thought you were just trying to drive me crazy." What to me had been an exciting opportunity to push each other to hone and develop ideas had been to him an excruciating exercise in one-upmanship. This drove home the importance of providing a clear explanation up front about the purpose of debate and creating a positive space in which it can occur—not to mention the importance of knowing the people I was debating with well enough to recognize when I was driving them nuts without meaning to!

Be clear when the debate will end

One of the reasons that people find debate stressful or annoying is that often half the room expects a decision at the end of the meeting and the other half wants to keep arguing in a follow-up meeting. One way to avoid this tension is to separate debate meetings and decision meetings. Another way to ease the anxiety of the people who want to know when the decision will get made is to have a "decide by" date next to each item being debated. Then at least they know when the debate will end and the decision will be made.

I recommend setting up a weekly "big debate" meeting. In my staff meeting we identified the most important debate each week, and who needed to be involved (see "'Big Debate' Meetings" in chapter 8).

Don't grab a decision just because the debate has gotten painful

It's tempting to end debates and make a decision too soon when a debate becomes too painful. You might be creeping up on a topic that's been a subject of great contention. At times like this, people often look to the boss to end the suffering and make a decision. My instinct is to be a peacemaker, or to get to a decision quickly. But a boss's job is often to keep the debate going rather than to resolve it with a decision. It's the debates at work that help individuals grow and help the team work better collectively to come up with the best answer.

I once made a preemptive decision about what seemed like a small thing—a seating chart—that ended badly. We didn't even have cubes, just tables. As the team grew from ten to sixty-five people, we eventually had to rearrange the space and move everyone's desk. Everybody had an opinion about what the layout should be, and a young project manager volunteered to herd the cats. They were hard to herd. The angst about who sat next to whom and how far they were from a window went on for the better part of a week. Frustrated, I came in on a Sunday and moved everyone's desks myself. The result was near mutiny on Monday morning. "We were this close to a decision!" exclaimed the project manager. "And you just set us back a week." He was an unusually levelheaded person, but there were tears of real frustration in his eyes.

The right thing to do would have been to set a "decide by" date, so everybody would know that they couldn't lobby the project manager endlessly. If the debate seemed too rancorous, I could have asked him how I could help. For example, I could have suggested the people whose differences he was having a hard time reconciling try to wrap it up over a meal or a walk, or that they switch roles and argue for each other's positions. But grabbing the decision away from him and making it myself was not only overbearing; it simply didn't work.

DECIDE
Push decisions into the facts, or pull the facts into the decisions,
but keep ego out

YOU HAVE LINED up decisions and facts and shoved all ego—especially your own—out of the way. Now is the time, as Twitter and Square CEO Jack Dorsey put it, to "push the decisions into the facts." Here is what I've learned about what that means—how to help a team make the best possible decisions—or to "always get it right."

You're not the decider (usually)

I once had an impromptu conversation with a woman on one of my teams. At lunch one day, I asked her how it was going. She rocked back and forth, clutching her head.

"What's wrong?" I asked, alarmed.

"I thought I was hired for my brain, but I have not been allowed to use it a single time since I got here! But Mark"—and here she winced visibly at uttering her manager's name—"makes all the decisions, even when he doesn't really understand the situation."

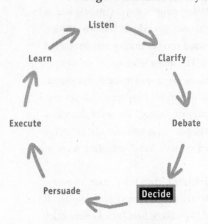

I attended Mark's next staff meeting, at which he was reviewing the team's quarterly OKRs (objectives and key results). As he flashed up the first slide, I felt optimistic. I had taken the job only three weeks before so I didn't know much, but his plan looked *great*. The deck he'd built to explain the goals for the quarter had everything I looked for: objectives that were clear and ambitious, key results that were measurable.

Then I saw that the person sitting to my right was slouching a little in her chair. Looking around the room, I registered arms crossed, faces stony, and a silence so loud that it penetrated even Mark's well-prepared speech. Mark's response was to speak even more animatedly and enthusiastically about the OKRs. He finished up by telling me how proud he was of "his" team. Clearly he meant to pay homage to them, but instead he sounded belittling and patronizing. *My* skin started to crawl, so I could only imagine how the people working for him felt.

"Any questions?" Mark concluded.

All hands and eyes were cast firmly downward, so I asked the room. "If Mark hadn't decided on these OKRs, what would you all have planned to do next quarter?"

There was a collective exhale. Reluctantly, the young woman who'd clutched her head at lunch spoke up. While Mark's vision was inspiring, she worried that it just wasn't realistic. She calculated how much time it would take to do what he was suggesting, and it became clear that everyone would be working eighty-five hours a week. Others chimed in. He had badly underestimated the lag time in a system that made work less efficient than it should be. They'd been trying to fix it, but the problem was proving intractable.

A conversation started. It seemed that, while Mark's proposed goals made sense in theory, his team knew that there were major obstacles that made his plan impracticable. He had dismissed those obstacles as mere "implementation details," but, after *listening* to his team, it was clear that he'd skipped the important steps of "listen," "clarify, "debate," and "decide" and instead gone straight to "persuade" mode. It was pretty clear to me that 1) his decisions were not grounded in the facts 2) even if his decisions were the right ones, nobody was going to execute on them and 3) he was in danger of losing his team, if he hadn't already. I proposed that we finish going around the table, just to hear everyone out. Then we could regroup the following day.

This is a common mistake that is not limited to new managers. George W. Bush famously said, "I am the decider." Part of the reason it was so funny was that he wasn't in fact the decider, and he seemed to be the only one who didn't know it. If being elected as president of the United States doesn't grant you automatic decision-making power, becoming a manager or even CEO of your start-up definitely doesn't grant you "decider" status.

In his book *A Primer on Decision Making*, James March explains why it's a bad thing when the most "senior" people in a hierarchy are always the deciders. What he calls "garbage can decision-making" occurs when the people who happen to be around the table are the deciders rather than the people with the *best information*. Unfortunately, most cultures tend to favor either the most senior people or the people with the kinds of personalities that insist on sitting around the table. The bad decisions that result are among the biggest drivers of organizational mediocrity and employee dissatisfaction.

That is why kick-ass bosses often do not decide themselves, but rather create a clear decision-making process that empowers people closest to the facts to make as many decisions as possible. Not only does that result in better decisions, it results in better morale.

The decider should get facts, not recommendations

When collecting information for a decision, we are often tempted to ask people for their recommendations—"What do *you* think we should do?"—but as one executive I worked with at Apple explained to me, people tend to put their egos into recommendations in a way that can lead to politics, and thus worse decisions. So she recommended seeking "facts, not recommendations." Of course "facts" come inflected with each person's particular perspective or point of view, but they are less likely to become a line in the sand than a recommendation is.

Go spelunking

As the boss, you do have the right to delve into any details that seem interesting or important to you. You don't *have* to stay "high level" all the time. Sometimes you *will* be the decider. And even when you've delegated the key decisions, you can still plunge into the details of some other, smaller decision from time to time. You can't do that for every decision, but you can do it for some of them. I call this "spelunking" in your organization, and it is a good way to find out what's really going on. It's also a good way to put bosses and their direct reports on more equal footing—to show that nothing is "above" or "below" anyone's concern.

Also, when you are the decider, it's really important to go to the source of the facts. This is especially true when you're a "manager of managers." You don't want the "facts" to come to you through layers of management. If you ever played the game "telephone" as a kid, you know what happens to "facts" when they get passed around too many times.

In order to make sure they were able to understand and challenge facts as presented, leaders at Apple were expected to know details many "layers" deep in their organizations. If Steve Jobs was making an important decision and wanted to understand some aspect of it more deeply, he'd go right to the person working on it. There were numerous stories about relatively new, young engineers who'd return from lunch to find Steve waiting in their cube, eager to ask them about a specific detail of their work. He didn't get this information filtered to him through the person's boss or through the person's boss's recommendation; he went straight to the source. The more often you can do that, the more empowered your whole organization feels.

PERSUADE

"Emotion. Credibility. Logic."
—ARISTOTLE, *RHETORIC*

YOU'VE MANAGED TO drive your team to a decision, but there are still people who don't agree with it—the same people who will be responsible for helping to implement it. If you're working efficiently, not everybody on your team is involved in every step of the listen-clarify-debate-decide process for everything—just the relevant people. Now that a decision has been reached, it's time to get more people on board. This isn't easy, and it's vital to get it right.

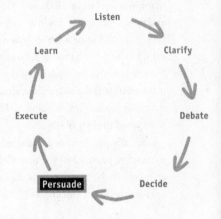

Persuasion at this stage can feel unnecessary and make the decider resentful of people on the team who aren't fully in agreement. The decider has painstakingly gone through the listen, clarify, and debate steps and made a decision. Why doesn't everyone else get why it's obvious we should do this—or at least be willing to fall in line?

But expecting others to execute on a decision without being persuaded that it's the right thing to do is a recipe for terrible results. And don't imagine that you can step in and simply tell everyone to get in line behind a decision, whether you have made it or somebody else has. Even explaining the decision is not enough, because that addresses only the logic; you have to address your listener's emotions as well. And you must establish that the decider, whether that's you or somebody else on your team, has credibility if you expect others to execute on the decision.

Authoritarian bosses tend to be particularly weak persuaders; they don't feel a need to explain the decision or their logic—"Just do it, don't question me!" And, because they usually don't know or care how the people on the broader team feel, they don't address their emotions. They fail to establish their credibility because they expect people to do what they say simply because they're the boss.

But even more democratic, open bosses often get so lost in explaining the rationale for a decision that they forget how people must feel about it, or vice versa. If you have done the basic work of Radical Candor—of getting to know each of your direct reports personally and establishing a norm of open exchange—it will be easier. But even then, being persuasive doesn't come naturally to a lot of people.

Many leaders I've worked with fail to be persuasive because they don't want to come across as manipulative, and the line between persuasion and manipulation can be a fine one. Aristotle was troubled that so much rhetoric and persuasion came down to manipulating people's emotions. He thought that there had to be a better way to get an idea across to a large number of people who don't have the time or knowledge to understand it completely. He resolved this by explaining that to be legitimately persuasive a speaker must address the audience's emotions but also establish the credibility and share the logic of the argument. These are the elements of persuasion that have stood the test of time.

To help you be more persuasive, and to teach the "deciders" on your team to be more persuasive, the rest of this section will cover, briefly, Aristotle's elements of rhetoric—pathos, logos, and ethos, which I'll translate loosely as emotion, logic, and credibility.*

Emotion
The listener's emotions, not the speaker's

You might have a strong emotional connection to a decision. It might be that you see it leading to a change that is likely to help a large group of people. But if you fail to take into account your *listener's* emotions, too, you won't be persuasive.

I had a colleague named "Jason" who was responsible for making his product usable for deaf people. He couldn't have been more passionate about his work—his mother was deaf—but he was unable to persuade the engi-

---

* I feel sheepish covering such well-trodden territory in such a few pages. But, despite two fancy degrees from two fancy schools, I'd never learned about this model until I spent time at Apple University, and I found it really helpful, so I share it, briefly, with you. Many tens of thousands of books have been written on Aristotle's *Rhetoric*. For another quick but more academic reference, see The Stanford Encyclopedia of Philosophy (http://plato.stanford.edu/entries/aristotle-rhetoric/). Probably the most-cited twenty-first-century look at persuasion is Robert Cialdini's book *Influence*. A quick search will reveal many other great sources.

neering team to prioritize certain key features in time for launch. When I showed him Aristotle's framework, he exploded.

"I don't know how I could have put any more emotion into my arguments," he said, his voice choked with frustration. He'd explained to them his personal connection to the project. They'd seemed moved, but they still hadn't gotten it done.

"What were the emotions on the engineering team like?" I asked.

"Oh. They were just exhausted. They'd been pulling all-nighters for weeks. It was like a death march over there."

"What did you do to address *their* emotions?"

Jason smacked his forehead, seeing clearly now where he'd gone wrong.

When Steve Jobs made his 2003 announcement that Apple would launch iTunes for the Windows platform, he knew he was doing more than just announcing a new product. For the Mac faithful, any accommodation to Microsoft was nothing short of betrayal. The logic behind the decision to launch iTunes for the Windows platform was sound: to win the music industry, Apple had to be on the platform that had over 90 percent market share—not just Mac, which had under 5 percent. But leading with this logic only would have made the Mac faithful angrier. So instead he acknowledged their incredulity and disbelief—with the headline "Hell froze over"—and took their emotional response seriously by reassuring them that Apple would remain true to its core.

Dick Costolo, when he was CEO of Twitter, was the master at connecting with the emotions of "Tweeps," people who work at Twitter. I have scrutinized many employee engagement surveys. I thought it was impossible to do better than Steve Jobs. Well over 90 percent of Apple employees reported feeling positive about their CEO when I was at Apple. But an even higher percentage of Tweeps felt positive about Dick as their CEO.

Dick's warm sense of humor helped him connect to people's emotions and earn their trust, which made him a persuasive leader. Dick often had everyone at Twitter's company all-hands meetings doubled over with laughter, most especially with his unexpectedly candid responses to somewhat hostile impromptu questions. I asked him how he came up with these responses, and he replied, with a characteristic smile, "Unfortunately, they just come to me."

If you don't happen to have experience as a stand-up comedian, you can still borrow a page out of Dick's book. He recommended several great improv classes to other leaders in Silicon Valley, to help them find a way to have fun answering all the awkward questions at all-hands meetings instead of dreading them.

Credibility
Demonstrate expertise and humility

Credibility is one of those things that is hard to articulate but you know it when you see it. Part of it is obviously knowing your subject and demonstrating a track record of sound decisions. But it also requires a third component—humility—which is sometimes in short supply.

Steve Jobs, not always thought of as a model of humility, had a knack for inserting some "aw, shucks" elements into product announcements. For example, at the 2010 iPad launch, Jobs started by saying, "We started Apple in 1976. Thirty-four years later we just ended our holiday quarter . . . with \$15.6 billion of revenue. I don't even believe that. Now what that means is that Apple is an over-fifty-billion-dollar company. Now I like to forget that, 'cause that's not how we think about Apple. But it is pretty amazing."* Behind him was an image of two geeks with a clunky box, a reminder of Apple's humble beginnings and the fact that Apple was driven by a zeal for building products that could change the world, not just a desire for profit. This added context allowed Jobs to point out that Apple had the expertise and resources to create a whole new category of computer without losing his audience. Note in particular the carefully chosen language in this sentence: "Now I like to forget that, 'cause that's not how we think about Apple." The "we" here is an important part of establishing humility for himself and for the entire company.

But how do you establish your credibility if you don't happen to be Steve Jobs with a track record of so-called Schumpeterian change, or if you're so new that you don't have much of a track record at all? Focus on your expertise and past accomplishments. Be humble and invoke a "we" not an "I" whenever possible. Bragging doesn't work, but neither does false humility. Don't forget to establish your credibility or to help the deciders on your team to establish theirs when it's time for them to persuade others to execute on a decision.

---

* https://www.youtube.com/watch?v=jj6q_z2Ni9M

Logic
Show your work

Most people expect that the "logic" part of persuasion will be easiest, since it doesn't present the personal awkwardness of establishing credibility or require the psychological finesse of addressing the collective emotions of a group of people. And yet it contains its own traps. Sometimes, the logic may seem self-evident to you, so you fail to share it with others. When you know something deeply, it's hard to remember that others don't.

The good news is that you learned the secret to sharing your logic in high school math class: show your work. When Steve Jobs had an idea, he wouldn't just describe the idea; he'd share how he got to it. He showed his work. This signaled that if there was a flaw in his reasoning, he wanted to know about it. And if there wasn't, people would be more likely to accept his idea. Showing his work was what strengthened his logic and ultimately made him not only persuasive but "always getting it right."

EXECUTE
Minimize the collaboration tax

AS THE BOSS, part of your job is to take a lot of the "collaboration tax" on yourself so that your team can spend more time executing. The responsibilities you have as a boss take up a tremendous amount of time. One of the hardest things about being a boss is balancing these responsibilities with the work you need to do personally in your area of expertise.

Here are the three things I've learned about getting this balance right: Don't waste your team's time; Keep the "dirt under your fingernails"; and Block time to execute.

Don't waste your team's time

In four years of working for Sheryl, I can honestly say she never wasted a single moment of my time, and in fact she saved enormous time for everyone who worked for her. She expected us to come to our 1:1s with a list of problems she could help us resolve. She'd listen, make sure she understood, and then she was like a sapper, an explosives expert. She defused some political situations that could have blown up in my face and she dispensed with seemingly insurmountable obstacles. No unnecessary meetings, no

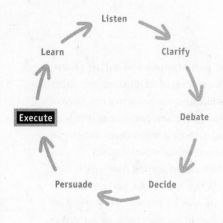

unnecessary analysis. She was never late to a meeting with me, and she wouldn't tolerate anyone being late to one of her meetings. She'd make us have debates as a team, but just before they started to feel tedious, she'd identify a "decider," and ask that person to come back to the rest of us with a decision by a particular date. She was one of the most persuasive people I've ever met, and she taught those of us on her team to be more persuasive as well. When some ridiculous time-wasting mandate would come down from on high at Google, Sheryl would figure out a way to shield us from it. All of that protection gave everyone who worked for her a lot more time to execute. And when the results came in, they didn't escape Sheryl's sharp analytical mind—we had to learn from what we'd done, whether we succeeded or failed.

The reason why Sheryl's teams were so productive was that she was constantly putting us through our paces on the GSD wheel, but she was also constantly clearing the decks for us so we could spend as much time as possible getting stuff done.

Keep the "dirt under your fingernails"

Even though the burden of the collaboration tax falls on you as the boss, the tax shouldn't be 100 percent. In order to be a good partner to the people on your team, and in order to keep the GSD wheel spinning efficiently, you need to stay connected to the actual work that is being done—not just by observing others executing but by executing yourself. If you become a conductor, you need to keep playing your instrument. If you become a sales manager, you need to keep going on sales calls yourself. If you mange a team of plumbers, fix some faucets. Of course, you need to spend time listening to people in 1:1s, leading debates, and so on. But you need to learn to toggle between leading and executing personally. Don't abandon the first for the second; integrate the two. If you get too far away from the work your team is doing, you won't understand their ideas well enough to help them clarify, to participate in debates, to know which decisions to push them to make, to teach them to be more persuasive. The GSD wheel will grind to a halt if you don't understand intimately the "stuff" your team is trying to get done.

Block time to execute

Often, execution is a solitary task. We use calendars mostly for collaborative tasks—to schedule meetings, etc. One of your jobs as a manager is to make sure that collaborative tasks don't consume so much of your time or your team's time that there's no time to execute whatever plan has been decided on and accepted.

LEARN

"Consistency is the hobgoblin of little minds."
—RALPH WALDO EMERSON, *SELF-RELIANCE*

BY THE TIME you've reached this spot on the wheel, you and your team have put in a ton of work, you've achieved something, and you want it to be great. And it is human nature for us to become attached—often unreasonably attached—to projects we've invested a lot of time and energy into. It can take almost superhuman discipline to step back, acknowledge when our results could be a lot better or are simply no good, and learn from the experience.

Drew Houston, cofounder and CEO of Dropbox, is the most committed and humble learner I've ever encountered in my career. The reason why Dropbox has hundreds of millions of users is because the company, led by Drew, has been relentless in making the product intuitive and easy to use. Drew has been singularly willing to try things, admit they didn't work as well as he'd hoped, and pivot. Hard as it is to launch and iterate with your company's products,

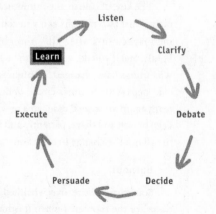

though, it's much harder to do the same with one's self. But what really impressed me about Drew was that he is even more relentless in reshaping *himself* as CEO than he is in improving upon the product his company builds. Drew has probably read and reread every book on management ever written. He has thought extremely deeply about what kind of company he wants to build, and what kind of leader he wants to be.

In his book *Denial*, Richard Tedlow writes about dozens of painful failures that have resulted when otherwise brilliant and successful people refused to see, let alone admit to, their mistakes. A colleague of mine once built a team that was getting absolutely *terrible* results, but he just couldn't admit it. Those of us who were trying to point it out to him were mystified. When we finally got through to him, he exclaimed, "It's unbearably painful to admit it when you have an ugly baby!"

It's obvious that good bosses learn from mistakes and successes alike and keep improving. And yet, denial is actually the more common reaction to imperfect execution than learning. Why is learning so rare? When managing a large team, I found there were two enormous pressures that tempted me to quit learning.

Pressure to be consistent

We are often told that changing our position makes us a "flip-flopper" or "erratic" or "lacking principles." I prefer John Maynard Keynes's idea that "When the facts change, I change my mind."

The key, of course, is communication. Someone might reasonably complain, "Just two months ago you convinced me of X and now you're telling me maybe not-X after all?" You obviously can't change course like this lightly, and if you do, you need to be able to explain clearly and convincingly why things have changed. I'd often revisit the listen, clarify, debate, and decide steps with an inner circle. When it was time to persuade the broader team again after we'd reached a new conclusion, it was important to take a deep breath and share, patiently and repeatedly, how we'd gotten there, and to call out the change in direction explicitly.

Burnout

Sometimes we're overwhelmed by our work and personal lives, and these are the moments when it is hardest to learn from our results and to

start the whole cycle over again.
That's why you are at the very
center of the wheel that moves
you forward as a manager.
You've got to take care of yourself, first and foremost. That's
easier said than done, of course.

Dick Costolo showed a re-
markable ability to remain centered. While I was his coach,
the press took Dick on a hero-
shithead roller-coaster ride the
likes of which I've never seen.
Watching from the sidelines
stressed me out more than it

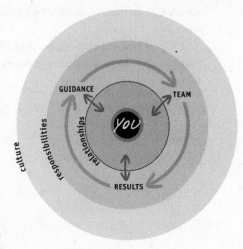

stressed him out, even though he was at the center of the storm and I was
at a safe distance. After a particularly horrible day of bad press, I woke up
in the middle of the night after having a dream that the Twitter office
building was on a launchpad and that we were blasting into space without
our space suits. I woke my husband up with a shout and then couldn't
go back to sleep. Dick told me he'd slept soundly through the night.

When everybody was singing Dick's praises as if he were the Second Coming, he reacted with characteristic self-deprecating humor. Every
celebrity you could imagine was offering Dick invitations that most of
us would have given our eyeteeth to have, and he declined most to make
sure he could both focus on operations at Twitter and get home to have
dinner with his family. When everyone went on the attack, he quoted
his daughter: "Dad! Bad news and good news. Bad news: you're on the
Yahoo! Finance list of five worst CEO's this year. Good news: you're number five."

But Dick didn't pretend that nothing was wrong, either. This was not
just a difficult time for him, it was a difficult time for Twitter. He gave a
talk to the company about the "mental toughness" required to remain confident in the face of a barrage of bad press. I felt awkward as I got weepy
listening to him talk, but then I looked around and saw I was far from alone.
I think a lot of Dick's mental toughness came from his ability to stay

centered, to do things like block two hours of think-time on his calendar every day.

Chapter Five, the next chapter in this book, begins with some specific things you can do to make sure you are staying centered, both at work and in life.

PART II

TOOLS & TECHNIQUES

I hope Part I of this book has alleviated some of the fear, anxiety, and self-doubt that can be the constant companion of any boss. Chapters One through Four explained the core ideas I learned from twenty-five years of leading teams—from diamond cutters in Moscow, to Google and Apple. I wrote them because too many good people become bad bosses, and bad bosses are a major source of unhappiness in our world and dysfunction in our workplace. I hope that these ideas will help you find your own way to be a better boss, have more success at work, and make the world a little happier.

Now you understand how building Radically Candid relationships with each of your direct reports will help you guide your team to achieve results. And even though relationships don't scale, culture does. Your relationships and your responsibilities reinforce each other, and from that interaction your success flows and your culture grows. But how to enact these principles?

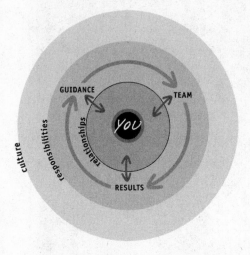

What, exactly, do you do differently when you go to work tomorrow?

Part II of this book will describe some tools and techniques you can use to put the ideas from Part I into place immediately. I've organized these chapters around the core ideas of the book, not around what you should do first, second, third. Please read for understanding now. But rest assured, the very last chapter will offer you the step-by-step set of things you can do to roll out Radical Candor. There are few greater joys than doing work you love with people you care about and achieving great results. That's not a pipe dream. You *can* create that kind of environment, and I'll describe how.

RELATIONSHIPS

An approach to establishing trust with your direct reports

HOW DO YOU CREATE A climate in which Radically Candid relationships can flourish? In this chapter, you will begin to see that your role as boss is far more meaningful than the usual Dilbert stereotype. When I was at business school, I was taught that my job as a manager was to "maximize shareholder value." In life, I learned that too much emphasis on shareholder value actually destroys value, as well as morale. Instead, I learned to focus first on staying centered myself, so that I could build real relationships with each of the people who worked for me. Only when I was centered and my relationships were strong could I fulfill my responsibilities as a manager to guide my team to achieve the best results. Shareholder value is the result. It's not at the core, though.

As I've said before, there's a chicken-and-egg interaction between your relationships and your responsibilities. You can't fulfill your responsibilities without good relationships, but the way in which you fulfill your responsibilities is integral to those relationships. They're built from the outside in *and* the inside out. This chapter will focus on inside out. Chapters Six to Eight will focus on outside in. In this chapter I'll talk about staying centered, staying on an equal footing with the people who report to you, and the art (and dangers) of socializing at work.

STAY CENTERED
You can't give a damn about others if you don't give a damn about yourself

IT MAY SEEM strange at first, but I always begin my efforts to coach CEOs in building a Radically Candid workplace by looking first at how that person has structured their life and is dealing with the pressures of their job. What we bring to work depends on our own health and well-being. It's a

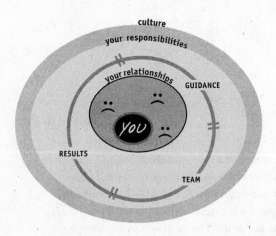

measure of how far we've come as a society that this claim no longer feels overly "soft." And it's a great boon to business, because managers who create a stable foundation for themselves are invariably more effective at building teams on which people can do the best work of their lives.

Think for a moment about hard times at work. *You're* stressed out. *You're* not sleeping. Your problems at work and at home are compounding each other. Hard times are made much harder when you're not at your best. And they can make it particularly hard to "care personally" about the people you work with, not to mention those you live with. You're too busy dealing with your own suffering. But "caring personally" is integral to building the relationships that drive everything else. The essence of leadership is not getting overwhelmed by circumstances.

You can't give a damn about others if you don't take care of yourself. And when you don't care about yourself or those around you, everything else—including your results—gets out of whack. But you already know that. What am I recommending you *do* about it?

Work-life integration

Be relentlessly insistent on bringing your fullest and best self to work—and taking it back home again. Don't think of it as work-life balance, some kind of zero-sum game where anything you put into your work robs your life and anything you put into your life robs your work. Instead, think of it as work-life integration. If you need to get eight hours of sleep to stay centered, those hours are not something that you do for yourself at the expense of your work or your team. Your work and your life can give each other a "double bounce." The time you spend at work can be an expression of who you are as a human being, an enormous enrichment to your life, and a boon to your friends and family.

Figure out your "recipe" to stay centered and stick to it

The world is full of advice here, and what is enormously meaningful for one person is pure crap for another. I once saw a movie where a New York cop was showing a Moscow cop the fish tanks and special lights and elaborate meditation rituals he used to manage stress. "How do you cope?" the New Yorker asked. The Muscovite replied with one word: "Vodka."

Do whatever works for you. The key, I've found, is to prioritize doing it (but not overdoing it) when times get tough. It's even more important to focus on making time for whatever keeps you centered when you are stressed and busy than when things are relatively calm. A very successful entrepreneur I knew went to the gym both before and after work during crunch times.

Here's what I need to do to stay centered: sleep eight hours, exercise for forty-five minutes, and have both breakfast and dinner with my family. If I skip one or two of those things for a day or two, it's OK. But that's the routine. Also, every so often I need to read a novel (ideally one a week), go away for a romantic weekend with my husband (ideally four times a year), and take a two-week vacation with siblings and parents (once a year). If I can manage to do those things, I can usually stay centered no matter what storms are raging around me. If I can't manage to do those things, I'll usually go a little nutty even if everything is pretty serene all around me.

Calendar

Put the things you need to do for yourself on your calendar, just as you would an important meeting. If you are having trouble leaving the office in time to get home for dinner, put your commute time in your calendar. Pretend you have a train to catch.

Show up for yourself

Don't blow off those meetings with yourself or let others schedule over them any more than you would a meeting with your boss.

FREE AT WORK

OK, NOW YOU'RE centered and bringing your best self to work. The next step is to think about how to give your team a sense of autonomy and agency so that they, too, can be centered and bring their best selves to work. You can guide your team to get results if you've built a trusting relationship with each person reporting to you, and there can only be real trust when people feel *free at work*. The first rule of building the kind of relationship with the people that will make them feel free at work is to relinquish unilateral authority. If you're a manager at Google, it got laid down for you. If you're a manager at almost any other company, you're going to have to relinquish it voluntarily. That will take enormous discipline. It's natural to crave a little control. But power and control are illusory and won't get you where you really want to go. Relationships are more effective, and more satisfying.

The basic premise here is that when everyone on your team is able to bring the best of what they've got mentally, emotionally, and physically to their work, they are more fulfilled in their jobs, they work better with one another, and the team gets better results. You can't get that out of people with power, authority, or control. Twitter and Square CEO Jack Dorsey explained why succinctly in an email he sent out to the whole company. "If you have to use someone else's name or authority to get a point across, there is little merit to the point (you might not believe it yourself). If you believe something to be correct, focus on showing your work to prove it. Authority derives naturally from merit, not the other way around."

If you can build a trusting relationship with people so that they feel free at work, then they're much more likely to do the best work of their lives.

But you're not "getting it out of them"; you're creating the conditions for them to bring it out of themselves.

As discussed in Chapter One, there are few things more damaging to building a trusting relationship with another person than unilateral authority or a sense of superiority. The way you treat people determines whether you'll get their best effort, a perfunctory effort, or an effort to sabotage you. When you treat people like cogs in a machine, you'll get no more than you demand, and you create an incentive to break the machine. I'll never forget the time I did a consulting project at a steel mill when I was in business school. I designed what I thought was a very clever compensation system that treated the workers as if they were "coin-operated." The foreman said to me, "With a system like that, guys who can't write their names will learn calculus to figure out how to screw me!" I realized he was exactly right.

Of course, the only thing worse than tyranny is anarchy, which is, as Hobbes put it in *Leviathan*, "nasty, brutish, and short." In anarchy, bullies get away with optimizing for their narrow self-interest and the overall results are often nonexistent. A Russian anecdote about the dictator and the lawless warlord explains this perfectly. The warlord visits the home of the dictator, who shows him the spectacular view outside his window. "You see that road?" the dictator asks and then beats his chest. "Ten percent for me. Ha ha ha ha!" When the dictator visits the warlord, the warlord has an even more spectacular view to show off. "You see that road?" ask the warlord. "What road?" asks the dictator. The warlord beats *his* chest. "One *hundred* percent for me. Ha ha ha ha!" In a state of anarchy, the warlord's authority is even more unchecked than the dictator's in a totalitarian regime.

Shona Brown, who wrote *Competing on the Edge: Strategy as Structured Chaos* before she joined Google's Executive Management Team to lead Business Operations, wanted to avoid creating dictators or permitting the rise of warlords. She carefully constructed a hiring process, a promotion process, and a performance review process with this in mind. All those processes were not to control employees. Rather, they were aimed at replacing unilateral authority, which is easily hijacked by expediency or narrow self-interest, with a process that required the input of the whole team. By forcing managers to lay down unilateral control, Google encouraged them to build good relationships with their direct reports and ensured that everyone could feel free at work. It also dramatically improved decision-making at Google.

Google's distrust of unchecked managerial authority played out in virtually all of its procedures. Managers couldn't just hire people—they had to put candidates through a rigorous interview process that then sent "interview packets" all the way up to Larry Page to approve or disapprove. Promotions were decided not by the managers but by a committee of peers. Performance ratings were influenced by 360-degree feedback on each employee, not just the manager's subjective opinion, and then calibrated across teams to make sure standards were similarly upheld across teams. That made it pretty hard to play favorites or hold people back unfairly. And so on.

Whether or not Google's extreme approach would work for your company, you can see how it gives people a sense of fairness and autonomy simply by reducing the odds that any individual can be at the mercy of a single person. Bosses can't become petty bureaucrats. When you have too much unilateral authority, you'll inevitably do things that will erode trust, ruin your relationships, and make your direct reports want to escape from their jobs the way they'd want to break out of jail. Sometimes even just a tiny bit of unilateral authority is enough to make people behave badly. Think about your last trip to the Department of Motor Vehicles. That's why the first rule of building the kind of relationship with the people that will make them feel free at work is to lay down unilateral authority.

Again, I'm not recommending abdication or anarchy. I'm not talking about simply ignoring the people who report to you, or letting them do whatever they want. You have a job to do. You have to guide your team to achieve results, and to do that you're going to have to break ties and make tough decisions, often unpopular ones. That's part of why building relationships based on trust and in which people feel free at work is so important.

I recommend that you look for places where you can let go of some of the traditional sources of a boss's control, thereby signaling to your reports that you want them to be more autonomous. Much of the advice you'll read about in the next three chapters is aimed at encouraging you to give up your unilateral authority and to focus instead on building trust-based relationships.

MASTER THE ART OF SOCIALIZING AT WORK

SOME COMPANIES PUT a lot of effort into bringing employees together outside of the office. It might be a happy hour, or a holiday party, or an off-site event. While retreats and parties can be productive if people on your team really want them, it is best to remember that mostly you get to know the people you work with on the job, every day, as an integrated part of the work rhythm, not at the annual holiday party.

Spending time with people from work in a more relaxed setting, without the pressure of work deadlines, can be a good way to build relationships. It doesn't have to be expensive. You can take a walk together or have a picnic. Meeting each other's families can also have a big impact. More memorable than the extravagant carnival set up at Google for "bring your kid to work" day was the fact that Alan Eustace, a senior vice president of Engineering, wore a pink bunny suit. Inviting your team and their families or significant/insignificant others over to your home for a meal can be a great way to open yourself up and show you care.

Sometimes, though, when these events are introduced by management, they can feel both obligatory and forced—unintentionally undermining a culture of freedom and autonomy. You already spend a lot of hours every day with your colleagues and direct reports. Use *that* time to build relationships. For the most part, it's better to use the time after work to keep yourself centered than to socialize with work colleagues.

When you do organize a social event at work, bear these warnings in mind: even non-mandatory events can feel mandatory. And booze can land you in dangerous territory.

Even non-mandatory events can feel mandatory

Fun events *can* be a good way to get to know the people on your team, and to help them get to know one another. But be aware that if you organize it, the social pressure will drag some people into situations they'd rather avoid. I'll never forget talking to Marissa Mayer when she was at Google about a whale-watching trip that her boss had organized to help the team bond. Marissa gets seasick. She knew she'd wind up blowing chunder over the side of the boat if she went. But her boss pressured her, saying she should go anyway, to be a good team player. You shouldn't have to barf over the side of a boat to demonstrate you're a good team player.

It's important to avoid those ironic moments when attempts to team-build and improve morale actually make things worse. I once worked with a leader whose team was working eighty hours a week. At their off-site retreat, work-life balance was on the agenda—at 9 P.M. at night, after riding go-carts. The truth was, they would all rather have skipped the go-carts, but they thought they *had* to do "fun" things to "bond." Sometimes, the greatest gift you can give your team is to let them go home.

Booze

A drink or two can be a social lubricant. But it can also backfire, and badly. Here are just a few of the nightmares that I have personally witnessed or have firsthand knowledge of that were a result of too much alcohol at work:

A woman vomited on her salad plate at a client dinner. A man punched a police officer and spent the night in jail. An office couch had to be removed because it was clear people had had sex on it. Another office couch was ruined when somebody who was drunk vomited on it. A woman drank so much that she passed out in the office, and her boss's boss got a call at 3 A.M. from security. Emotional agony and marriages destroyed by unwanted drunken sexual advances. Rape allegations. A suicide attempt. These are, needless to say, not good ways to build relationships.

RESPECT BOUNDARIES

BUILDING RADICALLY CANDID relationships requires you to walk a fine line between respecting other people's boundaries and encouraging them to bring their whole selves to work. There is not one "right" place for these boundaries to be or one way to push them open a little more. You'll need to negotiate boundaries differently with each person you work with. And you've got to respect these boundaries while also getting to know the people you work with better over time, in order to build the best relationships of your career. Here are some things I've learned about walking this line. I hope they will help you negotiate yours.

Building trust

Building trust in any relationship takes time because trust is built on a consistent pattern of acting in good faith. It's a big mistake to assume too much trust too quickly (e.g., by prying into deeply personal questions when you barely know a person). On the other hand, you do need to start somewhere. If you never ask a single question about a person's life, it's hard to move up on the "care personally" axis. Probably the most important thing you can do to build trust is to spend a little time alone with each of your direct reports on a regular basis. Holding regular 1:1s in which your direct report sets the agenda and you ask questions is a good way to begin building trust. (See "1:1 Conversations," chapter eight.) The way you ask for criticism and react when you get it goes a long way toward building trust—or destroying it. (See "Soliciting Impromptu Guidance," chapter six.) Having annual "career conversations" is also an excellent way to strengthen your relationship with each person who reports directly to you (see chapter seven).

Sharing values

When I was working with the team developing *Managing at Apple*, a number of people advocated strongly for starting the course with an exercise that required managers to write down and share their "personal values." Their rationale was not bad. Your values are what keep you centered. But I'm extremely wary of these kinds of exercises. First, developing one's personal values is the work of a lifetime. It can feel cheapened by a forty-five-minute exercise. Second, while some people find it helpful to articulate their values explicitly, others feel that it's impossible to do this in a meaningful way. Third, and most important, many people feel that their values are a deeply private set of beliefs that they don't want to discuss with colleagues. Others may take the exercise as an invitation to proselytize, and the way they talk about their values may highlight differences that are actually irrelevant to their ability to work together. An exercise that requires people to talk publicly about their values may drive a wedge rather than help people find what they have in common.

Why would I object to asking people to write down their values since I am all about "bringing your whole self to work" (i.e., feeling free enough to pour everything you've got intellectually, emotionally, and physically into your job)? A student in one of my classes once told a story that explained why succinctly. He was a gay man from the Midwest, and he felt certain that if he had come out in his previous job he would have been ostracized by many of his colleagues. Doing a values exercise at that company, therefore, might have required him to lie about his values.

The important thing to do is to stay in touch with your personal values, and to demonstrate them in how you manage your team, not by writing down things like "hard work," "honesty," and "innovation" on a piece of paper. Live your values. Don't try to list them like an HR exercise from the show *The Office*.

Demonstrating openness

That brings me to an important precept at the heart of Radical Candor: openness. You don't have to share the same deeply personal values to build good relationships at work; and it's a terrible idea to try to convince your colleagues that your values are "right" and theirs are "wrong." But you do need to *respect* other people's values when they do share them with you.

You might imagine that in liberal places like San Francisco, where I work, or New York, people are wide open to difference. But I've had several colleagues who've complained that they have to keep their conservative political views to themselves or face ostracism here in San Francisco. They have to bite their tongue whenever people make comments that take for granted that they agree all conservatives are stupid or venal. Think about it—whether it's the gay man forced to weather anti-gay jokes or the conservative forced to weather anti-conservative jokes, the result is the same—some part of them is negated, and they can't help feeling alienated, not free at work.

That's why it's crucial to remind people that an important part of Radically Candid relationships is opening yourself to the possibility of connecting with people who have different worldviews or whose lives involve behavior that you don't understand or that may even conflict with a core belief of yours. It's possible to care personally about a person who disagrees with your views on abortion or guns or God. The fastest path to artificial relationships at work, and to the gravitational pull of organizational mediocrity, is to insist that everyone have the same worldview before building relationships with them. A radically candid relationship starts with the basic respect and common decency that every human being owes each other, regardless of worldview. Once again, the *work* is the bond everybody on a team *does* share, and the most productive way to strengthen that bond is by learning how to work together in ways that benefit everyone involved.

Dick Costolo spent a lot of time and effort thinking about how to make Twitter a more inclusive, open environment. When he took the Implicit Association Test (IAT) that measures unconscious bias, his scores revealed him to have essentially no unconscious bias. Per the IAT he's less gender-biased than I am, and I consider myself a real champion for women.

One of my favorite stories about Dick and diversity was his effort to eliminate the phrase "you guys" from his vocabulary. I told him a story about my twins—one a boy and one a girl—who were in kindergarten. Both of their teachers were speculating why boys raise their hands more often than girls. Then I attended a class and heard the questions: "OK, you guys, who knows what four plus one is?" No wonder the girls weren't raising their hands! Children are literal, and girls are not guys. I told Dick that story, and confessed that I'm literal too and feel annoyed whenever somebody addresses a mixed group as "guys," or "you guys." Most people look crossways at me when I launch into my "you guys" diatribe, but Dick smacked his forehead. "Of course! There's nothing worse than being invisible. I can't believe I never thought of that! There's no worse way to make a group of people feel excluded than to use language that pretends they are simply not in the room."

"Yes, like *Invisible Man*," I said. Dick and I had recently discussed Ralph Ellison's novel about an African-American man whose color renders him invisible.

"Yes, exactly! OK, you've convinced me. I'm going to start saying *you all!*" Dick said.

It's not easy to change your reflexive idiom, but Dick spent real energy training himself to say "you all" instead of "you guys."

Physical space

Is touching a colleague ever a good idea? A lot of people would say any sort of physical contact at work other than a super-professional handshake is inappropriate or dangerous. I think we've thrown the baby out with the bathwater on this one. When a colleague's spouse has been killed in a car accident or an employee has just announced their engagement, a super-professional handshake just doesn't cut it, and real hug may be the world's most effective way to show you care personally.

Stacy Brown-Philpot, TaskRabbit's CEO, learned a lot about hugging—and navigating physical space—from much-loved Silicon Valley coach Bill Campbell. The first time Stacy ever met Bill was when he came up to her after a talk and told her that she flapped her hands in front of her face when she spoke and that she would have more credibility if she'd stop it. She said it was the most useful public speaking advice she's ever gotten.

"Were you a little mad that this man you'd never met before came up and criticized you?" I asked her.

Stacy thought about it for a moment. "Well, no I wasn't. Because before he said anything to me he gave me a great big bear hug and a kiss on the cheek. So I knew he was coming from a place of warmth. It was immediately obvious that he cared and was just saying it to help me."

"Were you weirded out that a strange man hugged and kissed you?"

"No, because it seemed just so natural coming from him. I wish more people would hug like that."

My husband, who coached Bill's son's Little League team, said, "He hugged all the coaches and all the parents and all the kids. He just hugged everybody! More people should do that."

Like Stacy and my husband, I wish more people gave hugs like that. Not just little one-arm side swipes, but the kind of six-second hugs that Gretchen Rubin writes about in *The Happiness Project*. Gretchen, who has research for EVERYTHING, explains why a longer hug is more effective than a shorter one.

> **"Interesting fact: to be most effective at optimizing the flow of the chemicals oxytocin and serotonin—which boost mood and promote bonding—hold a hug for at least six seconds."**

Of course, a hug or a touch *can* go wrong. Early in my career, I had a boss who gave me a big hug when I was upset about something, and then started grinding into me in a sexual and most unwelcome way. Now I was *really* upset. I had relied on him as a mentor and now I would forever see him as just another sleazebag. If a hug is sexual or belittling or obviously unwanted, it's obnoxiously aggressive. If all you ever give is hugs and you never challenge the other person, then your hugs may be ruinously empathetic. Conversely, don't feel bad when the other person doesn't want to be hugged. And if you are not comfortable with a hug, it's OK too. When Russ Laraway read these pages, he immediately asked me not to hug him.

To show that you "care personally" with your hugs, you have to obey the "platinum rule." The "golden rule" says do unto others as you'd have them do unto you. The "platinum rule" says, figure out what makes the other person comfortable, and do that. If most people on your team are comfortable with hugs but a couple are not, you need to figure out a way to make sure that they don't feel excluded from all those hugs they don't want. Use your words!)

But if you *can* do what Bill Campbell did for Stacy, and offer the kind of Radically Candid hug that opens a person's mind and heart to learning something new, or to growing in some way, you'll leave the world just a little bit happier.

Go ahead. Try it. I dare you! It's fine to push yourself past your comfort zone, but not fine to make others uncomfortable, so try it only with people who *want* to be hugged!

Recognizing your own emotions

"I know what kind of day I'm gonna have by the kind of mood you're in when you walk in the door," Russ told me one morning when we worked together at Google. I've rarely felt so ashamed. I thought I was pretty even-keeled and that I had a good poker face during tough times. He saw I was upset and gave me some credit without backing off his direct challenge: "You at least *try* not to take it out on us. But still, we all notice what kind of mood you're in. Everybody notices what kind of mood the boss is in. We have to. It's adaptive."

What did I need to do to make sure that my whole team didn't have a worse day just because I was having a bad one? It's here that the imperative to bring your whole self to work can collide with the negative impacts of doing just that. But repressing those feelings tends not to work, either. You can't successfully hide how you feel from people who work closely with you. You don't want to take your bad days out on your team, but nor can you hide the fact you're not at your best. The best you can do is to own up to how you feel and what's going on in the rest of your life, so others don't feel your mood is their fault.

I learned simply to say something along the lines of, "Hey, I'm having a shitty day. I'm trying hard not to be grouchy, but if it seems like I have a short fuse today, I do. It's not because of you or your work, though. It's because I had a big argument with a friend [or whatever]."

If you have a truly terrible emotional upset in your life, stay home for a day. You don't want to spread it around any more than you'd want to spread a bad virus around the office, and emotions are just as contagious as germs. Mental-health days should be taken more seriously than they are.

Master your reactions to others' emotions

Many people cross a dangerous emotional boundary when they become the boss. They try to manage other people's emotions. This is a big overstep. All people, including the people who report to you, are responsible for their own emotional lives. There are fewer faster paths to Manipulative Insincerity than imagining you can control another person's emotional reactions or maneuver around them. To build Radically Candid relationships, do not try to prevent, control, or manage other people's emotions. Do acknowledge them and react compassionately when emotions run high. And do try to master your reactions to other people's emotions.

You already know how to react to emotion with compassion. You do it all the time in your personal life. Somehow, at work we are primed to forget these basics. Here are some pointers on reacting with compassion—things you probably do instinctively with other relationships but may not be doing at work:

Acknowledge emotions. Emotional reactions can offer important clues to help you better understand what's really going on with the people you manage. They can offer you a shortcut to the heart of the matter. So don't respond to outbursts or sullen silences by pretending they are not happening. Don't try to mitigate them by saying things like, "It's not personal," or "Let's be professional." Instead say, "I can see you're mad/frustrated/ elated/_____"

Ask questions. When somebody is frustrated or angry or upset enough about a situation at work that they react emotionally, this is your cue to keep asking questions until you understand what the real issue is. Don't over-direct the conversation; just keep listening and it will become clear.

Adding your guilt to other people's difficult emotions doesn't make them feel better. People I've managed or coached have often come to me distraught after they gave guidance to somebody who started crying. "What should I have done differently?" they ask. Maybe they handled the situation perfectly. Just because somebody is crying or yelling doesn't mean you've done anything wrong; it just means they are upset. If you feel guilty about the fact that they are upset, you're more likely to have a defensive reaction than a compassionate one. Your defensive reaction can lead you, in turn, to unintentionally patronizing or cold behavior. People spend a huge portion of their lives at work. They generally care about their work. *Of course* they get upset when things go wrong. When somebody is upset, it's not necessarily your fault. Their upset may have nothing to do with you. Focus on them, not on yourself.

Telling other people how to feel will backfire. Here are some of the most counterproductive words you can utter: "Don't be sad"; "Don't be mad"; "No offense, but." If you're tempted to use these phrases, think about that Meatloaf song, "I want you, I need you, there ain't no way I'm ever gonna love you, now don't be sad." That just makes it sadder! If you're a person who can't bear emotion, don't put the burden on the other person *not* to cry or yell or get defensive. If you tell somebody they can't have a particular emotional reaction, it becomes almost inevitable they will have that reaction; your injunction is likely to elicit the very emotions you most fear. It's like Tolstoy's brother telling him he couldn't leave the corner of the room until he quit thinking about a white bear. The white bear occupied Tolstoy's mind for *hours*. I once had a boss who told me I couldn't cry in front of him. So I cried *all the damn time* with that man! It was terrible for both of us.

If you really can't handle emotional outbursts, forgive yourself. You don't have to sit there watching somebody cry or yell if it's unbearable for you. If somebody starts to have an emotional reaction you can't deal with, it's fine to say, "I am sorry you're upset. I'm going to step out for a moment and get you some water. I'll be right back." Then, when you get back, you can say, "I'd like to change the topic for now and discuss this later. I promise I'll come back to it, because I can see it's important. But I'm having a hard time right now."

Keep tissues a short walk away from your desk. I used to keep a box of tissues in my office in case of tears. Then a person I worked with made a habit of coming into my office and crying every Friday afternoon. This was an exhausting way to end the week. I went to a colleague who was deathly afraid of tears for advice. He pointed out to me that offering a Kleenex at the first sign of tears sometimes can really turn on the waterworks. If he saw somebody start to tear up, he'd excuse himself to leave the office and go get Kleenex. That little respite was often enough to allow the crier to regain composure. I tried this technique the next Friday, and it worked!

Keep some closed bottles of water at your desk. Another good piece of advice I heard from an HR business partner was to have some unopened bottles of water at hand. If you see that somebody is getting upset, offer a bottle of water. Often, the simple pause to unscrew the top and take a sip of water is enough to help the person feel calmer. If you are a crier, you can use the bottle of water!

Walk, don't sit. When planning a difficult conversation, try taking a walk instead of sitting and talking. When you're walking, the emotions are less on display and less likely to start resonating in a destructive way. Also, walking and looking in the same direction often feels more collaborative than sitting across a table and staring each other down.

BUILDING RELATIONSHIPS WITH your direct reports takes time and real energy. Sometimes, especially when things are not going well, this will be the most depleting part of your job. Remembering that it is central to your job will help. And if you can power through these times, you may find as I have that these relationships give your work meaning far beyond the results that you achieve together.

6.

GUIDANCE

*Ideas for getting/giving/
encouraging praise & criticism*

I N CHAPTER TWO, I DESCRIBED how Radically Candid relationships create the trust that enables you to give better guidance and how giving better guidance in turn further develops those Radically Candid relationships. Guidance is the "atomic building block" of management, but it is profoundly uncomfortable for most people. What follows are specific tools and techniques that will make it easier for you to create a culture of guidance on your team.

In order to build a culture of Radically Candid guidance *you need to get, give, and encourage both*

GUIDANCE=	Praise	Criticism
Get from		
Give to		
Encourage between		

praise and criticism. The graphic I developed to help keep the balance right is shown on the previous page.

SOLICITING IMPROMPTU GUIDANCE
Embrace the discomfort

ONE OF THE key insights I received about creating a culture of guidance came from watching the argument between Larry Page and Matt Cutts

GUIDANCE=	Praise	Criticism
Get from	✔	✔
Give to		
Encourage between		

that I described in the Introduction. Before Larry criticized Matt's proposal, he encouraged Matt to challenge with gusto by grinning encouragingly when Matt started to get passionate. Larry never said, "Don't get emotional." The more intense Matt's criticism got, the wider Larry's grin got. How can you foster an environment in which this becomes unremarkable? What are the things you can *do* to get criticism from your team?

It's not so easy, because when you are the boss people *really* do not want to criticize you or to tell you what they really think. Along with the position, you inherit a bunch of assumptions that have nothing to do with who you really are. The role often changes people's impression of you in ways that can be bewildering. For example, I am five feet tall, have blonde hair, and speak with a Southern accent. All my life I'd fought the "dumb blonde" stereotype. So when I became a manager and somebody told me I was intimidating, I thought she was joking. Then, I overheard somebody else describe me as tall. Even though one guy on the team was *seventeen* inches taller than I am.

Don't think for a minute that because you're a nice person, or because you used to eat lunch every day with the people you now manage, that people won't see you differently now that you're the boss, or that they will automatically trust you. Take a look at the many colorful definitions of boss like this one in Urban Dictionary: "Bosses are like diapers: Full of shit and all over your ass." "Boss: Disingenuous form of address used by insolent little twats, which although ostensibly deferential, actually implies that they don't actually have any respect for you at all." To some degree, the minute you assume the role of boss you'll be fighting preconceptions. And the authority that comes with the role is, in fact, likely to bring out some of your worst instincts—so it may not *just* be a matter of unfair perception!

That's why when you become the boss it's important to work so hard to earn your team's trust. You may be worried about earning their respect, and that's natural. Unfortunately, though, being overly focused on respect can backfire because it'll make you feel extra defensive when criticized. If, on the other hand, you can listen to the criticism and react well to it, both trust *and* respect will follow.

Here are some tips/techniques I've seen work to get the conversation flowing:

You are the exception to the "criticize in private" rule of thumb. Michelle Peluso, CEO of Gilt Groupe, explained the benefits of criticizing herself publicly. In an interview with *The New York Times* she said, "I've always taken a slightly different approach with 360 reviews. We'll share them with each other on the executive team, and I'll start with mine—'Here is where I'm good, and here is where I'm not doing so well.' I'll even tell the whole company and say, 'Here is where I want your help.' That makes it a bit safer for other people to do the same, and you can build trust."

Once I figured out who on my team was most comfortable criticizing me, I would ask that person to do it in front of others at a staff meeting or an all-hands meeting. They were always reluctant at first—"What about 'criticize in private'?" But when you are the boss, that rule doesn't apply to you. When you encourage people to criticize you publicly, you get the chance to show your team that you really, genuinely want the criticism. You also set an ideal for the team as a whole: *everyone should embrace criticism that helps us do our jobs better.* The bigger the team, the more leverage you get out of reacting well to criticism in public.

Also, the bigger your team, the harder it is for people to get on your calendar. If you have more than sixty or so people working for you and you make them wait till they can get a private moment with you to share some criticism, you'll probably never hear it. Airing it in public has another benefit as well: it saves you from having to hear the same thing over and over.

Too many managers fear that public challenge will undermine their authority. It's natural to want to repress dissent, but a good reaction to public criticism can be the very thing that establishes your credibility as a strong leader, and will help you build a culture of guidance.

Have a go-to question. When you're the boss, it's awkward to ask your direct reports to tell you frankly what they think of your performance—even more awkward for them than it is for you. To help, I adopted a go-to question that Fred Kofman, author of *Conscious Business* and my coach at Google, suggested. "What could I do or stop doing that would make it easier to work with me?" If those words don't fall easily off your tongue, find words that do. Of course, you're not really just looking for one thing; that opening question is just designed to get things moving.

Embrace the discomfort. Most people will initially respond to your question with something along the lines of "Oh, everything is fine, thank you for asking," and hope that's the end of the conversation. They probably didn't see your question coming, and so they feel immediately wary. Their discomfort will make *you* feel uncomfortable, and you may find yourself reassuring them by nodding and offering an "I'm glad to hear that." *Don't do this.* It's essential that you prepare yourself for these scenarios in advance and commit to sticking with the conversation until you have a genuine response.

One technique is to count to six before saying anything else, forcing them to endure the silence. The goal is not to be a bully but to insist on a candid discussion—to make it harder for the person to say nothing than to tell you what they're thinking. If they can't come up with anything on the spot, you can always arrange a time to meet again. If counting to six doesn't do the trick, ask the question again. And again if necessary. One of the bankers who led Facebook's IPO told me about a time that Sheryl asked him for feedback after a meeting with potential investors. "What could I have done better?" she asked him. He couldn't think of anything. The presentation had been a home run. Sheryl wouldn't let him off the hook, though. "I know there was *something* I could have done better in there." He still couldn't think of anything. Now, he was getting nervous. "You have a reputation for being great at giving feedback," Sheryl encouraged him. "I bet if you think about it you can come up with *something*." Now, he was sweating. But still she didn't let him off the hook. She smiled expectantly, and stayed silent. That was when he finally thought of something, and told her. "Thank you!" She said. "I'll do better next time!"

Another way to embrace the discomfort is to point out when people's body language is at odds with what they're saying. Imagine you're at a meeting with a colleague with whom you've just shared a big, possibly impractical idea. He responds, "Oh! Great idea," but you notice that he hunches over and crosses his arms defensively. Ignoring that sort of nonverbal cue is a lost opportunity. Without being obnoxious, try saying something like, "Then why are you folding your arms and hunching down in your seat? Come on, tell me what you're really thinking!"

Listen with the intent to understand, not to respond. You've finally gotten the other person to offer some criticism. Once again, you have to manage your response. Whatever you do, don't start criticizing the criticism. Don't start telling the other person they weren't Radically Candid! Instead, try to repeat what the person said to make sure you've understood it, rather than defending yourself against the criticism that you've just heard. Listen to and clarify the criticism—but don't debate it. Try saying, "So what I hear you saying is . . ." If you find my language too programmatic, find another way to say it.

If you're not one of those people who instinctively welcomes criticism as an opportunity to improve, you'll of course feel a strong urge to act defensively—or at the least to explain yourself. This is a natural response, but it pretty much kills any chance that you'll get the person to offer you the gift of candor again. So don't feel bad that you are having this very normal human reaction. Manage your feelings rather than letting them manage you. Remind yourself going in that no matter how unfair the criticism, your first job is to listen with the intent to understand, not to defend yourself.

Reward criticism to get more of it. Once you've asked your question and embraced the discomfort and understood the criticism, you have to follow up by showing that you really did welcome it. You have to reward the candor if you want to get more of it. If you agree with the criticism, make a change as soon as possible. If the necessary change will take time, do something visible to show you're trying. For example, my cofounder Russ once complained that I interrupted him. It was true; I am an inveterate interrupter. I tried not to do it, but I knew I wouldn't succeed in eradicating this bad habit just because he'd mentioned it. Telling Russ that I couldn't help myself was hardly a good way to reward his candor. So I said, "I know, it's a problem. Can I ask you to help me stop interrupting?" I pulled a fat, blue rubber band out of my drawer and put it around my wrist. I asked him to snap the rubber band every time I interrupted him. Russ thought this was funny, and agreed. I wore the rubber band, which I now think of as my "radical bander," to my staff meeting. I asked everyone present to help me by snapping it. Sure enough, others started snapping the rubber band. Then, I mentioned it at an all-hands meeting. Additional snapping *did* help me interrupt less. But equally important was that it sent a strong signal that I had heard the criticism and was taking action, and that I wanted to hear more criticism.

In some cases, of course, you may disagree with the criticism. It's here that your Radical Candor skills become essential. It is never enough to simply acknowledge the other person's feelings—that invariably feels passive-aggressive and insincere. Instead, first, find something in the criticism you can agree with, to signal that you're open to criticism. Then, check for understanding—repeat what you heard back to the person to make sure you got it. Then, let them know you want to think about what they said, and schedule a time to talk about it again. *It's essential that you do get back to it.* The key then is to explain exactly why you disagree. If you can't make a change, giving the employee a thoughtful, respectful explanation of why not, is the best reward you can offer for their Radical Candor. Sometimes they'll come around, sometimes not. Sometimes they may even spot flaws in your reasoning that causes you to reconsider. Or the reward for their candor might have to be a full explanation of why you disagree, an openness which invites them to poke some more at your logic, and a clear idea of when it's time to stop arguing and commit.

Gauge the guidance you get. Try keeping a tally. How many times each week do the people reporting to you criticize you? How often do they praise you? If it's all praise and no criticism, beware! You're having smoke blown up your rear end. You need to work harder to get them to criticize you. Try teaching the people on your team about the idea of Radical Candor. Explain why you don't want them to be ruinously empathetic or manipulatively insincere with you. Tell them you'd welcome Radical Candor, but you'd prefer Obnoxious Aggression to silence. Print out the Radical Candor framework on page 299), and when you're having a conversation and you feel like somebody is pulling their punches, point to Radical Candor and ask them to go there. In the first edition I mentioned a software gauge. This did not work well. Looking the person in the eye when you're talking to them works much better than an app! When you give guidance, watch the other person's response, and adjust how you are talking based on what you see. For more on how to do this, see the section "Gauge Criticism": "Using this framework like a compass" in the Afterword.

ORANGE BOX
Make it not just safe but natural to criticize you

JOHNSON & JOHNSON'S ORIGINAL credo had an interesting line: "Employees should have an organized system for suggestions and complaints." When it got rewritten, this intention got watered down into a much vaguer and less useful statement: "Employees must feel free to make suggestions and complaints." If you're the boss, you have to do much better than announce how employees "must" feel. Employees *won't* feel free if you don't take specific actions to ensure that it's not just safe but expected to make suggestions and complaints. You have to organize a system. But it needn't be elaborate.

Michael Dearing, who defined product marketing at eBay in 2002 and is now the CEO of the successful seed-stage fund Harrison Metal, used a simple but effective technique for getting people to criticize him. He put an orange box with a slit on the top in a high-traffic area so that people could drop questions or feedback into it. At his all-hands meeting he'd reach into the box and answer off the cuff. A good friend of mine, Ann Poletti, who

GUIDANCE=	Praise	Criticism
Get from		✔
Give to		
Encourage between		

used to work on Michael's team, said that no matter how banal the question, he was "always amazingly respectful and took on each question thoughtfully."

Here's how Ann described it: "Taking Q&A with a team of 200-plus when the business was very turbulent and eBay was in the midst of switching CEOs . . . must have worn him out—he's an introvert. I know he hated doing it, but he never seemed annoyed or impatient, in fact he made it look like he enjoyed the questions." By proving to the team that he would fix problems when people pointed them out rather than shoot the messenger, Michael eventually built a culture where people would challenge him directly. Over time the orange box emptied out. When people had an issue, they would stand up and ask direct questions, or simply drop by his cube.

MANAGEMENT "FIX-IT" WEEKS

ENGINEERING ORGANIZATIONS OFTEN do the equivalent of spring cleaning. Everyone will stop working on new features for a week and fix bugs in the current product. Engineering teams are constantly tracking and evaluating bugs, so that they have a prioritized list to tackle when the so-called "fix-it" week comes around. A bug fix-it week is sort of the opposite of a Hack Week; instead of a chance to work on new and exciting ideas people usually don't have time to get to, it's a chance to fix old and annoying problems that have been bothering people for months. It's like cleaning out the utensil drawer into which you spilled a little honey three months ago but somehow never found the moment to take all the knives and forks out to scrub the bottom of the drawer properly. Fix-it weeks can be deeply satisfying in a totally different way from hack weeks.

GUIDANCE≠	Praise	Criticism
Get from		✔
Give to		
Encourage between		

At some point, a team at Google decided that it would be good hygiene to have regular management fix-it weeks. (Later, another team did a similar thing but called it "bureaucracy busters.") Here's how it worked: a system was created where people could log annoying management issues. If, for example, it took too long to get expense reports approved, you could file a management "bug." And you could do the same if performance reviews always seemed to take place at the worst possible time of year, or if the last employee survey took too long to fill out, or if the promotion system seemed unfair, and so on.

The management bug tracking system was public, so people could vote to set priorities. Somebody was assigned the job of reading through them all and grouping duplicates. Then, during management fix-it week, managers would have bugs assigned to them. They'd cancel all regularly scheduled activities (or most of them) and focus on fixing the management issues that were most annoying to the organization.

GIVING IMPROMPTU GUIDANCE

SO FAR WE'VE dealt with getting your team to give you feedback. I put that first because I wanted to emphasize that it has to be a two-way street. But in fact, it starts with you. If you don't have the courage to *give* Radically Candid guidance, the people who report to you won't believe you really want to get it from them, so you won't hear about it when your team thinks you're veering off course. And if you don't lead by example, the people on your team are unlikely to guide each other.

GUIDANCE=	Praise	Criticism
Get from		
Give to	✔	✔
Encourage between		

Be humble

I start with being humble because it's absolutely essential when delivering both praise and criticism. We're all naturally defensive when first criticized, but if you deliver criticism humbly, it breaks down the natural resistance to what you're saying. Being humble is just as important when delivering praise. Otherwise, you sound patronizing or dishonest. Furthermore, a common concern that people raise about giving feedback is "What if I'm wrong?" My answer is that you may very well be wrong. And telling somebody what you think gives them the opportunity to tell you if you are. A huge part of what makes giving guidance so valuable is that misperceptions on *both* sides of the equation get corrected.

Here are some techniques I've found helpful to make sure I'm being humble when giving praise and criticism:

Situation, behavior, impact. The Center for Creative Leadership, an executive-education company, developed a technique called "situation behavior impact" to help leaders be more precise and therefore less arrogant when giving feedback. This simple technique reminds you to describe three things when giving feedback: 1) the situation you saw, 2) the behavior (i.e., what the person did, either good or bad), and 3) the impact you observed. This helps you avoid making judgments about the person's intelligence, common sense, innate goodness, or other personal attributes. When you pass blanket judgments, your guidance sounds arrogant.

A simple example from everyday life: instead of yelling, "You asshole!" when somebody grabs your parking space, try saying, "I've been waiting for that spot here for five minutes, and you just zipped in front of me and took it. Now I'm going to be late." If you say this, you give the person a chance to say, "Oh, I'm sorry I didn't realize, let me move." Of course, the person might also just flip you off and say, "Tough shit." *Then* you can yell with more justification, "You asshole!" :)

Situation, behavior, and impact applies to praise as well as to criticism. Praise can feel just as arrogant as criticism. When somebody says, "You're a genius," it begs a question: "Who are you to judge my intelligence?" When somebody says, "I'm so proud of you!" it's natural to think, "Who are you to be proud of me?" Better to say, "In your presentation at this morning's meeting (situation), the way you talked about our decision to diversify (behavior) was persuasive because you showed everyone you'd heard the other point of view (impact)."

It's the fear of sounding arrogant or patronizing that sometimes makes me hesitate to give praise to people properly. Using these three touchstones helps.

Left-hand column. Chris Argyris, a professor at Harvard Business School, and Donald Schön, a professor of philosophy and urban planning, developed an exercise called the "left-hand column." This method also helps leaders avoid letting arrogant snap judgments seep out into their guidance.

Here's how it works. Think of a conversation you had that was frustrating. Take out a clean sheet of paper and draw a line down the middle. Write down what you actually said in the right-hand column. Write down what you thought in the left-hand column. Now think about when the conversation went sideways. Did what you think spill out into what you said? The point is not just to say whatever is in your left-hand column; it's to have the humility to question what you're thinking—"Is Sally really hoarding information, or did she just forget to tell me?" "Is Sam really unreliable, or did I just not define the requirements clearly enough?"

"Ontological Humility." Fred Kofman argues for the importance of reflecting your core values in the way you work. His book *Conscious Business* includes a chapter titled "Ontological Humility," which reminds us not to confuse objective reality with our subjective experience. He explains by quoting his daughter: "Broccoli is yucky. That's why I don't like it." This is funny in a three-year-old, but when adults confuse subjective tastes with objective reality, it's arrogant. "He is an idiot. That's why he's wrong." The idea is that when you are mindful that your subjective experience is not objective truth, it can help you challenge others in a way that invites a reciprocal challenge.

Be helpful

It's obvious that being helpful is a great way to show that you care personally, and that the whole point of challenging directly is to be helpful.

Still, it's hard to do. You're really busy, and besides, you don't have all the answers—you're humble, right? The good news is that being helpful doesn't mean you have to be omniscient or do everybody else's work for them. It just means you have to find a way to help them clarify the challenge they're facing—that clarity is a gift that will enable them to move forward. Here are some tips and reminders:

Stating your intention to be helpful can lower defenses. When you tell somebody that you aren't trying to bust their chops—that you really want to help—it can go a long way toward making them receptive to what you're saying. Try a little preamble. For example, in your own words, say something like, "I'm going to describe a problem I see; I may be wrong, and if I am I hope you'll tell me; if I'm not I hope my bringing it up will help you fix it."

Show, don't tell. It's the best advice I've ever gotten for story-telling, but it also applies to guidance. The more clearly you show *exactly* what is good or bad, the more helpful your guidance will be. Often you'll be tempted not to describe the details because they are so painful. You want to spare the person the pain and yourself the awkwardness of uttering the words out loud. But retreating to abstractions is a prime example of Ruinous Empathy. Further, it can actually unintentionally signal that the behavior in question was so bad/shameful that you can't even talk about it, thereby making it hard for the person to move on. I once had to say, "When we were in that meeting and you passed a note to Catherine that said 'Check out Elliot picking his nose—I think he just nicked his brain,' Elliot wound up seeing it. It pissed him off unnecessarily, made it harder for you to work together, and was the single biggest contributing factor to our being late on this project." The whole situation was so ridiculous that it was tempting just to say, "What you did in the meeting was juvenile." But that wouldn't have been as clear or as helpful.

And again, the same principle goes for praise. Don't say, "She is really smart." Say, "She just gave the clearest explanation I've ever heard of why users don't like that feature." By *explicitly describing* what was good or what was bad, you are helping a person do more of what's good and less of what's bad—and to see the difference.

Finding help is better than offering it yourself. When Sheryl Sandberg offered to get me a speaking coach, she did have to budget for it, but she didn't have to sit there watching me practice presentations for hours. It took some of her time but not too much.

You won't always be so lucky to have the budget for coaches that Sheryl had at Google. But more often than not you will have a colleague or acquaintance who can help. All you have to do is to make the introduction and help your direct report structure the conversation.

Guidance is a gift, not a whip or a carrot. It took me a long time to learn that sometimes the only help I had to offer was the conversation itself. Adopting the mindset that guidance is a gift will ensure that your guidance is helpful even when you can't offer actual assistance, solutions, or an introduction to someone who can help. Don't let the fact that you can't offer a solution make you reluctant to offer guidance. Think about times that guidance has been most helpful to you, and offer it in that spirit.

Give feedback immediately

Giving guidance as quickly and as informally as possible is an *essential* part of Radical Candor, but it takes discipline—both because of our natural inclination to delay/avoid confrontation and because our days are busy enough as it is. But this is one of those cases where the difference in terms of time spent and impact is huge. Delay at your peril!

If you wait too long to give guidance, everything about it gets harder. You know how it is when you kick things down the road—you notice a problem and note that you need to deal with it, but you don't take the time to write it down. Then it occurs to you, and you need to sit and remember what precisely the problem was. Then you need to remember to schedule the meeting. You're beginning to need a list of the things you've intended to say but haven't. And then before the meeting, you need to find time to remember what's on the list of random things you've been intending to say but failing to jot down. The list of things won't really hang together—you will no longer be able to remember clear examples of the problem—so you won't be able to use the "situation behavior impact" model, and you'll end up with a confused, frustrated colleague. What, exactly, are you criticizing? Putting criticism off is simply daunting and exhausting. It's much more effective and less burdensome to just say it right away!

Of course, there are times when you should wait to praise or criticize somebody. Generally, if either you or the other person is hungry, angry, or tired, or for some other reason not in a good frame of mind, it's better to wait. However, this is the exception not the rule, and too often we use the exception as an excuse not to do what we know we should do. Finally, there is a difference between saying it right away and nitpicking. If it's not important, don't say it right away or at all.

Say it in 2–3 minutes between meetings. Just saying it right away in a minute or two, three at most, will take less time than scheduling a meeting for later, let alone having it—and it won't stick around in your mind, worrying you at odd moments. When I teach classes on Radical Candor, the single most common question people ask is, "How do I find the time?" At first, I took this as a sign that they hadn't bought my argument about how important guidance was. But after more conversations, I realized that people actually don't believe it can be quick. They think it's an hour-long conversation they need to schedule. They think giving good guidance is going to add *hours* of meetings to each week. They think of it like a root canal. Try thinking of it as brushing your teeth instead. Don't write it in your calendar; just do it consistently, and maybe you won't ever have to get a root canal.

So let me reiterate: impromptu guidance really, truly is something you can squeeze in between meetings in three minutes or less. If you give it right away in between meetings, you will not only save yourself a subsequent meeting but also deliver the guidance in less time than it would take you to *schedule* the subsequent meeting. And the quality of your guidance will be much better. The best guidance I've gotten in my life generally happened in super-quick conversations on the fly, like my exchange with Sheryl. If you have five direct reports and you want to offer each praise three times a week and criticism once a week, this is far more impromptu feedback than most managers offer. And it will just take you a maximum of sixty minutes per week—all those minutes grabbed from the time you'd otherwise spend just walking between meetings. But doing it does require energy and consciousness.

Keep slack time in your calendar, or be willing to be late. Prioritizing something generally means making time in your calendar for it. But how do you make time in your calendar for something that is "impromptu"? You can't. Better to talk to the person right away. But in order for that to happen, you must do one of two things. One, keep slack time in your calendar, either by not scheduling back-to-back meetings or by having twenty-five- and fifty-minute meetings with hard stops, not thirty- and sixty-minute meetings. Or, simply be willing to be late to your next meeting.

Don't "save up" guidance for a 1:1 or a performance review. One of the funniest things about becoming a boss is that it causes an awful lot of people to forget everything they know about how to relate to other people. If you have a beef with somebody in your personal life, it would never occur to you to wait for a formally scheduled meeting to tell them. Yet, management has been bureaucratized to the point that we throw away effective strategies of everyday communication. Don't let the formal processes—the 1:1 meetings, annual or biannual performance reviews, or employee happiness surveys—take over. They are meant to reinforce, not substitute, what we do every day. You'd never let the fact that you go to the dentist for a cleaning a couple times a year prevent you from brushing your teeth every day. Don't use performance reviews as an excuse not to give impromptu in-person feedback.

Guidance has a short half-life. If you wait to tell somebody for a week or a quarter, the incident is so far in the past that they can't fix the problem or build on the success.

Unspoken criticism explodes like a dirty bomb. Just as in your personal life, remaining silent at work for too long about something that angers or frustrates you makes it more likely that you will eventually blow up in a way that makes you look irrational, harms your relationship, or both. Don't let this happen to you. Unless you feel you're in a rage, just say what you're thinking right away!

Avoid black holes. Be sure to let people know immediately how their work is being received. If you ask somebody to do work to help you prepare for a meeting or a presentation where that person won't be present, be sure to let them know the reaction to their work. If you don't, the person who did the work feels as if their efforts have gone into a black hole. It is important to pass on both praise and criticism for the contributions they made. Better, of course, is to let people present their own work whenever possible so they can get guidance first-hand. Even at nonhierarchical Google, praise from my boss always meant more to the people working for me than guidance from me.

In person (if possible)

Remember, the clarity of your guidance gets measured at the other person's ear, not at your mouth. That's why it's best to deliver guidance in person. You won't really know if the other person understood what you were saying if you can't see the reaction. If you don't know whether what you said was clear to the other person, you may as well not have said it. And most communication is nonverbal. When you see a person's body language and facial expression, you can adjust how you are delivering the message so they can best hear it. It is far easier to tell if the other person understood you clearly when you can look into their eyes, notice if they are fidgeting, folding their arms, etc.

Often the reason why you'll be tempted not to deliver guidance in person is that you are trying to *avoid* seeing the other person's emotional reaction. This is natural. But the quality of your guidance will improve if you're present for these feelings. If somebody is upset, this gives you an opportunity to show compassion—to go up on the "care personally" dimension of the Radical Candor framework. The emotional response of the other person will help you better understand how your message landed, and to adjust. When somebody is blowing you off (as I did Sheryl when she first told me I said "um" a lot), you know you have to go further on the "challenge directly" dimension of the Radical Candor framework. But when someone is upset or angry, focus on showing that you care personally, don't let the emotions knock you off your good intention to challenge directly.

Unfortunately, giving guidance in person is not always possible. When that is the case, here are some things to keep in mind:

Immediate vs. in person. If the person is in another city and giving guidance in person means waiting more than a few days, then optimize for immediacy unless what you're talking about is a big deal. (Don't fire somebody via text.) If the person is down the hall, and doing it in person means just taking a little walk, then get off your butt!

Hierarchy of modes. A video call, if you have high-speed internet access, is second best. If the connection is spotty, use phone for voice and video as a bonus, muting your computer. Phone is third best. Email and text should be avoided if at all possible. It always feels faster to fire off an email or text, but when I think about all the times I had to spend hours clearing up a misunderstanding that arose from an email that was misunderstood, I realize that it's actually faster to walk down the hall or if the person is remote pick up the phone.

Multiple modes. I found that praising people at a public all-hands meeting was a great way to share significant accomplishments. However, I often found that following up in person at a 1:1 carried more emotional weight, and following up with an email to the whole team carried more lasting weight.

Reply All do's and don'ts. If you *must* criticize or correct somebody over email, do *not* Reply All. Never. Even if there's a small factual error that went out to a lot of people, reply just to the person who made the factual error and ask *that* person to Reply All. For praise on small things, I found that a quick Reply All email worked pretty well. This kind of praise takes only a moment, and it shows that you are noticing and appreciating what's going on around you. If you can remember to mention it in person when you pass the person in the hallway or walk by their desk, so much the better. But don't let perfection be the enemy of the good.

Being in a remote office is hard. If you are in a remote office, or if you are managing people in remote offices, it's really important to have quick, frequent interactions. This will allow you to pick up on people's most subtle emotional cues. I learned this from Maurice Tempelsman, my boss when I lived in Russia. He made a point of calling me every day from New York, if only for a three-minute check-in call. He had operations in Africa in the 1970s and had learned the importance of frequent communication to pick up on emotional cues from people in far-flung locations. In fact, he claimed he could sense a person's mood even when phone calls were impossible and he had to rely on telex—but only if he got in the habit of telexing daily. (Telex was the technology used in between the telegraph and the fax machine.)

Praise in public, criticize in private

A good rule of thumb for guidance is praise in public, criticize in private. Public criticism tends to trigger a defensive reaction and make it much harder for a person to accept they've made a mistake and to learn from it. Public praise tends to lend more weight to the praise, and it encourages others to emulate whatever was great. However, this is a rule of thumb, not a hard and fast rule. Here are some things to think about.

Corrections, factual observations, disagreements, and debates are different from criticism. It's vital to be able to correct somebody's work, to make a factual observation, or to have a debate in public. But criticizing a *person* should be done in private—"There's a typo on slide six," or "There are a lot of typos in this presentation, and given the nature of our work we need to be 100 percent accurate," or "There are a bunch of typos here but they don't matter too much at this stage," or "You missed your number by 5 percent," or "I disagree with what you just said." Those kinds of corrections could go out over email or be said in a public meeting. Here is an example of criticizing the *person*: "When you give several important presentations that are all riddled with typos that a simple spell-checker would catch, I start to wonder what's going on. Can you explain?" That sort of thing needs to be a private conversation.

Adapt to an individual's preferences. While the majority of people do like to be praised in public, for some any kind of public mention is cruel and unusual punishment. When you're praising people, your goal is to let them know what they did well as clearly as possible and in the way that will make *them* feel best—not the way you'd like to hear it. When you care personally about each individual working for you, when you've taken the time to get to know each person, being aware of these preferences is natural.

Group learning. I've rarely encountered anyone who will *admit* that they like to be praised publicly. So whenever I praised in public I would explain that I wasn't doing so because the person wanted public praise, but so that everybody could learn from what had happened. Something like, "Not because I want to embarrass Jane, but to make sure all of you learn from what she did, I'm going to tell you what she just accomplished, and how she did it." When I wanted to encourage public criticism so that everyone learns from one another's mistakes, I'd let it be self-reported. (See "Whoops the Monkey" later in this chapter.)

Don't personalize

There is a big difference between caring personally and personalizing when giving praise and criticism. Caring personally is good. Personalizing is bad. Here are some tips that can help you avoid personalizing but accept it when people take what you say personally:

The "fundamental attribution error" will harm the effectiveness of your guidance. This phrase was coined by Lee Ross, a social psychologist from Stanford. We've touched on this already, but it's useful to repeat because it is so central to healthy human relationships, whether with spouses, children, friends, or the people who report to you. Making a fundamental attribution error is using perceived personality attributes—"You're stupid, lazy, greedy, hypocritical, an asshole," etc.—to explain someone else's behavior rather than considering one's own behavior and/or the situational factors that were probably the real cause of the other person's behavior. It's a problem because 1) it's generally inaccurate and 2) it renders an otherwise solvable problem really hard to fix since changing core personality attributes is so very difficult and time-consuming. In the story I told in chapter two the problem with the AdSense policy was *not* that Larry was greedy; it was that I didn't understand his proposal. But it was so much easier and more satisfying in the moment to just accuse Larry of being greedy. Try to catch yourself when you think or say, "You are _____." Use situation, behavior, impact, or the left-hand column techniques to be humble and to avoid personalizing.

Say "that's wrong" not "you're wrong." I once worked with a Radically Candid guy who had an unfair reputation for being an a-hole. Once people got to know him well, they realized he wasn't a jerk, he was just super intense; in fact, he cared as deeply about his colleagues as he did about the quality of the work they did together. His work was so good that the short-term impression he made didn't stop him from being successful. But the fact that he rubbed people the wrong way often created a lot of unnecessary stress for both him and his team. I moved from New York to California, and I lost touch with him for a few years. Then I happened to meet somebody who'd just joined his team. I braced myself for a request for advice about how to work with him, but all I heard was, "Oh, he's such a great guy! I love working with him. He has a reputation for being one of the most supportive people at our company." I called up my friend to pass along the compliment, and to ask how he'd pulled this off. He told me that a simple suggestion had helped him turn things around. What was it? He stopped saying, "You're wrong," and instead learned to say, "I think that's wrong." "I think" was humbler, and saying "that" instead of "you" didn't personalize. People started to be more receptive to his criticism.

All too often, an argument over something simple—"Should we go left or go right? Should we put the button at the top or at the bottom?"—becomes a contest of egos: "You are a moron! You are an arrogant jerk!" When an argument is about an issue, keep it about the issue. Personalizing unnecessarily will only make the issue harder to resolve.

The phrase "don't take it personally" is worse than useless. I've warned against personalizing, but even when you take the steps outlined above—even when you don't personalize—feedback *is* personal for the person receiving it. Most of us pour more time and energy into our work than anything else in our lives. Work is a part of who we are, and so it is personal. Thus when you try to soften the blow by saying, "Don't take it personally," you are in effect negating those feelings. It's like saying, "Don't be sad," or "Don't be mad." Part of your job as a boss (and as a human being) is to acknowledge and deal with emotional responses, not to dismiss or avoid them.

How not to personalize even when it really *is* personal. It's easier to understand how to avoid personalizing guidance when you're talking about a person's work. But when you're talking about something that is more personal, it's even harder. One woman I worked with had body odor to the point that it undermined her effectiveness. But how to raise the issue? I tried hard to make the conversation about her colleagues' noses, not her armpits. She wasn't American, but we were working in the U.S., so I laughed a little bit about American culture. I tried not to be prescriptive about the solution— maybe she had an allergic reaction to deodorant, or a health concern—but I did make clear that the status quo was undermining her otherwise strong performance. She looked embarrassed, but she fixed the problem. Five years later, she wrote me a note thanking me. A manager now, facing a similar situation, she finally understood how hard raising the issue must have been for me. But she had also noticed a remarkable increase in people's willingness to work with her once she addressed the body odor problem. So she knew how important it was to overcome her own reluctance, and find a way to explain the problem to the person reporting to her.

GAUGE YOUR IMPROMPTU GUIDANCE, GET A BASELINE, TRACK YOUR IMPROVEMENTS

I'VE EMPHASIZED THAT Radical Candor gets measured at the listener's ear, not at the speaker's mouth. But how is a speaker to know what's going on in the listener's ear? Do you really have to get guidance on your guidance? The bad news is, yes. The good news is that it can take fifteen seconds.

GUIDANCE=	Praise	Criticism
Get from	✔	✔
Give to	✔	✔
Encourage between		

Visual cues that make you aware of when you're moving toward Radical Candor or away from it are invaluable. One of the most effective ways to become more Radically Candid is to explain the framework to your team and then ask them to gauge your guidance each week. Track your progress over time. Are you moving toward Radical Candor, or away from it?

A low-tech way to do this is to put a copy of the framework near your desk. Leave some stickers by it—one color for praise, another for criticism. Ask people to put stickers in the quadrant they feel best describes your most recent interactions. If somebody feels you were unnecessarily harsh, they should put a criticism sticker in the Obnoxious Aggression quadrant. If they feel you pulled your punches, they'll put a criticism sticker in the Ruinous Empathy quadrant. If they feel you dished out too many meaningless "atta boy"s or "good job"s or "I'm so proud of you"s just to make them feel better, they'll put a praise sticker in the Ruinous Empathy quadrant. If they feel you told them they did a good job but then told somebody else they did a bad job, then they put a praise sticker in the Manipulative Insincerity quadrant.

Asking your team to gauge your guidance will help make Radically Candid guidance feel more natural. (I saw this play out at Apple, where we printed out a version of the Radical Candor framework on beautiful cardstock, and many managers put it up near their desks.)

One, it exposes people daily to the Radical Candor framework. That helps them understand that when you're challenging them, you're doing it because you care, not because you're a jerk who wants to make their lives miserable. Two, when you have a shared vocabulary, colleagues are likely to ask you to be Radically Candid, which makes getting over the "if you don't have anything nice to say don't anything at all" syndrome much easier. Three, the visual cue is a reminder that will help push you to be Radically Candid when the heat of the moment is pulling you in a different direction. In my experience, most bosses *fear* being jerks but employees fear their bosses are not shooting straight. When a boss sees clearly that the employee wants to hear it straight, it's *much* easier to say it straight. Four, if you ask them to do this but they don't, or if they submit ratings anonymously in the app, you've got a good signal that they don't trust you to react well. You'll need to start proving to your team that you won't punish them if they criticize you. You need to go back and work on soliciting Radically Candid guidance.

For example, if you saw that a number of people were tagging both your praise and your criticism in the Ruinous Empathy quadrant, you'd know that you were not challenging people directly enough with your praise or your criticism. You'd need to focus on giving praise that is more specific and more sincere and to "just say it" when criticizing people. It's scary the first time you try it. But the vast majority of people I've coached have been pleasantly surprised. They gear up to just say it, expecting the worst kinds of emotional reactions, and then the person *thanks* them. After that happens, Radical Candor becomes easier.

The transition from Ruinous Empathy to Radical Candor may be a direct path, and relatively comfortable. When people move directly over to Radical Candor, the transition will feel good right away. But sometimes people have to overcorrect to get it right. They must go from Ruinous Empathy toward the very quadrant they fear most—Obnoxious Aggression—before they can achieve Radical Candor. Since the main reason people are being ruinously empathetic in the first place is that they hate to feel like a jerk, that can result in a transition that feels scary. If that's you, don't despair.

You're actually moving in the right direction. But certainly don't stop here—push on up to Radical Candor!

Getting from Ruinous Empathy to Radical Candor requires changing behavior, and that is never easy. But the good news is that it's like brushing your teeth. If you weren't taught as a child to brush your teeth, adopting the habit would take some effort, even though it only takes a couple of minutes twice a day. Once you're used to brushing your teeth, though, not brushing your teeth feels gross. You can't bear to go to sleep or leave the house in the morning if you haven't brushed.

And even when you do give guidance, you'll have good weeks and bad weeks. There are going to be times when you are overwhelmed or distracted by things at home, and Ruinous Empathy and/or Obnoxious Aggression will take over. You won't always be 100 percent sincere. Guidance is hard, and there will always be pressure on you not to be Radically Candid. You can't "fix" yourself once and for all; you have to manage yourself, daily. Getting a signal from others about whether you are moving toward or away from Radical Candor will really help.

Getting a gauge report can be painful for people when they are in the Manipulative Insincerity or Obnoxious Aggression quadrants. It can also be motivating, though, since very few people actually *want* to be a manipulative or obnoxious.

Getting a "Ruinous Empathy" gauge report is also painful, though it's especially effective. Getting a reminder that challenging directly is actually kind can have a big impact on behavior quickly. It's not that hard to "just say it" with criticism and "be specific" with praise. Since the majority of management mistakes happen in the Ruinous Empathy quadrant, gauging guidance can quickly improve quantity and quality of guidance that people get, and move you and your whole culture toward Radical Candor. If we can move from Ruinous Empathy to Radical Candor more often, the world will be not only more productive but happier. Obnoxious Aggression leads to more success than Ruinous Empathy but is also extremely unpleasant.

The most important thing is figuring out how others experience your guidance. Listen to how they feel about the guidance you're giving them. Help them understand that when you're challenging them it's because you care about not just their professional growth but them as human beings. A regular visual prompt that shows you where your guidance is landing from other people's perspective can really help. For more advice see the section in the Afterword, "Gauge Criticism": "Using this framework like a compass (page 252).

BEING RADICALLY CANDID WITH *YOUR* BOSS

IN A TALK I gave recently I said that when you are the boss, it is not just your job but your moral obligation to be Radically Candid. A couple days later, somebody who'd watched the talk Tweeted me: "Tried Radical Candor on my boss. Got Fired." I felt terrible and offered to help him find another job. He assured me it was all for the best and he already had a few other options.

Nevertheless, let me clarify. If you are *not* in a position of authority, I do recommend that you try being Radically Candid—but proceed with caution. It is not your moral obligation to criticize your boss if it will cost you your job. If you find you cannot be Radically Candid with your boss, I recommend that you consider finding a new job with a new boss. But do it on your own terms. Don't get fired. Protect yourself.

How can you practice safe Radical Candor with your boss? Do you have to get permission to start trying it? Not surprisingly, since I believe that unilateral authority doesn't work, I'd say no. Take the initiative on your own. Once you start rolling out Radical Candor with your team and seeing good results, explain what you're doing and why to your boss. Give your boss a chance to challenge you, but assume good intent. If you get some positive signals, try getting and then giving some guidance.

Happily, you can approach Radical Candor with your boss in much the same way you did with your team. Start by asking for guidance before you give it. You want to make sure you understand the other person's perspective before you start dishing out praise or criticism, no matter who the person is—your boss, your employee, your peer, or anyone else in your life. When you get the guidance, don't offer a critique of the criticism, and don't accept bland praise; focus on rewarding the candor if you get it and on embracing the discomfort if you don't. If your boss is already rolling out Radical Candor and is explicitly asking you to gauge their feedback, that's an exception to the don't-critique-the-criticism rule of thumb.

If your boss is being ruinously empathetic, and asks to be gauged, gauge with candor.

Next—and here is a slight modification if you're talking to your boss instead of your employee—ask *permission* to give guidance. Say something like, "Would it be helpful if I told you what I thought of X?" If your boss says no, or that's not your job, let it drop and polish up your résumé! If your boss says yes, start with something pretty small and benign and see how they react. If they react well and reward the candor, keep going. If they don't, give up immediately or assume ill intent. Try again, carefully, but if you get the same reaction the next time, it may be time to move on. You deserve a better boss.

When offering guidance to your boss, use the same tips above: be helpful, humble, do it immediately and in person, praise in public (if it doesn't look like kissing up), criticize in private, and don't personalize.

The ability to be Radically Candid with your boss is crucial to your success. One of the most difficult things about being a middle manager—and, since most CEO's report to a Board of Directors, pretty much *all* managers are middle managers—is that you often wind up responsible for executing decisions that you disagree with. This can feel like a Catch-22. If you tell your team you *do* agree with the decisions, you feel like a liar—or at the very least, inauthentic. If you tell your team that you *don't* agree with the decisions, you look weak, insubordinate, or both.

Radical Candor is the way out of this dilemma. If you are able to tell your boss that you disagree with a decision, then at least you can have conversations that will allow you to better understand the rationale behind it. And once you understand the rationale more deeply, you can explain it to your team—even if you don't agree with it. When they ask, "Why are we doing this, it makes no sense to us, didn't you argue?" you can reply, "I understand your perspective. Yes, I did have an opportunity to argue. Here's what I said. And here is what I learned about why we are doing what we are doing." If they insist on knowing whether you agree, you can tell them in all honesty that your boss listened to your point of view, that you were given an opportunity to challenge the decisions, and that now it's time to commit to a different course of action than the one you were arguing for. Andy Grove had a mantra at Intel that we borrowed to describe leadership at Apple: Listen, Challenge, Commit. A strong leader has the humility to listen, the confidence to challenge, and the wisdom to know when to quit arguing and to get on board.

GENDER AND GUIDANCE

GENDER DIFFERENCES MAKE guidance harder to give for both men and women, but in very different ways. Both bias and what I call "gender politics" can foil efforts to be Radically Candid with someone of a different gender. I'm focusing on gender here because this book is rooted in my first-hand experiences and I'm a Caucasian woman. But there are important parallels in race, and any instance where relationships cross group boundaries.

Why Radical Candor may be harder for men managing women

Most men are trained from birth to be "gentler" with women than with men. Sometimes this can be very bad for the women who work for them. The most sexist man I ever worked for was invariably far more reluctant to criticize me than the men who worked for him. He lived in mortal fear of making me cry. He made plenty of men who worked for him cry, but that didn't seem to register with him. I'd be willing to bet that women don't actually cry more often than men at work. I've never seen data on this, but in my experience, men cry too, and just about as often. But, nevertheless, this boss was afraid to criticize the women on his team because he was sure we'd cry, and I felt he looked down on us with arrogance and pity as a result.

I don't want to be too harsh here. Lots of men are more reluctant to criticize the women who report to them than the men, and most of them are not misogynists. If you find you have this reluctance, don't beat yourself up. Just remember, if you're a boss, it's your job to manage your fear of tears and *not* pull your punches when criticizing women. Criticism is a gift, and you need to give it in equal measure to your male and female direct reports.

Gender politics is another factor that makes it harder for some men to be Radically Candid with women. I was recently talking to a physics professor whose student didn't know the quadratic equation. (I don't remember it from high school algebra either, but I'm not majoring in physics.) Stunned, and wondering how she'd gotten this far with such a gaping hole in her knowledge, the professor told her she needed to learn it immediately. Furious at the criticism, she slammed him in his rating as a teacher.

This didn't start out as a gender issue. The initial problem was that this young person, like so many others, was unused to criticism—a phenomenon explored well in an *Atlantic* article titled "The Coddling of the American Mind." But the professor's colleagues—some of them well-meaning men trying to be sensitive to gender issues—allowed the rift to become a gender question. Suddenly, telling a student majoring in physics that she needed to learn the quadratic equation became a risky thing for professors at this institution to do.

This situation was not only bad for the student who resisted what she needed to know to succeed, but also for all the female students this professor taught after her. Understandably, he became more hesitant to criticize the work of his female students than of his male students. And yet to grow in their field these young women, like their male counterparts, needed his criticism. The situation wasn't much fun for the professor, either.

This scenario illustrates an anti-guidance trend that's creating a perfect storm in higher education—and blowing through all companies where millennials are working today. But if teachers and bosses become wary of exposing students or employees to facts that might be perceived as "threatening" or "disturbing" due to their fear of reprisals, both schools and companies are in trouble. Combine that with gender politics, and learning takes a real hit. Will the tone of the current "campus conversation" (or lack thereof) backfire and reduce mentorship and learning for women?

The strange case of the quadratic equation is extreme, but milder examples happen every day. And not just with college students, but with middle-aged people working at companies that pride themselves on being data-driven.

Recently, I was talking to a close male friend, who's an engineering leader, about the issue of women in tech. I suggested he ask a woman who works for him—a person whose career he's supported and nurtured for years—what she thought. He looked up at me with real surprise. "I can't talk to her about that!" he exclaimed, genuinely surprised I'd suggest it.

This came from a man who's not just unbiased but truly sensitive to bias and determined to stamp it out. He catches things even I miss. So if he can't have a Radically Candid conversation about gender issues with a woman he knows well, we've hit a real low. But the problem is not him, nor the woman who works for him. I know them both, and I'm pretty sure that the conversation would've gone well. It's that the pervasive atmosphere of anxiety around gender issues has everybody walking on eggshells and avoiding important truths.

Another male colleague recently got caught in a firestorm by making an important and logical point about gender in the workplace. Phrases he used got taken out of context and blown up in the press and throughout social media. This is another man who's committed to treating everyone he works with fairly and who regularly throws extra energy into fostering the careers of his female colleagues. But after this kerfuffle, he decided he wasn't going to talk about gender publicly anymore. I couldn't blame him. But it was another blow to Radical Candor and to civil discourse on an important topic where he was, for my money, on the right side.

We must stop gender politics.

Why gender bias makes Radical Candor harder for women

Gender bias makes it difficult for women to be Radically Candid with both men and women.

One common bias women often fall prey to: the "Abrasive Trap."

Here's my personal experience with the Abrasive Trap. One day, my boss called me into his office and asked me if I was familiar with recent competence/likeability literature. I wasn't, and he explained point-blank that the more competent a woman is, the less her colleagues tend to like her. There were a couple of people I worked with who, perhaps because of gender bias, simply didn't like me, my boss said. Rather than asking these people to re-evaluate their attitudes, he asked me to work on my "likeability."

Naturally, I thought he should address the gender bias, not tell me to work around it by baking cookies for people who resented my competence. But I loved the work I was doing. I was close friends with the men sitting in the offices to the right and left of me. And, in my heart, I knew I could be obnoxiously aggressive sometimes; I don't know anyone in a leadership position who doesn't fall into that quadrant a little more often than they'd like to. Plus, I thought I knew which of my colleagues didn't like me and why the situation was driving my boss nuts. So I did everything I could to make peace with him (short of baking cupcakes).

I was pretty sure I'd fixed the problem when my boss called me into his office once more. He said things were better, but he had an idea that would totally put the issue to rest. I was all ears. His suggestion? A demotion for me. That way, he explained, my colleague would not be so jealous of my position. That would make it easier for me to be more "likeable." Less than three weeks later, I found another, better job and quit.

I was lucky. This happened late enough in my career that I had lots of other options. If it had happened earlier, though, I might have accepted the demotion along with the bitterness that came with it. Or I might have quit without the benefit of other job offers and been set back in my career.

Kieran Snyder, cofounder of Textio, applied linguistic analysis to performance reviews, and she found that when women challenge directly—which they must do to be successful—they get penalized for being "abrasive." (That word actually comes up verbatim a lot.) The "abrasive" label gets placed on women by other women as well as by men.

Snyder wrote an article about her findings for *Fortune* which sparked some of the longest, most impassioned email threads I've seen at several companies that I advised. Why did this article strike such a nerve? Every professional woman I know has many, many stories of being called abrasive, or of being disliked for being too competent—and of paying the price emotionally and professionally.

Let's examine an abstract case, and show why the "abrasive" label holds women back and contributes to fewer female leaders, even in organizations that start out with a fifty-fifty gender balance. Take Snyder's example of two colleagues who perform at the same high level. Here's the feedback they received from their reports:

- "Jessica is really talented, but I wish she'd be less abrasive. She comes on too strong."

- "Steve is smart and great to work with. He needs to learn to be a little more patient, but who doesn't?"

These comments will translate into performance ratings, and the ratings will affect promotions. Let's assume that Jessica gets a slightly lower rating than Steve as a result of her so-called "abrasiveness." Not such a big deal in a given quarter, perhaps. But a series of lower ratings will eventually cost Jessica a promotion. And even if the ratings aren't lower, selection for promotion and leadership roles depend heavily on "likeability."

When bias plays out over a whole organization, the impact on female leadership is profound. Researchers ran a simulation of what happens to promotions over the course of several years when bias impacts ratings just a little bit. When gender bias accounts for just 5 percent of the difference in performance ratings, an organization that starts out with 58 percent of the entry-level positions filled by women winds up with only 29 percent of the leadership positions filled by women.*

Of course, that's only part of the story. Let's look at what happens to Jessica personally over the course of her career. If she's early in her career, she'll probably get promoted eventually despite her alleged "abrasiveness," but now she's a year or so "behind" Steve. Fast forward another five to seven years. Now Steve is two levels ahead of Jessica. Since pay increases steeply with each promotion, he may be getting paid a lot more than Jessica is. If Steve and Jessica get married, and they have a child, guess whose career is more important for family income, and who's more likely to stay home from work when the baby is sick?

But that's not even the worst-case scenario for Jessica. Let's imagine that she takes the "abrasive" feedback to heart and quits challenging her reports directly. She adjusts her behavior so that she's more likeable but less effective at work. Instead of being Radically Candid, which gets her unjustly accused of being obnoxiously aggressive, her feedback tends to be ruinously empathetic or manipulatively insincere. This makes her less effective as a leader. So now, in addition to gender bias, there are real performance issues to contend with. In this case, Jessica is never going to get ahead. Frustrated beyond measure and feeling that she must choose between being liked and being successful, she decides that this is not a game worth playing—and quits.

Some version of this dynamic has played out in the life of every woman I know. Some have fought it successfully but we've all experienced it. We must stop this madness, too.

What can you do?

These issues have gotten too hot to handle. Many men—even the men who genuinely care about addressing gender bias—have understandably

---

* Martell, R.F., D.M. Lane, C. Emrich. "Male-female differences: A computer simulation." *American Psychologist 51*, 2 (Feb. 1996).

decided it's not worth the risk to talk about anything remotely related to gender. The risk doesn't necessarily come from the women they work with. It sometimes comes from other men who stir the pot in an effort to use gender issues to advance their careers. It sometimes comes from an overzealous HR department. It sometimes comes from the law, which can so often be absurdly inappropriate in a specific instance. It sometimes comes from the pressures of social media, or a one-sided story in the press—these stories are too often low-hanging fruit for reporters looking for something sensational. Context matters, but the context of gender politics and gender bias is becoming untouchable—to everyone's detriment.

It doesn't have to be this way. I have a few thoughts on how individuals can take action to cool things down where they work on a daily basis.

Men: don't "pull punches" with women

If you're a man and worried that you might be pulling your punches with female employees because you're wary of gender politics or afraid she'll cry, it can be helpful to become aware of how the woman feels about your guidance; just ask her. Try explaining the Radical Candor framework, and then when you're giving feedback simply say, "I'm trying to be Radically Candid, and I want to check in with you to see how my feedback is landing for you." Ask her to gauge your praise and criticism. (Even if you're *not* worried about gender politics, it is a good idea to find out!) You may not even be aware you're going easy on some people and not others.

Women: demand criticism

Similarly, if you're a woman and worried that your male boss is hesitant to criticize your work, it can be helpful to make him aware that you want more feedback.

Try saying, "What can I do or stop doing to make it easier for you to be Radically Candid with me?" or "I'm worried you're so concerned about my feelings that you're hesitant to give me the feedback I need to improve," or "The thing that I most need from you is to tell me what you really think." Then, pause. Count to six in your head. Embrace the discomfort. Do whatever it takes to drag a candid assessment out of your male colleagues or boss. Review the section above on getting guidance, and double down!

Men and women: things to think about when you feel a woman is being "too aggressive"

Before you give feedback like that, try these tactics to make sure you're not falling into the competence/likeability trap. And don't imagine you won't fall into the trap just because you're a woman! Both genders are equally guilty here I've found, unfortunately.

Switch genders. If the woman were a man who did the exact same thing, would the criticism "you're too aggressive" turn into "you really know how to get things done"? Really imagine a man on your team doing exactly the same thing the woman did. Now, how would you react? If you'd react differently, you're about to fall into the trap.

Two improv actors I know who do role plays to help people practice giving good guidance at some major Silicon Valley companies did the following experiment: they both used the word "fucking" when talking to their "boss" in the role play. Participants, male and female, reacted with extreme offense when the female actor used the word, but didn't blink when the male actor did. One participant, a woman, didn't care when the male actor used the word, but exclaimed, "I want to fire that bitch!" when the female actor did.

Be more specific. Feedback like "you're too aggressive" is too abstract and thus subject to the abrasive trap. If you describe specific examples of how this manifests itself, it will become more clear whether there is a real problem, or if this is your unconscious bias at work.

Don't use gendered language. Notice the words you use. Do you use words like "abrasive," "shrill," "screechy," or "bossy," that are rarely used to describe a man? If so, you may be about to fall into the trap. One of the things I appreciated about working with Dick Costolo was that he challenged the use of words like "abrasive," especially in performance reviews. He often caught nuances I myself had missed, and he always spoke up when he heard something that seemed inappropriately gendered.

Never just say, "Be more likeable." Make sure you address the situation by giving women specific suggestions for changing their behavior and becoming more effective. And remember that though gender bias is a fact of life, it's your job as the boss not to advise women how to navigate around it, but instead to help your entire team *recognize and eliminate it*—to create a more just working environment where unfair bias doesn't hurt anyone's career.

Things to think about if you're a woman who's being told, "You're abrasive."

Before you react to feedback that you're too aggressive/abrasive/etc., consider the following four rules of thumb:

Never stop challenging directly. Too often, the advice to women who are perceived as abrasive (or worse) is to stop challenging directly. This is almost always the wrong answer. You must challenge directly to be successful.

Care personally—but kill the angel in the office. Too often, in order to move up on the "care personally" dimension, women expend too much energy picking up the office housework or otherwise being the angel in the office, to paraphrase Virginia Woolf. Self-abnegation is never an effective way to show you care. You don't have to bake cookies or get coffee or make the copies or spend a lot of time and money on your clothes while the guys wear jeans and company t-shirts if you don't want to!

The competence/likeability research has not concluded that you weren't out of line. Remember: it is possible that you *have* been obnoxious. Don't be the angel in the office, but remain open to the possibility that you may have hurt somebody unnecessarily.

Just because it's wrong to kiss up and kick down doesn't mean it's right to do the opposite. I've coached many, many women who make the same mistake I made with my "clutter" email to Larry in Chapter Two. They are Radically Candid with their teams, but obnoxiously aggressive with their bosses. I don't have any research to show that this is more common for women than for men but it's been pronounced enough in my personal experience that I mention it here.

Don't write men off. When I told my father about my boss who offered me a demotion as a way to avoid the competence/likeability trap, he asked me what I meant. I described for him the now-infamous case of Heidi/Howard Roizen, in which a business school professor gave two different classes of students the same case study about the real-life actions of real-life entrepreneur Heidi Roizen—but he changed the gender of the protagonist for one of the classes. When he surveyed students, they thought that Heidi and Howard were equally competent, but that Heidi was a bitch and Howard was a great guy. (My words!)

My father replied, "Yeah, I know what you mean, I work with a lot of women who are just more aggressive than they need to be." Now, my father is one of the most intelligent people I've ever met, and he's supported my ambitions and my career every step of the way, starting with taking me out to look at the stars through a telescope every night when I was ten and wanted to be an astronaut. But neither his intelligence nor his love for me and desire to see me succeed were strong enough to silence his unconscious bias. He still tumbled right into the competence/likeability trap. I explained it to him again, though, and we both had a good laugh. Luckily, he is my father and I knew how deeply he cared. But if he'd been another man, I might have been tempted to commit the fundamental attribution error—to write him off as hopeless, a misogynist, a sexist pig, or some other epithet. Don't do that. Because it won't help you solve the problem. Just keep challenging directly and showing you care personally it until they get it.

FORMAL PERFORMANCE REVIEWS

IT'S SAFE TO say that performance reviews rank up there with root canals, though in this analogy, they're probably just as painful for the dentist as for the patient. To some degree this is unavoidable. If, like me, you are reflexively suspicious that such processes are overly corporate, artificial, and dehumanizing, you're not going to look forward to them.

That is why GE—which pretty much invented performance reviews—and a number of other companies are abolishing them. As long as these companies take specific measures to create a culture of good guidance, and as long as they figure out some other way to make the logic for decisions about who gets salary increases, bonuses, and promotions transparent, abolishing performance reviews may work. If your company

GUIDANCE=	Praise	Criticism
Get from	✔	✔
Give to	✔	✔
Encourage between		

doesn't do formal performance reviews, it's especially important to double down on impromptu guidance.

However, if your company does do performance reviews, don't dismiss them out of hand. I've found time and again that a formal performance review with a rating sometimes clarifies in a way that impromptu feedback does not. Imagine you've told one of your direct reports that his negativity is hurting his ability to work well cross-functionally. He may hear you, but he may not understand how much that matters until he gets a low performance rating. Time and again, the miscommunication that performance ratings revealed was nothing less than astounding to me. If handled correctly, they offer an important opportunity to improve your guidance.

The "if handled correctly" is a big part of making them work. If your company has a formal performance review process, here is my advice for delivering a performance review well.

No surprises. There should never be any surprises in a formal performance review, and if you've been diligent about offering regular impromptu guidance, you'll lower the odds of this happening considerably.

Don't rely on your unilateral judgment. Even if your company doesn't require a 360 process so that you learn what other people think of your direct report's performance, you can still do a sanity check. One manager I know does this by simply asking each person on the team to give their peers a $\sqrt{-}$, $\sqrt{}$, $\sqrt{+}$. Most people get a $\sqrt{}$, and if they do that's the end of the conversation. If one person gives a peer a $\sqrt{-}$ or a $\sqrt{+}$, he asks a couple more questions. This takes about five minutes out of everyone's 1:1 time twice a year, right before performance reviews, and offers him a great sanity check to make sure he's being fair and seeing a broader perspective. In an ideal world, these ratings would be transparent and attributed. However, building that system would take time he doesn't have. And everybody knows why he's doing this, so giving somebody a $\sqrt{-}$ doesn't feel like "dirty escalation."

Solicit feedback on yourself first. Asking each of my direct reports to give *me* a performance review before I gave them one was helpful. The main advantage here was that it made the review feel more like a two-way conversation and less like an arrogant one-way judgment. Also, when I got a review before I gave one, I understood how each of my reports was thinking before I launched into their review. Sometimes, that made me re-evaluate what I'd planned to say, or how I planned to say it.

Write it down. Writing is painstaking and time-consuming, and so a lot of companies don't require written performance reviews. But it's happened to me dozens of times that writing things down changes the review. I think I know what I want to say during a review, and then when I start to write it down, I realize that the situation is much more nuanced, upon reflection. Taking the time to articulate your thinking on paper beforehand can spare you the awkwardness of having to backpedal in the middle of a review, or after you've delivered it.

I've also found that after I have written something down, it becomes almost impossible for me to wimp out of saying it in the course of the review. Sometimes the heat gets turned up pretty high during a performance review and there's the temptation to retreat into Ruinous Empathy. If I've explicitly made note of an important criticism beforehand, I'm already one step closer to Radical Candor.

Finally, a written review offers people a useful way of clarifying points made during the meeting later on. There's an awful lot to take in during a performance review, and having a document to look back at later can be really helpful. I carried the performance reviews that Sheryl wrote for me around in my bag for months after the actual review, as a way to remind myself of what I needed to work on.

Make a conscious decision about when to give the written review. There is no right timing here. Some people are *much* better able to have a productive conversation if they already know the substance of the review. Generally, these are the people who really like to prepare, who hate surprises. Send it the night before to those people. Others tend to read too much into what you write, so it's better to be there when they read it so you can clarify. If you wrote, "Your team gets frustrated when you cancel your staff meeting at the last minute," they might interpret this to mean, "My team hates me, and I'll probably be fired tomorrow." For people prone to such reactions, you need to deliver the review orally, to check and recheck for understanding, before giving it to them in writing. After you give these people a printout of the written review, go get a cup of tea while they read it, and then return to talk. No matter how you decide to deliver the review, commit to being Radically Candid—and to being sure that what you have to say has been fully understood by the other person.

Schedule at least fifty minutes in person, and don't do reviews back-to-back. I was always tempted to schedule a bunch of reviews back-to-back, thirty minutes each, and knock them out quickly. But whenever I did reviews that way, they went badly. The conversations often went longer than expected, so a line of people waiting for their reviews would form outside my office. That wasted people's time (a cardinal sin for a boss) and made them unnecessarily nervous. And, even when I scheduled more time, doing them back-to-back was a bad idea. These conversations are often emotionally draining, and I always needed more than a ten-minute break between them.

Spend half the time looking back (diagnosis), half the time looking forward (plan). When I wrote performance reviews, I focused on being extremely clear about how each person did over the past quarter/half/year. In the conversation, however, I tried not to spend more than about half of the time talking about the past, because it was more important to start engaging people on the future. I didn't come up with the plan—I asked them to. How would they parlay success into even more success, or how would they address an area of poor performance? Focusing on the future discourages people who did well from resting on their laurels and prevents people who did badly from wallowing in despair. Focusing on what each person plans to do differently as a result of the review is also a great way to check for understanding—I often thought I had been clear and realized the person hadn't understood me only when I heard the plans they were formulating as a result of the review.

Schedule regular check-ins to assess how the plan is working. Once I'd helped the person whose performance I was reviewing to come up with a plan, it was important to make it real by planning regular check-ins and marking them in my calendar. This was often as simple as an agenda item in a couple of future 1:1s in which the person reports progress to me. But some sort of follow up was key.

Deliver the rating/compensation news after the performance review. If your company gives formal ratings and/or ties those ratings to compensation, you need to think clearly about how to sequence the information you're giving them. Many people are so focused on how their rating will affect their compensation that it's very hard for them to have a real conversation during the performance review. It can therefore be helpful to separate the two, and to deliver rating/compensation information *after* the conversation. I found that when I announced the rating at the beginning, all too often the person tuned out everything else I said. Sometimes this meant giving them the rating/comp info at the end of the conversation. Other times I'd delay by a day or more, asking them to come up with their thoughts and a plan for the future first. Many companies separate "development conversations" from "rating conversations" by a quarter or more. This is fine, as long as the "development conversations" don't substitute for regular impromptu guidance, which should be happening on a weekly cadence.

PREVENT BACKSTABBING

You are a boss, not a diplomat. Shuttle diplomacy won't work for you.

ONE OF THE most important ways to create an environment in which Radical Candor trumps political BS is to never let one person on your team talk to you about another behind their back. It feels like you're being empathetic to listen, but actually you're just stirring the political pot. Instead, insist that they talk directly to each other, without you. Hopefully, they'll work it out. But if they can't, offer to have a three-way conversation, ideally in person but at worst on the phone. This must be a live conversation (i.e., not over email or text). When you have the conversation, help them come up

GUIDANCE=	Praise	Criticism
Get from		
Give to		
Encourage between		✔

with a solution they can both understand and live with. I read an article about a CEO who would come up with the worst possible solution for both people when they couldn't work things out without his intervention. He did it because he hated mediating conflict. But that solution just created more conflict, not less. Your job is to be supportive, not punitive, when people come to you together with a conflict they cannot resolve. Open, fair, and fast conflict resolution is one of the services you owe your direct reports.

PEER GUIDANCE

REMEMBER THAT GOOD guidance should happen in a *conversation*, in *person*. There are a number of tools springing up that promise to replace the need to give feedback by asking users to write little snippets of text; these then get sent around and recorded, with analytics layers put on top. They look slick, but in the end they are a giant step in the wrong direction for relationships—a little bit like breaking up over text message. It's important that you, as the leader, encourage your team to take the time to *talk* to one another.

GUIDANCE=	Praise	Criticism
Get from		
Give to		
Encourage between	✔	✔

"Whoops the Monkey." Dan Woods, who was CTO at a start-up where I worked in the 1990s, developed the lowest-tech, cheapest, most effective system for encouraging praise and criticism on a team that I've seen. It involved two stuffed animals: a whale and a monkey. At every all-hands meeting, he invited people to nominate each other to win the "Killer Whale" for a week. The idea was to get people from the team to stand up and talk about some extraordinary work they'd seen somebody else do. The winner of the whale the previous week decided who deserved the whale this week. Next, people nominated themselves for "Whoops the Monkey." If anyone screwed up that week, they could stand up, tell the story, get automatic forgiveness, and help prevent somebody else from making the same mistake. When we first started doing this at both Juice and Google, there was silence. You could hear crickets. Not knowing what else to do, I put twenty dollars on Whoops's head. Once people could pretend that they weren't copping to my corny stuffed animal but simply wanted that twenty dollars, the stories started pouring out. This practice not only made it safe to make mistakes—and therefore to innovate—it also speeded up resolution to problems that otherwise would have festered. I once learned that somebody on my team had mortally offended an executive and that I needed to do some damage control. I knew the executive and could help. Another time I discovered that a mistake made by my team had infuriated a customer who now needed appeasing. I knew the customer and now that I heard about the problem I could help. The stories that the Killer Whale and Whoops elicited became my favorite part of most all-hands meetings. We all learned a lot in fifteen minutes.

Of course, that approach won't work everywhere. Apple, for example, was a "measure twice, cut once" kind of place, very different from Google's "launch and iterate" ethos. A practice like Whoops the Monkey would have been false advertising, and the stuffed animals would definitely not have met the design ethos at Apple!

In some industries, like aviation, sharing mistakes is so important that joking about Whoops the Monkey would simply be inappropriate. When a pilot makes a mistake, it could cost the lives of hundreds. Yet, pilots are human and will make mistakes. The more they can learn from one another's mistakes, the safer air travel can be. The Federal Aviation Administration (FAA) wanted to figure out how to get pilots sharing information freely after near-misses or crashes. Because the FAA has the authority to revoke licenses from pilots, it was unlikely that pilots would be forthcoming about mistakes they'd made. So, the FAA funded a program that NASA administers: the Aviation Safety Reporting System. Retired pilots talk to pilots involved in safety incidents, to figure out what happened. As long as the pilots hadn't been careless or reckless, they were granted immunity for their mistakes. This made it safe for them to share information, and as a result we are all a lot safer when we fly.

Imagine if there were a similar Medical Safety Reporting System. What if, instead of suing doctors who made honest mistakes we gave them immunity, collected and shared the information, and came up with ways to help other doctors avoid making the same mistakes? If we made it safer for doctors to give each other guidance, and to learn from each other's mistakes, the impact could be enormous.

Peer gauging. Another good way to get people talking to each other is to explain the Radical Candor framework to your team. Explain how you ask your team to gauge the guidance you give them, so that you can improve your guidance. Encourage them to gauge their peer guidance. Having a shared vocabulary will help your culture move toward Radical Candor.

SPEAKING TRUTH TO "POWER"

ROXANE WALES, WHO worked first at NASA and then in Learning and Development at Google, once told me that one of the most important things any manager of managers could do to foster a culture of guidance was to have so-called "skip level meetings." In these meetings, which need to happen only once a year to be effective, you will meet with the people who work for your direct reports,

GUIDANCE=	Praise	Criticism
Get from		
Give to		
Encourage between	✔	✔

without your direct reports in the room, and ask what they could do or stop doing to be better bosses.

This sounds super hierarchical, but let's face it: the "flat" organization is a myth. Hierarchy is an inescapable fact of life. The best way to lower the barriers that hierarchy puts between us is to admit that it exists and think of ways to make sure everyone feels they are on an equal footing at a human level despite the structure. To make sure everyone feels free to "speak truth to power."

The rationale for skip level meetings is that most people are very reluctant to criticize their boss. Plus, managers, especially new managers, will consciously or unconsciously seek to repress criticism rather than to encourage it. Finding out when this is happening and stamping it out will preserve a culture of Radical Candor and prevent a whole world of misery for the people who work for such a manager.

You have to be really careful with skip level meetings. They can turn into gripe sessions, and it must be clear that you aren't automatically presuming that the boss, your direct report, is guilty, or that you're unwilling to hear any criticism of your direct report. The intent of these sessions is to be supportive of the managers who report to you, not to undermine them. And part of being supportive is knowing when they are screwing up, and helping them address the situation. Also, for your own sanity, as well as for the sake of building a Radically Candid culture, it's important that these meetings not encourage people to come running to you instead of talking directly to their boss. Here are a few rules of thumb I learned for conducting them.

Explain it. Show it. Explain it again. Explain to each of your direct reports that you have two goals: 1) to help each of them become better bosses and 2) to make sure people on their team feel comfortable giving them feedback directly.

Show you mean what you just said. Start by asking your boss or somebody who has time to do a skip level on you. If you're the CEO, ask a coach or an advisor or board member to do it.

Never have a skip level meeting without prior consent of your direct report. Instead, ask the managers who report to you to explain the whole thing to their teams beforehand. It's vital that everyone understands that the meeting with you is in support of, not an attack on, their boss. Then, when you begin the meeting, reiterate that the goal of the meeting is to help the boss get better. Remind people that the goal is to create a culture where everyone always feels comfortable giving guidance, especially criticism, directly to their bosses—and that this meeting is a step in that direction, not a substitute for that goal.

More importantly, never have skip level meetings for some of the people who work for you but not others. It must be clear that this is a routine process undertaken for anyone who has direct reports. If you have skip level meetings only when there are problems on a team, then they will become a punishment rather than a welcome tool to help people develop their management skills.

Ensure the meeting is "not for attribution." Ensure everyone understands that, while the goal is to get everyone comfortable giving feedback directly to their boss, this is a "not for attribution" meeting. In other words, everything of import will be shared with their boss, but not who said it.

Take notes and project them. Project the notes you take during the meeting, and let people know that you will share them with the manager. Encourage people to say something if they find the notes inaccurate. When people speak up, be sure to change the notes and double check they are OK before proceeding. *It is important to take the notes yourself, rather than asking somebody else to do it.* First, it shows you are listening and engaged. Second, it's a great way to learn when you misunderstand something.

Kick-start the conversation. The first of these meetings is often incredibly awkward. You'll have to work hard to earn the trust of everyone in the room. Generally, it's easiest to start with praise to get people talking, "What is your manager doing well?" Then, "What could your manager be doing better?" Then, "What really sucks?" As problems emerge, try to get people to think about solutions, so it doesn't devolve into a gripe session. But if you're getting a lot of complaints, remind yourself it is a good thing not a bad thing. You are failing only if it is all sweetness and light.

Prioritize issues. Once things get flowing, remind people that often far more issues will get raised than will get fixed. The goal is to make things better—making them perfect is unrealistic. Push the people in the room to decide what the most important issues are and to prioritize those.

Share notes right after the meeting. When there are about eight minutes left in the meeting, ask everyone to look at the notes, reminding them that you'll be sharing the document with their boss momentarily. This has a way of focusing the conversation and making people feel accountable for their suggestions. The immediacy—you're going to share this with the person you were talking about eight minutes from now!—makes the conversation feel less like it is happening behind the person's back. It also means you don't have to remember to send the notes out to all the participants to double-check that everybody is comfortable with them, and then remember to share it with your direct report. You do all that in the meeting and spare yourself the unnecessary "next steps" that too often clutter your brain or just don't happen. This also alleviates the anxiety of the person who is being evaluated. They want to know what was said right away!

Ensure that your directs make and communicate changes. Once your direct reports have read the notes you've gathered, work with each to come up with one or two specific things they can immediately change. It mustn't be something big and vague like, "Improve my relationships." Much better if it's something smaller but more tangible like, "I will disagree in person, not over email." Encourage each of your direct reports to send an email out to their teams explaining what they have learned and what they are going to do differently as a result, and to cc you on the note. Then, encourage them to follow up in the next staff meeting to get a sense of whether people feel this has gone far enough. The more visible the change, the better. Review these changes in a follow-up to the skip level meeting, and encourage the team to tell you whether or not they made a difference. If people feel that no changes were made, or that the meeting didn't make a difference, treat this *very* seriously. In extreme cases, you may want to remove the manager in question from the team—either to return to an individual contributor role, to manage a different team, or to be fired.

Have these meetings once a year for each of your direct reports. The biggest problem with skip level meetings is that when they start going well, everybody wants them all the time, and you can get skip level proliferation. At one point at Google, I felt like I had a skip level meeting every other day. They take a lot of energy and focus and can lead to burn-out if you have to do too many of them. I recommend doing it once per year for each of your direct reports, and, if you manage managers, insist that they do the same. That way, the process scales and takes you just about seven to eight (an hour per skip level, half an hour per skip-level follow-up) hours a year if you have five direct reports.

Skip level meeting FAQs

I've worked with dozens of people who've become managers of managers for the first time, and these skip level meetings were always a source of great interest and anxiety. Here are some of the questions people have asked me most often.

What if it becomes clear that an entire team has lost faith in their manager? This will rarely happen—in years of doing these meetings, this has only happened to me three times. In each case, I started digging into the problems and found that the manager in question absolutely should not have been managing people.

What if people won't talk? Break the ice with them. "So everything is perfect?" Also, try to have a couple of issues you have heard about and offer those up. Ask, "If you could change one thing . . ." and then go around the room and put everyone on the spot to answer. Embrace the discomfort!

What if people won't shut up? If one person is doing all the talking, read faces carefully. If somebody looks as though they agree or disagree strongly, ask what they think. If somebody looks bored, ask, "So, this issue doesn't seem to resonate for you. Are there others on your mind?" If there seem to be more problems than you can cope with, focus the conversation on prioritizing them. Remind people that personality transplants are not available.

How do you strike the right balance between being supportive of the boss you're hearing about and being open to the team's thoughts? Be careful not to judge or defend the manager about whom you are soliciting feedback. If it feels as though you are fishing for reasons to punish the boss in question, either people will clam up or a gripe session will ensue. Make it clear that your role is not to judge but to pass along the feedback. If you encounter a really big problem, promise to look into it more deeply. Do not judge anything on the spot. Don't defend or malign the boss you're hearing about. That doesn't mean you can't sympathize with the way people feel, though. There's a world of difference between saying, "Wow, I can tell this is stressful. I'm sorry about that. Let's see what we can do to improve the situation," and saying, "Wow, your boss is a micromanager. Don't worry—I'm going to put a stop to this!"

* * *

THE KEY TO success when implementing any of these suggestions is to return to core principles, rather than following step-by-step instructions. Remember: if you are being Radically Candid, you are demonstrating, in a day-to-day way, that you are *seeing* the individuals on your team and the work they are doing. Even when you have particular criticisms, that level of attention is implicitly complimentary. And if you are demonstrating daily that you care personally, your Radically Candid responses are taken far more seriously, even embraced. Whenever you feel yourself getting lost in the weeds, simply return to these two questions: "Am I showing my team that I care personally?" and "Am I challenging each person directly?" If the answer to both questions is yes, you're doing just fine.

TEAM

Techniques for avoiding boredom and burnout

C HAPTER THREE ("UNDERSTAND WHAT MOTIVATES Each Person on Your Team") discussed the importance of getting to know each person who reports to you well enough that you can put the right people in the right roles, avoiding both boredom and burn-out. Ideally, you want everyone on your team to achieve exceptional results. But you don't want 100 percent of them to be gunning for the next job—or to be content with their current role. Instead you want a balance, so that you have both people who push for change and those who offer stability. And to understand what motivates the different people you work with, you need to have Radically Candid relationships with each.

Of course, the real world is rarely ideal. Typically, some people on your team will be achieving just mediocre results, and some may be failing altogether. You'll get the biggest bang for your buck spending time with the people who are doing the best work, but you still need to figure out how to manage everybody else. What follows are some specific techniques for doing just that.

CAREER CONVERSATIONS

Understand people's motivations and ambitions to help them take a step in the direction of their dreams

AS DESCRIBED IN Chapter Three, all people have their own growth trajectories, and it's a mistake to push everyone to be either a "superstar" or a "rock star." You need to balance growth and stability. To understand a person's growth trajectory, it's important to have career conversations in which you get to know each of your direct reports better, learn what their aspirations

are, and plan how to help them achieve those dreams. You should have these conversations with each person who reports directly to you, regardless of where they are in the team framework described in Chapter Three.

Once you've gotten the hang of these conversations, you'll look forward to them. They are your single biggest opportunity to move up on the "care personally" axis of the Radical Candor framework. In fact,

these conversations are the very first thing I recommend you do when rolling out Radical Candor on your team. Yes, they do take time, but they can occur in your usual 1:1 slots. And they will generate some of the most enjoyable conversations you have as a boss.

Russ Laraway, the cofounder of our company, Candor, Inc., is the very best manager I've ever worked with in my career. He developed a particularly effective approach during a difficult period at Google. At the time, Russ was a Director of Sales, and he had taken over a team that had come in via an acquisition. The new arrivals were thoroughly demoralized: pessimistic about their growth opportunities at Google and convinced their managers didn't value them. Very few reported that they expected to be working at

Google in three years. But Google had spent over a billion dollars to acquire their company, and it needed the team intact if the investment was to be worthwhile. Russ realized if he didn't do something fast he wasn't going to have much of a team left. He knew his first step was to show them that the company cared about them. But of course it's *bosses* who give a damn—companies can't care personally any more than governments or any other institution can.

Russ knew that the single biggest concern of employees at Google—both on his team and generally—was their career prospects. This was partly a money-driven problem—the cost of housing is so absurdly high in Silicon Valley that few people could afford to buy a house, even though they were working at Google. It was also an age issue. Google had an extremely young employee base, and a critical mass of people were about to turn thirty; many of them felt that they were barreling toward midlife crises. At an off-site retreat with her whole team during this period, Sheryl decided to address this company-wide anxiety about so-called "career growth". "You need a long-term vision and an eighteen-month plan," she advised.

This struck Russ. How could he help everyone who worked for him articulate their long-term vision and their eighteen-month plan? And how could he teach them to help their direct reports, and so on, cascading to all seven hundred people on his team? The existing solutions that were offered were called "personal development plans," and they weren't that useful. Some pretty much told everyone their careers were their own responsibilities; others focused minutely on the steps one had to take to get a promotion. They were either a blank canvas or an uninspiring paint-by-numbers picture. What was needed here was some education, in the literal sense—the latin root *educo* meaning "to lead out." People knew what they wanted. Russ felt it was a boss's job to help them articulate it, and then achieve it.

Russ tried asking "Todd" to describe his long-term vision for his career. Todd said what he thought Russ wanted to hear—essentially, he wanted to be just like Russ when he grew up. Russ laughed. "That's not ambitious enough! I'm not even sure I want this job. You want more. You deserve more!" Todd wasn't budging. Russ tried another tack. "OK. That's one vision. But nobody really knows what they want to do when they grow up. Give me another vision." This time, Todd confessed he wanted to be more like a mini Jack Welch than a Russ Laraway (i.e., to be a CEO, but perhaps not a Fortune 500 CEO). Russ knew he was getting somewhere now.

Something similar happened when he tried this again with another person, "Sarah." First she said she wanted to be like Russ, then she talked about another, larger ambition. "What about another vision," Russ asked. "A CAD—crazy-ass dream." Now, Sarah said what she *really* wanted to do was to start a spirulina farm. Whoa, what? Spirulina, Russ learned, is a super-food: a bacteria rich in protein and iron.

Now Russ was intrigued. How was a job persuading people to use Double-Click to serve their ads going to help Todd become a mini Jack Welch or Sarah to manage a spirulina farm? Russ decided not to worry about that right away but instead simply to get to know each of his direct reports better. Russ had thought that he knew them all pretty well, but clearly he didn't. The next time they talked, Russ asked each more about their life story.

When Sarah talked about previous transitions she'd made—quitting one sport and focusing on another, for example—Russ asked more questions. By the end of the conversation, he understood much better what motivated Sarah at work. He then wrote down each of her motivators (e.g., "financial independence," "environmentalism," "hard work," "leadership") and explained how the stories she'd told him about her life had led him to choose these words. This was an important check for understanding. For example, Russ had chosen the word "leadership" as a key motivator for Sarah, based on a story she'd told him about volunteer work she'd done to preserve California's open-space preserves. But she didn't like that word, preferring "stewardship." Russ realized how valuable this conversation was, and decided that going forward he'd ask people about their past before moving on to their future.

Now, Russ was ready for the task of connecting what Sarah was doing right now to what she wanted to be doing at the very peak of her career. Russ, who's very analytical, put each of Sarah's dreams into columns. Next, he asked Sarah what skills she thought were most important to achieve each dream. Finally, he asked Sarah what skills she felt she had the most competence in.

This analysis helped Russ and Sarah figure out what skills were most important for her to begin developing or to continue deepening. For example, it became clear that the most important thing that Sarah could work on now was getting management experience. She'd been thinking she needed to develop her analytical skills and her presentation skills. And if her goal were to be a director at Google, that would've been important. But management skills were much more important to a spirulina rancher than presentation skills. Furthermore, Sarah hated making presentations, and she didn't want to develop her analytical skills. But she *was* interested in getting some real management experience. Now it was more clear to both Sarah and Ross why.

Together, she and Russ came up with a plan to make sure she got increased management responsibility and also some mentorship from other great leaders at Google. While making the plan, it also became evident that Sarah could get the management experience faster by staying at Google than by leaving. Furthermore, Russ, her immediate boss, was one of the best managers in the company. Sarah decided to stay at Google for a few more years, where she became an enormously effective leader. She was getting the skills she needed, and saving money for her spirulina ranch. The work she was doing, which had seemed so separate from what she really wanted out of life, now made a lot more sense to her.

Realizing he'd come up with a good methodology for having career conversations, Russ held an off-site and taught his managers how to talk to their direct reports not just about their career goals or how to get promoted but also about their life stories and dreams. He taught every manager on his team to have a succession of three forty-five-minute conversations with each direct report over the course of three to six weeks.

Russ's approach was so successful that an internal survey of employee satisfaction showed the people on his team displaying a marked increase in optimism about their futures at Google and their positive feelings about their managers. Nobody from HR had ever seen such an improvement.

Conversation one: life story

The first conversation is designed to learn what motivates each person who reports directly to you. Russ suggested a simple opening to these conversations. "Starting with kindergarten, tell me about your life." Then, he advised each manager to focus on changes that people had made and to understand why they'd made those choices. Values often get revealed in moments of change. "You dropped out of graduate school after two years to work on Wall Street—please tell me more about that decision." Answers like, "I couldn't even afford orange juice on my grad school stipend, and I just wanted to make more money," or "I was bored with all that theory and no practical, tangible application of the ideas I was working on," enable you to begin to put together parts of the human puzzle. In the first case, you might write down "financial independence" as a key motivator; in the second, "see tangible results of work." If somebody says they quit running and started playing soccer because they liked being on a team, you might write down "being part of a team" as a motivator. If on the other hand somebody quit cheerleading to focus on swimming because they "were sick of the chitchat and preferred to focus on beating a personal best," you might write down "personal growth" as a motivator.

Remember, you're not looking for definitive answers; you're just trying to get to know people a little better and understand what they care about.

Many managers initially felt some discomfort with this kind of get-to-know-you conversation. It seemed like a boundary violation to ask people about their lives outside of work. Russ explained two things. One, most people are happy to have this conversation, as long as it takes place in an environment of trust and respect. If part of your job is to care personally, you have to get to know people personally. Two, there may be times when you touch on something that *is* too personal. If a person signals discomfort at a question, you have to respect that. For example, one person seemed profoundly uncomfortable with some basic questions about childhood. Sensing this, Russ let childhood drop, and the woman went on to describe her life after grad school, becoming much more confident. As he got to know her better, Russ learned that she'd had some significant trauma growing up. But she hadn't been comfortable telling Russ about it during a get-to-know-you conversation, and Russ hadn't pressed.

Russ has all of his managers practice these get-to-know-you conversations with each other, in order to get people more comfortable with having them, and also to be sensitive to not pressing beyond each person's level of comfort. Also, practicing these conversations helps to remind everyone that they have a goal: learning what motivates people at work.

The reason to pull these motivations out of a life story rather than to discuss them abstractly is that it's so easy to misunderstand abstractions. For example, an employee may say that financial independence is really important to her, and you may assume that's simply another way of saying that she's materialistic. If instead she tells you the following story, you might come away with a different impression: When she was twelve, her mother went back to work and the family was missing her full-time presence at home. They decided to take a trip to New Orleans to spend some time to-gether. As they strolled down Bourbon Street, your employee glanced into a strip joint and saw an almost naked woman twisted around a pole. She was horrified. Her father, who had already downed a couple of milk punches, noticed. "See that woman?" he said. "She makes more money in a single day than your mother makes in a year." Your employee felt so angry. On behalf of the woman on the pole, on behalf of her underpaid mother, at the whole world for all that her father's comment implied about being female. *That* is what she means when she says financial independence is important to her. It's not just selfish materialism.

Just this first of the three conversations will have a big impact. First, you've done more in forty-five minutes to get to know each person who reports to you than you could do in any other way. You've done something to show you care, and—invariably, after a conversation like that—you *do* care more. Next, you're already better equipped to figure out what kinds of opportunities would be helpful for each person. Finally, you're more prepared for the next conversation. When you understand what motivates a person and why, you're much better able to understand their dreams.

The second conversation: dreams

The second conversation moves from understanding what motivates people to understanding the person's dreams—what they want to achieve at the apex of their career, how they imagine life at its best to feel. Russ chose the word "dreams" very consciously. Bosses usually ask about "long-term goals" or "career aspirations" or "five-year plans," but each of these phrases, when used by a boss, tends to elicit a certain type of answer: a "professional," and not entirely human, answer. It also invites a response that the person imagines the boss wants to hear rather than a description of what the person really wants to achieve; a delicate balance between trying to appear suf-ficiently ambitious ("I want to be like you.") and yet not too ambitious ("But I don't want your job."). "What are your career aspirations?" doesn't invite a description of dreams that involve an entirely different career or employer—like the spirulina farm. Furthermore, questions about "career" tend to focus on promotions, and these conversations are never satisfying. People who want a promotion never feel they're getting one fast enough; people who don't want one feel lame for being insufficiently ambitious when you ask them about career aspirations.

When a personal development plan focuses too narrowly on the things a person has to do to get a promotion, it results in a conversation that leaves people worried they appear unserious about their current job and employers worried about encouraging people to leave. Maybe they don't want the next promotion, but the way the conversation is structured makes them reluctant to say so. Maybe they do want it, but for reasons they are not invited to share.

Giving space for people to talk about *dreams* allows bosses to help people find opportunities that can move them in the direction of those dreams. This makes work more satisfying and more meaningful and ultimately improves retention. But retention was the by-product—satisfying, meaningful work and productive relationships with the boss were the primary goals of Russ's "career conversation" process.

So what do you use in place of the standard questions? Russ recommends that you begin these conversations with, "What do you want the pinnacle of your career to look like?" Because most people don't really know what they want to do when they "grow up," Russ suggests encouraging people to come up with three to five different dreams for the future. This allows employees to include the dream they think you want to hear as well as those that are far closer to their hearts.

Ask each direct report to create a document with three to five columns; title each with the names of the dreams they described in the last conversation. Then, list the skills needed as rows. Show how important each skill is to each dream, and what their level of competency is in that skill. Generally, it will become very obvious what new skills the person needs to acquire. Now, your job as the boss is to help them think about how they can acquire those skills: what are the projects you can put them on, whom can you introduce them to, what are the options for education?

The final part of Russ's second conversation involves making sure that the person's dreams are aligned with the values they have expressed. For example, "If 'hard work' is a core value, why is one of your dreams to retire early?" Inquiring about the dreams people describe is an important way to push for candid, meaningful conversations. In one instance at Google, Russ's question revealed that the person had a special-needs child whose condition was expected to become especially acute in the teenage years. This father wanted to make sure he would be able to focus his entire attention on his child when the child was likely to need him most. That put his plans for early retirement in a whole different light.

You're not going to get the dramatic "spirulina ranch" story out of most people. I once worked with a man who had a baby with major health issues. The thing he cared most about at work during this period was getting home in time to take a thirty-minute walk with his wife during daylight hours. Given everything going on in his life, that seemed pretty ambitious, and I did everything I could to make sure he got out of the office in time for those walks.

Conversation three: eighteen-month plan

Last, Russ taught managers to get people to begin asking *themselves* the following questions: "What do I need to learn in order to move in the direction of my dreams? How should I prioritize the things I need to learn? Whom can I learn from?" How can I change my role to learn it? Once people were clear on what they wanted to learn next, it was much easier for managers to identify opportunities at work that would help them develop skills in the next six to eighteen months that would take them in the direction of at least one of their dreams. This translation of current work to future dreams was far more inspiring for people than "Here's how you climb the next rung on the ladder."

Here's what to do: make a list of how the person's role can change to help them learn the skills needed to achieve each dream; whom they can learn from; and classes they could take or books they could read. Then, next to each item, note who does what by when—and make sure you have some action items.

Helping people clarify values and dreams and then aligning them as closely as possible with their current work will invariably make your team stronger. Each individual will be more successful and happier, and together you'll achieve results "unexpected in common hours." Thoreau said it best in *Walden*:

> "If one advances confidently in the direction of his dreams, and endeavors to live the life which he has imagined, he will meet with a success unexpected in common hours. He will put some things behind, will pass an invisible boundary . . . If you have built castles in the air, your work need not be lost; that is where they should be. Now put the foundations under them."

It's *scary* to move confidently in the direction of one's dreams. Part of your responsibility as the boss is to help people find the courage to do just that. If you do it well, there are few more rewarding jobs.

THIS IS A high-level overview of three conversations that on the surface seem pretty straightforward. There's a lot riding on your ability to get them right: building trust with the people who report to you, figuring out what role each person is best suited for so that your team can achieve results. If you have additional questions about what you can do to ensure they go well, you can ask Russ directly at www.radicalcandor.com/contact. Your questions may very well become part of the book Russ is writing to help you better understand how to have these career conversations.

GROWTH MANAGEMENT
Figure out who needs what types of opportunities,
and how you're going to provide them

YOU'VE HAD YOUR three conversations and begun the process of lining up opportunities on your team with each person's aspirations. These efforts have moved you way up on the "care personally" dimension of Radical Candor. Now it's time to move over on the "challenge directly" dimension.

Once a year, you need to put together a growth-management plan for each person on your team. Take a look across your whole team and make sure that you understand how each individual's aspirations and growth trajectory is lining up with the collective needs of the team. Then, unless everyone on your team is both where they want and where they need to be, you're going to have to have some pretty challenging conversations.

Put names in boxes (temporarily!)

The first step is to identify your rock stars and superstars. Write their names in the correct boxes. Next, identify the people on your team who are

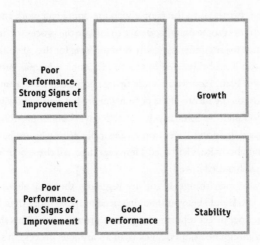

doing good, but not exceptional, work. This will probably be the majority of people. Then, identify the people who are performing poorly but whom you believe should do much better, either because they are demonstrating signs that they can improve or because their skills and ambitions suggest improvement is possible. Finally—and this is usually the hardest part—identify the people who are not doing good work and not getting any better. Don't obsess—spend twenty minutes, maximum, doing this exercise. Think fast.

Then, to make sure you are not biased, get an outside perspective. Find someone who is familiar with the work of the people on your team but not as emotionally attached as you are—your boss, a peer, an HR person. If they would put your people in different boxes, make sure you understand why, even if you disagree. *Especially* if you disagree.

Write growth plans

Next, come up with a three- to five-bullet-point growth plan for each person. Make sure that you have projects or opportunities that will stretch the superstars. Make sure that you're giving the rock stars what they need to be productive. Think of ways to push people who are doing good work to do exceptional work. What kind of new projects or education or help can you offer them? For the people who are doing bad work but show signs of improving: have you put these people in the wrong roles? Are expectations clear? Do they need additional training?

And that brings us to the people who are doing bad work and not getting any better. At some point, you have to initiate the process of firing these people—most bosses understandably wait too long for this. If you're at a big company, you'll probably need to talk to HR about a formal Performance Improvement Plan. How you handle firing people can have a tremendous effect not just on the future of the person you fire but also on how your team perceives you and the company. It can also have a big impact on you. Just the other day, Russ and I went on a sales call. Who was across the table from us? Somebody Russ had fired a few years ago. All three of us were glad that Russ had handled it well.

Back to happier things. If you are regularly thinking about personal growth, as you should be, you shouldn't need to spend more than five to fifteen minutes per direct report jotting down growth plans. This should feel more like a disciplined sanity check than an arduous process. It's a way to make sure you have the whole team's growth trajectory in your head.

Don't be an "easy grader" or a "hard grader"

If a lot of your peers are also doing growth-management plans, it's a good idea to compare notes. When you're part of a broader team, it's important to have a shared understanding of what exceptional work is, what good work is, and what bad work is. For example, if you have half your team in the rock-star box and nobody else has anyone there, it is more likely that you're out of step with your colleagues than that you have the best team.

If you are a manager of managers, find a simple way to keep everyone on the same page. For example, you can create a shared document and have all your directs put the names from their teams into the appropriate boxes, then get in a room together and discuss. If disputes erupt, ask people to resolve them in a separate meeting and then report back on what they decide, or to ask you to make a decision if they cannot agree on one. These are hard conversations, but worthwhile because they encourage more consistency among managers. Making sure that all managers are treating the different types of high performers similarly is important to making sure everyone feels the system is fair. It will also give your team the opportunity to be explicit about what they feel the right ratio of people on a steep versus gradual growth trajectory ought to be.

Ensure fairness by level

Because you care so much about your direct reports, you tend to see the best in them. This is a good thing, but it can turn into a form of unconscious bias on a really big team. If you're the leader of a team of five hundred people, you'll naturally tend to think most highly of your direct reports. And these direct reports think most highly of their direct reports. So if you're not careful, a disproportionate percentage of the people considered rock stars or superstars will be the most senior people in a hierarchy, even though that kind of grade inflation may not reflect reality.

Ensuring fairness across levels both cultivates growth throughout the organization and avoids unnecessary resentment. Too often, the people who have the most senior roles are given the highest ratings when in fact they are surfing on the productivity of the people working for them. Don't let that happen! In general, one would expect there to be the same distribution of excellent performance throughout, as well as a higher ratio of more senior people on a gradual growth trajectory and a higher ratio of more junior people on a steep growth trajectory. In practice, most management teams respond in the reverse manner—a greater percentage of senior rather than junior people get put in the superstar box. If this happens, ask some hard questions and make sure there's an identifiable, justifiable reason for it.

HIRING: YOUR MENTALITY AND YOUR PROCESS

WHEN HIRING, YOU'RE obviously looking for people who will be great at the job. But should you be hiring rock stars or superstars? The answer is, of course, "It depends." There are some jobs that require one or the other. Also you want to make sure you have the right ratio overall on your team. If you have too many superstars, hire a rock star next.

Process

Your hiring process is important; it's a vital part of building a great team. When you are growing really fast, you'll wind up spending a lot of your time hiring. At one point when I was at Google, I spent 25 percent of my time hiring people.

What follows are descriptions of the key things I've seen work (and not

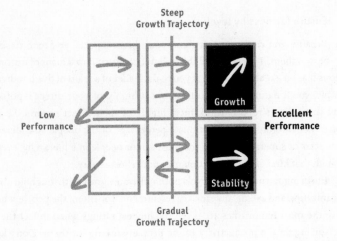

work) at Google, Apple, and elsewhere. These are the basic elements of a hiring process that is as rigorous as possible without being overly onerous. All hiring is flawed and subjective, and these drawbacks cannot be fixed; they can only be *managed*. Here are some simple things you can do to make sure you're hiring the right people:

Job description: define team "fit" as rigorously as you define "skills" to minimize bias. The hiring person—*not* a recruiter!—should write the job description, basing it on the role, the skills required for the role, and the team "fit" criteria. Defining team fit can be hard, which makes it tempting to leave out. Try to describe your culture in three to four words. It could be "detail-oriented," "quirky," and "blunt." Or maybe it's "big picture," "straight-laced," and "polite." Whatever you choose, be disciplined about interviewing for those things. This will help people avoid making gut decisions that are so often driven by bias. Also, if you take the time to define the growth trajectory required for the role, it can help the interviewers avoid one kind of hiring bias: hiring people who share your ambitions, which may not be desirable for the role. The written job description should then go to all interviewers, so they know precisely what they are interviewing for.

Blind skills assessments can also minimize bias. Interviewing takes time, filling out interview feedback reports takes time, and so it's important to be very selective about who gets invited to interview. A number of false positives and false negatives can be weeded out with a good prescreen. An example of a good prescreen is a skills assessment: ask potential candidates to do a project or solve a problem related to the job they're applying for. This will weed out a number of candidates who look good on paper but can't actually do the work. It will also give candidates who'd be great at the job but look bad on paper the opportunity to interview.

In an ideal world, this would be a blind skills assessment. Malcolm Gladwell tells a now-famous story about how orchestras that implemented blind auditions increased the percentage of women hired fivefold. Whenever possible, give candidates the opportunity to show the kind of work they can do without looking at who the person is.

Some companies have even experimented with asking candidates to do a skills assessment online, stripping out all personally identifying information. The people assessing the skills can't guess at the candidate's gender, race, etc. This is a brilliant idea, albeit very time-consuming and not always practicable. But increasingly services like hired.com offer a bias screen that filters out name and photo so that you're just looking at skills when seeing résumés.

Use the same interview committee for multiple candidates, to allow for meaningful comparisons. If you can avoid it, don't make unilateral hiring decisions. Because interviewing is so subjective and prone to bias, you'll improve your odds of making good decisions by getting multiple perspectives. However, this means you need to be consistent and thoughtful about who interviews with whom. If Bob, Charlene, and Dory interviewed and liked Xavier, but Ebert, Frank, and Georgia interviewed and liked Zan, how to decide whom to hire? This is a waste of eight people's time.

Four people is about the right size for an interview committee. Ideally, the interviewing committee is diverse. If you're a female candidate, it can be off-putting if everyone who interviews you is male. If you're an underrepresented minority, it can be frustrating if everyone who interviews you is of the same ethnicity. It's also helpful if at least one of the interviewers is on another team. This prevents "desperation hiring." When there's a "hole" on a team, people become so eager to fill the position that they ignore warning signals. Somebody who isn't feeling the pain of the hole on the team as acutely is more likely to point out these danger signs.

Casual interviews reveal more about team fit than formal ones. I am sure that there is good interview training out there somewhere, but I've never encountered it. My experience is that interviewing is a learning-by-doing skill. Let people develop their own style. I love stories, so my whole interview technique is just to ask people to "give me the oral version of your résumé."

Another good practice is to have people intentionally create more casual moments—take candidates to lunch, walk them to the car. Ask the receptionist and schedulers if they had any reaction to the candidate. In unguarded moments, candidates will do or say revealing things. An important part of my team's culture was Bob Sutton's "No Assholes" rule. One candidate I was about to hire was so rude to the scheduler that she cried. Another candidate was rude to a waiter. I didn't hire either of them. Another picked up napkins he hadn't dropped that were littering the floor. I did hire him. An executive I know who's a great hirer always walks candidates to the car. Here are a few of the things she's learned on these walks: one candidate divulged a drug habit, another bragged about his dominance at home with his family and said he had to keep his "women in line," another joked about how he liked to gossip about other colleagues and clients at lunch.

Make interviews productive by jotting down your thoughts right away. Write down your interview feedback; doing that is as clarifying for you as it is for the rest of the committee, and it will result in better hiring decisions. Write down your thoughts on each of the skills, if you're interviewing for skills, as well as for each of the team fit criteria identified.

I recently interviewed a candidate who was both charming and had an impressive résumé, but something was bothering me. I put my finger on it only when I sat down to write interview feedback: he had a tendency to make big assertions without having precise details at his fingertips. He talked about Company X's system as "able to scale to infinity," but when I pressed him he said they could handle a few million rows of data a day—hardly infinity, or even that impressive. He was also a little vague on what exactly Company X was *doing* to drive revenue, and what his role in driving it was.

I know, you're busy and you don't have time to write everything down. Here's a tip: schedule an hour, interview for forty-five minutes, and write for fifteen. This arrangement will force you to have a more focused interview *and* to make a better recommendation about whom to hire.

In-person debrief/decision: if you're not *dying* to hire the person, don't make an offer. The best advice I ever got for hiring somebody is this: if you're not dying to hire somebody, don't make an offer. And, even if you are dying to hire somebody, allow yourself to be overruled by the other interviewers who feel strongly the person should not be hired. In general, a bias toward no is useful when hiring.

Once three to four candidates have been interviewed for a role, the hiring committee should meet to discuss each one. These in-person conversations take real discipline to schedule, but if you believe that it makes sense to have multiple people interview each candidate, then talking about your assessments face to face is the fastest and soundest way to make a good decision.

Making all feedback visible to all interviewers after they've submitted theirs will help these hiring-committee meetings go more quickly, but it will require more prep from each person. A good way to ensure that everyone is on the same page is to schedule a one-hour meeting with a fifteen-minute "study hall" time at the beginning so everyone can read everyone else's feedback. If run well, the meeting should generally end early. If your team is empowered to make a decision without further ado, and if you are dying to hire the person and nobody has overruled you, do it immediately!! If not, make your recommendation to the powers that be at your company, and push them to make a decision fast.

FIRING

A necessary evil

SOME COMPANIES DON'T invest much time in the hiring process, on the theory that it's easy to fire people. This is a big mistake. Firing people is *not* easy, either emotionally or legally. At companies where it's too easy to fire people, bad/unfair firing decisions get made, with the result that even people who are great at their jobs start to get spooked. When people feel that kind of fear, they start to avoid taking risks. They learn less, they grow less, they innovate less, they become less than they could be. This is the opposite of personal growth management.

Other companies make the opposite mistake: they make firing people damn near impossible. In these companies, bosses have one hand tied behind their backs. Some address performance issues by foisting failing team

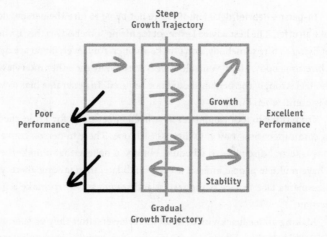

members on unsuspecting colleagues, which creates bizarre office politics. Those who are doing the best work also wind up having to carry people who are not able to contribute—and often quit in frustration as a result. Those who are not able to contribute realize it doesn't really matter and stop even trying. The gravitational pull of organizational mediocrity sets in.

Firing people is hard, and it ought to be hard. But if you do three things, you can make it far, far easier on the person you are firing—as well as on yourself and your team.

Don't wait too long

Virtually all managers I've ever worked with have been far too slow to admit when somebody on their team is starting to underperform. They don't admit it to themselves, let alone to their bosses or to HR. When I teach management classes, I often ask people to put names in quadrants on the talent management grid. I tell them there are no consequences. They don't have to share this with anyone. This is a purely mental exercise. After everyone has finished I ask, "How many of you think there are some underperformers at this company?" Generally, all the hands go up. Then I ask, "How many of you put a single name in one of the two 'poor performance' boxes?" Generally, only a couple of hands go up. A few people will laugh, but everyone is always very eager to move on. I force them to sit there until everyone has put names in the underperforming boxes.

There are four very good reasons to push yourself to identify underperformance early. One, to be fair to the person who's failing. If you identify a problem early, you give the person time to address it. You also reduce the shock if they can't or won't address it and you wind up having to fire the person. Two, to be fair to your company. If you identify and address problems early enough, you dramatically reduce the risk of getting sued or the chance that you'll have to keep them on the payroll for months of painful legal documentation. Three, to be fair to yourself. When you give somebody a good rating one quarter and fire them the next, word gets around, and it undermines trust with everyone else. Not to mention that you risk being sued by the fired employee. Although it is time-consuming and unpleasant to address performance problems, it takes a lot more time and is far more unpleasant to deal with a lawsuit. Four, and most importantly, you want to address underperformance early to be fair to the people who are performing really well. Tolerating bad work is unfair to the people who are doing excellent work.

Don't make the decision unilaterally

Once you've identified performance issues, take the time to get advice from your boss, to calibrate with your peers (if appropriate), and to get help from HR. Don't take the attitude that this is your decision alone. You don't want to fire a person out of anger, and you don't want to fail to fire a person out of denial. Many people get lost in their own heads around this highly charged issue; your boss and your peers can help you think more clearly. Good HR people can not only help you think more clearly but also make sure you do it in a way that won't get you or the company sued.

In an ideal world, your company has somebody in HR whose job it is to help you document properly. (If you run a company, identify such a person!) If that is not the case, find an employment lawyer or a seasoned HR person or an experienced manager and ask them for help. Don't just ask for advice; get them to edit what you write. Advice is far too abstract. I've seen dozens of cases where a manager has been advised how to write a Performance Improvement Plan (PIP). They are told to make it fair but not too easy, to make sure that it really addresses the performance issue. The managers hear the "fair" part but ignore the "not too easy" part. The person passes the PIP without addressing the core issue, and the performance problem drags on for another three or six months.

As a boss, you need to write the emails and other documents like

PIPs—but make sure that somebody who has done this before edits them carefully. It's going to take time—a lot more time than you want to spend on it. Again, it's worth taking the time because being sued is far worse!

Give a damn

Don't get too caught up in all the HR/legal advice, though. Take a deep breath and a big step back. You have a relationship with the person you're about to fire. You still give a damn about this person. Think hard about how to do it in a way that will make it easiest on them—even if it makes it harder on you, or if you have to take some risks.

When I was at Juice, I had to fire somebody and was worried it would be contentious. I got a bunch of advice from our lawyer about how to do it (we had no HR department). A lot of it was really helpful, but the lawyer kept advising me to hire a security guard to walk the person out. I knew the person I was firing would feel ashamed if I did it this way, and that it would make him more likely to go ballistic. "What is the risk of not walking him out?" I asked the lawyer. "He might go ballistic," she said. I realized I was likely to cause the very thing I was trying to prevent by following legal advice, so I did the opposite. I let him go back in, say good-bye on his own terms. He thanked me for that later, and I always had the feeling that following my gut instead of the legal advice spared everybody a lot of heartache—and probably avoided a lawsuit.

When you have to fire people, do it with humility. Remember, the reason you have to fire them is not that they suck. It's not even that they suck at this job. It's that this job—the job you gave them—sucks for them.

Follow up

I usually email people about a month after I've fired them to check in. I try to keep my ear to the ground about jobs they might be well-suited for. But even if I don't have anything to offer, I will reach out. Often, I'm the last person they want to hear from, and so if I don't hear back I don't push it, and I don't blame them. But sometimes the person is happy to take a walk, share a meal, or just have a quick exchange. I'll never forget one walk I took with a man who thanked me profusely for having fired him, and whose wife had asked him to pass along her thanks as well. It turned out that leaving the job was not just good for his career; it was also good for his marriage and for his relationship with his children.

It's hard to fire people, but it's hard to quit, too. Sometimes it's your job as the boss to be Radically Candid when something's just not working.

PROMOTIONS
Be fair

FEW THINGS CAN create a sense of injustice on a team like having a boss who promotes based on favoritism, or a manager who promotes people much faster than the manager sitting in the next office. Yet when a few managers get together to make sure their promotions are fair, the politics can get ugly very quickly. Disagreements can become overly personalized, silent disagreement can become toxic, and bizarre backroom bartering occurs—"I'll support your undeserving person if you'll support mine." A grudge held from the last cycle may kill the promotion of an otherwise deserving person the next time around.

Google's engineering team solved these problems with promotion committees, which were assembled off-site for one day twice a year. They debated the promotions of other people's direct reports, not their own, based on a packet of relatively objective information about each person's accomplishments. The debates were about the merits of a person's promotion, not "my person" versus "your person." But most importantly, the process was a solution to the age-old problem of manager favoritism. As a result, no engineer has ever been promoted at Google just by ass-kissing alone. (Unfortunately, other

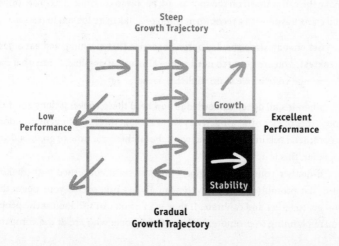

Steep
Growth Trajectory

Growth

Low
Performance

Excellent
Performance

Stability

Gradual
Growth Trajectory

teams at Google don't have as rigorous a promotion process as engineering does.)

That's not to say Google's system is perfect. It tends to reward people who do the most visible projects rather than those who make important breakthroughs behind the scenes. And recommendations from some people go further than they ought to. But it's still the best process I've seen, and worth emulating.

Even if your company doesn't go to these lengths to make promotions fair, you can confer with your peers, or if you're a boss of bosses you can require all your reports to calibrate their promotion plans with one another before any promotions get approved. Here are some tips for preventing the politics described above from ruining your calibration meetings.

Prepare. Ask everyone on your team to send in a list of people they are planning to promote, together with a justification. If you have an HR partner, ask that person to organize all names and justifications by level and pull together a presentation that makes the information easy to grasp and absorb. Go into the meeting having reviewed all the information and being prepared with your own point of view on each promotion—but also with an open mind.

Manage the time carefully, and don't let arguments go on too long. Go through all promotions by level, most senior to least. Plan for the more senior promotions to take up more time per person than more junior promotions, but don't let them take up *all* the time. When arguments go on too long, either make the call yourself on the spot, or ask people to continue the debate offline and come to you with a recommendation or a stalemate for you to resolve.

Get enough sleep the day before, exercise that morning, and eat a good breakfast. You are going to need to be calm and, if possible, funny that day. Encourage your whole team to do the same.

When it's all done, acknowledge how hard these conversations are. Plan some sort of clear-the-air activity—a walk together, etc. In general I don't recommend mixing alcohol and work, but if there is a time to go for a drink together, this is it.

If neither your company nor your boss seem concerned with making sure that promotions are fair, you can always propose to your peers that you get together and calibrate. If they won't, you can still look at the people you're planning to promote, look at other people who are at the company, and do a sanity check. You don't do people any favors by promoting them when the rest of the team feels they don't really deserve it.

REWARD YOUR ROCK STARS
Don't give all the glory to the superstars

Avoid promotion/status obsession

I once became totally paralyzed over my keyboard when trying to write the email I was supposed to send out to my whole team at Google to celebrate promotions. Ten years later, I finally understand what was wrong: I shouldn't have been writing that email at all. Announcing promotions breeds unhealthy competition for the wrong things: documentation of status rather than development of skill.

Most promotions come with increased salary, responsibility, and, in some companies, equity. That is a lot of external validation. Presumably, the people getting promoted have been praised in public for the work they've done along the path to getting the promotion. But when there are big public celebrations of promotions, the costs in terms of the organization's focus on hierarchy often outweigh the benefits of publicly recognizing those being promoted.

What about making roles clear and transparent? If a promotion includes a change of role, then announce it. But not every change of role signifies a promotion, and not every promotion signifies a change of role. Focus on

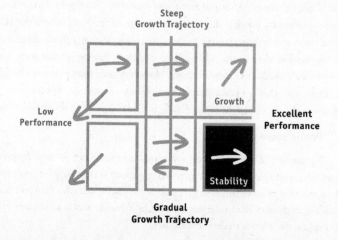

the work the person is doing, not the status they've achieved in the company for doing it.

What about public praise? Yes, by all means, praise in public. But think carefully about *what* you are praising. Praise the things you want more of: high-quality work, mind-boggling innovation, amazing efficiency, selfless teamwork, and so on. Do you really want such a focus on promotions? If not, then don't make such a big deal of them.

Say "thank-you"

Jim Ottaway, former SVP and Board Director of Dow Jones, once told me he'd been astounded to find a thank-you note he'd written a decade earlier still stuck on the wall of an employee's office. Realizing how much it meant, he wished he'd written a lot more notes like that. The importance of the simplest things, like thank-yous, are most often forgotten by bosses—even good bosses.

A thank-you goes beyond praise. Praise expresses admiration for great work. A thank-you expresses personal gratitude. In the case of a thank-you, you are explaining not just why the work matters, but why it matters to *you*. Take a moment to say thank-you. Do it in person, and do it in writing. Sometimes the thank-you has more meaning in private, other times in public. It rarely hurts to do both.

Gurus

Another great way to highlight how great people are at a job is to acknowledge them as gurus in their area of expertise. You might acknowledge their mastery by putting the person in charge of teaching others the skill. Give them a couple of months to develop a class, to really think about how to teach what they know. This can be deeply satisfying for the guru, and enormously productive for your team. Not everybody likes to teach, though, so make sure this is a reward not a punishment. Figure out another way to establish the person as the master in their field if they don't enjoy teaching.

Public presentations

Again, one of the most common complaints from people who do excellent work and are on a gradual growth trajectory is that they feel invisible. A simple way to solve this is to give people on your team who focus on tasks that are important but under-recognized or misunderstood an opportunity to explain their work to their colleagues.

AVOID ABSENTEE MANAGEMENT AND MICROMANAGEMENT

TO HELP YOU figure out when you're being a good partner rather than slipping into micromanagement or absentee management, I've developed a simple chart. I hope it will help you partner better with the people who report to you. One of the best ways to keep the people on your team engaged is by partnering actively with them.

ABSENTEE MANAGEMENT	PARTNERSHIP	MICROMANAGEMENT
Hands-off, ears off, mouth off.	Hands-on, ears on, mouth off.	Hands-on, ears off, mouth on.
Lacks curiosity. Doesn't want to know.	Displays curiosity. Recognizes when they need to know more.	Lacks curiosity. Pretends to know all.
Doesn't listen. Says nothing.	Listens. Asks why.	Doesn't listen. Tells how.
Is afraid of *any* details.	Asks about *relevant* details.	Gets lost in the details.
Has no idea what's going on.	Is informed because hands-on.	Asks for make-work presentations, reports, and updates.
Sets no goals.	Leads collaborative goal-setting.	Sets goals arbitrarily.
Remains unaware of problems.	Listens to problems. Predicts problems. Brainstorms solutions.	Tells people how to solve problems without fully understanding them.
Causes collateral damage by tripping on grenades unawares.	Removes obstacles and defuses explosive situations.	Tells people how to remove obstacles/ defuse situations, but watches from a safe distance.
Is ignorant of both the questions and the answers.	Shares what they know; asks questions when they don't	Pretends to know when they don't.
Is unaware of context.	Shares relevant context.	Hoards information.

SUMMARY

THERE ARE FEW pleasures greater than being part of a team where everyone loves their job and loves working together. You can build a team like that if you have career conversations with each of the people on your team, create growth-management plans for each person who works for you once a year, hire the right people, fire the appropriate people, promote the right people, and reward the people who are doing great work but who shouldn't be promoted, and offer yourself as a partner to your direct reports. It's absolutely within your power to build a team that looks forward to coming to work every day. Together you will accomplish things that you could never do individually, while each of you individually takes a step in the direction of your dreams.

RESULTS

Things you can do to get stuff done together—faster

THE ULTIMATE GOAL OF RADICAL Candor is to achieve results collaboratively that you could never achieve individually. You've created a culture of guidance. You've created an exemplary team that embodies the Radical Candor ethos of caring personally and challenging directly. As a result, the team is firing on all cylinders; and perhaps most importantly, it has developed a self-correcting quality whereby most problems are solved *before* you are even aware of them. It's not time to buy the yacht and sail off to the Caribbean, though. Now you get to use the gift of Radical Candor— all that freed-up time and energy—to focus your team on achieving great results.

Neuroscientist and academic Stephen Kosslyn once gave a talk in which he described how people who work together on a team become like "mental prostheses" for each other. What one person doesn't enjoy and isn't good at is what another person loves and excels at. Together, they are "better, stronger, faster." Getting better, stronger, and faster in this case means observing the steps of the GSD wheel described in Chapter Four. Your role will to be to encourage that process of listening, clarifying, debating, deciding, persuading, and executing to the point that it's almost as if your team shares one mind when it comes to completing projects, and then learning from their results. This is not true just at high-tech Silicon Valley companies. I recently talked to a man who was responsible for training new managers at New Jersey Transit. I asked him what was the first thing they taught. "Don't start by bossing people. They'll just hate you. Start by *listening* to them."

One of your most important responsibilities to keep everything moving smoothly is to decide who needs to communicate with whom and how frequently. This means meetings. Obviously, every meeting comes with a significant cost—time—so it is important to minimize the duration, frequency and number of people required to attend. The most important of these meetings is the 1:1 with each of your direct reports.

1. **1:1 Conversations**

2. **Staff Meetings**

3. **Think Time**

4. **"Big Debate" Meetings**

5. **"Big Decision" Meetings**

6. **All-Hands Meetings**

7. **Meeting-Free Zones**

8. **Kanban Boards**

9. **Walk Around**

10. **Be Conscious of Culture**

1:1 CONVERSATIONS

Employees set the agenda, you listen and help them clarify

1:1S ARE YOUR must-do meetings, your single best opportunity to listen, really *listen*, to the people on your team to make sure you understand their

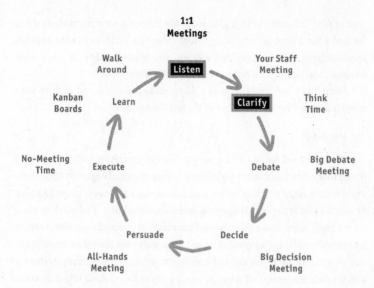

1:1 Meetings

Walk Around · Listen · Your Staff Meeting · Clarify · Think Time · Kanban Boards · Learn · Big Debate Meeting · No-Meeting Time · Execute · Debate · Persuade · Decide · All-Hands Meeting · Big Decision Meeting

perspective on what's working and what's not working. These meetings also provide an opportunity to get to know your direct reports—to move up on the "care personally" dimension of the Radical Candor framework. Remember: this is not the place to dump all of the criticism you've been saving up. That should come in those two- to three-minute impromptu conversations that you've already been having!

The purpose of a 1:1 meeting is to listen and clarify—to understand what direction each person working for you wants to head in, and what is blocking them. Sheryl once quickly helped me in a 1:1 meeting solve a problem that was enormously important to me and had seemed insurmountable until we talked. I was managing teams in ten different cities around the world and wanted to travel to each of them. At the same time, I was forty and trying to start a family. It's pretty hard to get pregnant when you're five thousand miles away from your husband. What to do? I brought my dilemma to Sheryl. "Oh, that's easy!" she said. I was all ears. "You can't. And you don't have any time to waste. You need to make getting pregnant your top priority." I was immensely relieved. It *had* seemed impossible to travel and get pregnant at the same time, and I was glad to hear Sheryl say what I had felt. But I also felt crestfallen. Did this mean I couldn't do my job? Of course not! "Remember that global off-site meeting your team wanted but we had a hard time getting budget for?" Sheryl asked. "Let's take another crack at getting the budget. That way you can fly everybody here. They want to come, and you don't want to go. Seems like a win-win."

Here are a few things you can do to make sure you and each of your reports are getting the most out of these 1:1 meetings:

Mind-set

Your mind-set will go a long way in determining how well the 1:1s go. I found that when I quit thinking of them as meetings and began treating them as if I were having lunch or coffee with somebody I was eager to get to know better, they ended up yielding much better conversations. If scheduling them over a meal helps, make them periodic lunches. If you and your direct report like to walk and there's a good place to take a walk near the office, make them walking meetings. If you are a morning person, schedule them in the morning. If you are a person who has an energy dip at 2 P.M., don't schedule them at 2 P.M. You have a lot of meetings, so you can optimize the 1:1 time and location for your energy. Just don't be a jerk about it. You may like to wake up at 5 A.M. and go to the gym. Don't expect the people who work for you to meet you there.

Frequency

Time doesn't scale, but it's also vital to relationships. 1:1s should be a natural bottleneck that determines how many direct reports a boss can have. I like to meet with each person who works directly for me for fifty minutes a week. But I can't bear more than about five hours of 1:1 time in my calendar. Listening is hard work, and I don't have an endless capacity for it every day. So I like to limit myself to five direct reports. When people are remote, I make sure that those conversations happen over video conference, and I try to supplement them with more frequent quick check-ins.

This is not realistic for a lot of companies—including some of the ones where I've worked. If you have ten direct reports, I'd shift 1:1s to twenty-five minutes a week. Plenty of people I know have twenty direct reports, and there's nothing they can do about it. It's just the nature of the way their companies are managed. If you're in that situation, I recommend twenty-five minutes every other week with each direct report. Also, see if you can cre-

ate some leadership opportunities for the people who work for you and reduce the number of direct reports you have.

Finally, to avoid meeting proliferation, I recommend that managers use
the 1:1 time to have "career conversations" (see chapter seven) and, if relevant, to do formal performance reviews.

Show up!

Probably the most important advice for 1:1s is just to show up. In an ideal
world, you have less than ten direct reports so that you can have a weekly 1:1
with each of them. Even in that ideal world, between your travel schedule,
the fact that you will inevitably get sick sometimes, and the occasional vacation, you will have to cancel at least two or three out of thirteen scheduled
1:1s. If you reserve some of those slots for special 1:1s (i.e., performance reviews, soliciting feedback, "career conversations"), you will have only seven
or eight "regular" 1:1s per quarter. And if your world is not ideal and you have
more than ten direct reports, you probably have 1:1s every other week. That
means you're having three or four 1:1s with each of your direct reports per
quarter. So, no matter what fires erupt in your day, do *not* cancel your 1:1s.

Your direct report's agenda, not yours

When your direct reports own and set the agenda for their 1:1s, they're
more productive, because they allow you to listen to what matters to *them*.
However, I recommend setting basic expectations for the agenda and how
it's delivered. Do you even want a structured agenda? If you do, and you want
to see it in advance, say so. If you don't, and you won't even look at it in advance, set expectations accordingly. Are you OK if they come in with a set of
bulleted items jotted on a napkin, or do you prefer they keep it in a shared
document so you can refer back to it? Whether you want a structured agenda
or you prefer a more free-flowing meeting, the agenda itself should be directed by your direct report, not you. Your job is to hold people accountable
when they come unprepared—or to decide that it's fine to have an agenda-less
1:1 from time to time.

Some good follow-up questions

Here are some follow-up questions you can ask to show not only that
you are listening but that you care and want to help, and to identify the gaps

between what people *are* doing, what they think they *ought* to be doing, and what they *want* to be doing:

"Why?"

"How can I help?"

"What can I do or stop doing that would make this easier?"

"What wakes you up at night?"

"What are you working on that you don't want to work on?"

> *"Do you not want to work on it because you aren't interested or because you think it's not important?"*

> *"What can you do to stop working on it?"*

"What are you not working on that you do want to work on?"

> *"Why are you not working on it?"*

> *"What can you do to start working on it?"*

"How do you feel about the priorities of the teams you're dependent on?"

> *"What are they working on that seems unimportant or even counterproductive?"*

> *"What are they not doing that you wish they would do?"*

> *"Have you talked to these other teams directly about your concerns? If not, why not?" (Important note: the goal here is to encourage the people to raise the issue directly with each other, not to solve the problem for them. See "Prevent Backstabbing" in chapter six.)*

Encourage new ideas in the 1:1.

It's worth keeping Jony Ive's quote, "new ideas are fragile," top of mind before a 1:1. This meeting should be a safe place for people to nurture new ideas before they are submitted to the rough-and-tumble of debate. Help them clarify both their thinking about these ideas and their understanding of the people to whom they need to communicate these ideas. The ideas may need to be described in one way for an engineer and another for a salesperson. Here are some questions that you can use to nurture new ideas by pushing people to be clearer:

"What do you need to develop that idea further so that it's ready to discuss with the broader team? How can I help?"

"I think you're on to something, but it's still not clear to me. Can you try explaining it again?"

"Let's wrestle some more with it, OK?"

"I understand what you mean, but I don't think others will. How can you explain it so it will be easier for them to understand?"

"I don't think 'so-and-so' will understand this. Can you explain it again to make it clearer specifically for them?"

"Is the problem really that they are too stupid to understand, or is it that you are not explaining it clearly enough?"

Signs you'll get from 1:1s that you're failing as a boss

1:1s are valuable meetings for your direct reports to share their thinking with you and to decide what direction to proceed with their work. They are also valuable meetings for you, because these meetings are where you'll get your first early warning signs that you are failing as a boss. Here are some sure signals:

Cancellations. If people who report to you cancel 1:1s too often, it's a sign your partnership is not fruitful for them, or that you're using it inappropriately to dispose of criticism you've been stockpiling.

Updates. If people just give you updates that could simply be emailed to you, encourage them to use the time more constructively.

Good news only. If you hear only good news, it's a sign people don't feel comfortable coming to you with their problems, or they think you won't or can't help. In these cases, you need to ask explicitly for the bad news. Don't let the issue drop till you hear some.

No criticism. If they never criticize you, you're not good enough at getting guidance from your team. Remember that phrase: "What could I do or stop doing that would make it easier to work with me?"

No agenda. If they consistently come with no topics to discuss, it might mean that they are overwhelmed, that they don't understand the purpose of the meeting, or that they don't consider it useful. Be direct but polite: "This is your time, but you don't seem to come with much to talk about. Can you tell me why?"

STAFF MEETINGS
Review metrics, study hall updates, and identify (but do not *make*) key decisions

LITERALLY EVERY CEO, middle manager, and first-time manager I have ever worked with has struggled to figure out how to run a productive staff meeting with their direct reports. All too often, the person leading the meeting comes to dread it; attendees view it as a waste of time; and those excluded feel sad and bad and left out. Although bloated staff meetings can be a drain on people's time and energy, the opposite is also true; a well-run meeting can save you time by alerting you to problems, sharing updates efficiently, and getting you all on the same page about what the week's shared priorities are.

An effective staff meeting has three goals: it reviews how things have gone the previous week, allows people to share important updates, and forces the team to clarify the most important decisions and debates for the com-

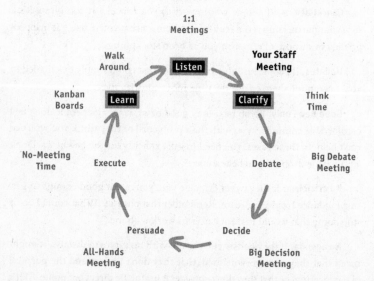

ing week. That's it. It shouldn't be the place to have debates or make decisions. Your job is to establish a consistent agenda, insist that people stick to it, and corral people who go on for too long or who go off on tangents.

Here's the agenda that I've found to be most effective:

- **Learn: review key metrics (twenty minutes)**
- **Listen: put updates in a shared document (fifteen minutes)**
- **Clarify: identify key decisions & debates (thirty minutes)**

Learn: review key metrics (twenty minutes). What went well that week, and why? What went badly, and why? This will go best if you come up with a dashboard of key metrics to review. By "dashboard" I don't mean some super sophisticated system set up by an IT department. I mean a spreadsheet with a few numbers on it. What are the most important activities and results you see each week that let you know if you are on track to achieving your goals? You can design the dashboard yourself; you don't need a corporate infrastructure to do it for you. Ideally it's updated automatically; if that's not possible, make sure everyone working for you updates their part the night before the staff meeting. If necessary, check it yourself and hound them till they get the updates in. If you can, put the dashboard in a place where the whole team can see it. Notes from this conversation should almost always be made public.

Listen: put updates in a shared document during a "study hall" (15 minutes). One of the most challenging aspects of managing a team is how to keep everyone abreast of what everyone else is doing so that they can flag areas of concern or overlap without wasting a great deal of time. Updates are different from key metrics. Updates include things that would never make it into the dashboard, like, "We need to change our goals for this project," "I am thinking of doing a re-org," "I'm starting to think I need to fire so-and-so," or "I have to have surgery next month and will be out for three weeks."

Some leaders have staff meetings that run for multiple hours to share this sort of information. Almost everybody hates long meetings, so some go the other direction and set up a public document where everyone jots down the key things they did last week and what they plan to do next week. Google did this and called these updates "snippets."

In theory, a snippets system for updates is easy to use and avoids interminable staff meetings; after all, it just takes a few minutes to write your own snippets and a few minutes more to read everyone else's. In practice, however, many people have enormous resistance to writing their snippets, and when some people don't do them, the whole system falls apart. I found that although I was all for avoiding an endless staff meeting, I was also one of those people who find it disproportionately burdensome to take the five minutes to input my snippets. For a while, I forced myself to do it anyway, but when I realized I wasn't alone, I decided to find a different solution. I made time for us all to do it in my staff meeting. This worked much better.

Here's the way study hall snippets work. Have everybody take five to seven minutes to write down the three to five things that they or their team did that week that others need to know about, and five to seven minutes to *read* everybody else's updates. Don't allow side conversations—require that follow-up questions be handled after the meeting. This simple rule will save enormous amounts of wasted time in your staff meeting. If you don't do this, most of the meeting will consist of two or three people talking while the rest watch on, uninterested.

Snippets works best with a shared document editable by multiple people simultaneously. You can use Google Docs, Office 365, Evernote. If your staff doesn't have laptops or smartphones, you can use paper and pen—everyone jots their notes down on a piece of paper, and then you do a round robin with the pieces of paper.

If you are a boss of bosses, these snippets should be made public to the broader team. That means people can't include things that need to be kept confidential: an individual's performance problems, contemplated salary adjustments, etc. You may want to keep a "confidential snippets" doc for your team, but make sure there are not too many items here. Most things you discuss should be shared with the broader team.

Clarify: identify key decisions/debates (30 minutes). What are the one or two most important decisions and the single most important debate your team needs to take on that week? If your team is fewer than twenty or so people, you can probably just list them and decide/debate in an ad hoc way.

If your team is bigger than twenty or so people, you will want to be more formal. Put these topics on the agendas of separate "big decision" and "big debate" meetings and identify owners for each. This may feel like meeting proliferation, but it's actually a way to get you *out* of meetings and get the people who want to be included in debates and decisions present for them. The debate and decision owners will generally not be you or the people reporting to you. These separate meetings are a way for you to delegate debates and decisions. Delegating debates and decisions pushes them into the facts, and avoids thinking that is hierarchical (and therefore disconnected from the details/reality).

The agenda for these two meetings should be communicated to the broader team. Anyone who wants to attend them is free to. At first they will probably be too big, but pretty soon people will go only if they really want or need to be there. Most people hate to be excluded from decisions relevant to them, but they hate attending meetings that are irrelevant to them even more. With a little transparency, it all sorts itself out.

THINK TIME

Block time to think, and hold that time sacred

YOU'VE JUST READ about adding 1:1 meetings and a staff meeting to your calendar. You'll probably have to attend some "big debate" and "big decision" meetings. In addition to all these regularly planned meetings, people are going to want to talk to you about this or that; urgent matters will arise that you must deal with. When are you supposed to find time to clarify your own thinking, or to help the people who work for you clarify theirs? If you don't take some action, you will hardly have time to go to the bathroom or grab water, let alone food. You will be tyrannized by your calendar. The only quiet moment to think you'll ever get is at home, late at night, when you really should be sleeping.

An extremely successful—and busy—CEO I know fought this by blocking two hours of think time on his calendar every day. He wouldn't move it for anyone. Once the president (I won't say which country) wanted to meet with him. The president didn't have any particular agenda, but most people would have taken the meeting for curiosity's sake. But not this CEO. Why? It would have interfered with think time. An enormously successful newspaper executive recounted walking into his CEO's office and seeing him leaning back in his chair just staring out at the sky. When he asked

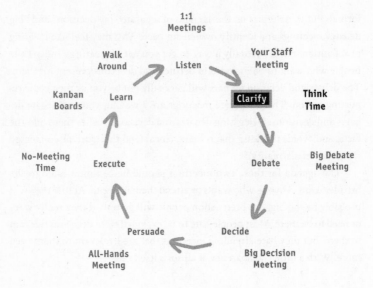

the CEO what he was daydreaming about, it turned out to be the idea that pivoted the company for the next decade.

It's not just CEOs who can pull this off. I did it when I worked as a middle manager at Google. My advice is that you schedule in some think time, and hold that think time sacred. Let people know that they cannot ever schedule over it. Get really, seriously angry if they try. Encourage everyone on your team to do the same.

"BIG DEBATE" MEETINGS

Lower the tension by making it clear that you are debating, *not* deciding.

"BIG DEBATE" MEETINGS are reserved for debate, but not decisions, on major issues facing the team. They serve three purposes:

They lower tension. At least part of the friction and frustration in a lot of meetings results from the fact that half the room thinks they are there to make a decision, the other half to debate. The would-be deciders are furi-

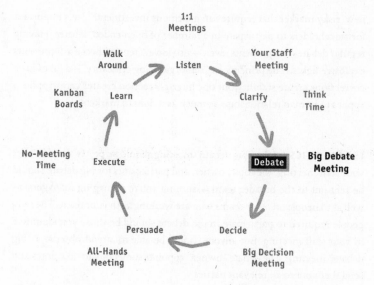

ous that the debaters don't seem to be driving toward an answer. The would-be debaters are furious that the deciders are refusing to think things through carefully enough, to consider every angle of the argument. When everybody knows that the meeting will end with no decision, this source of tension is eliminated.

They allow you to slow down key decisions when appropriate. When a topic is really important and there's a lot of disagreement about how to proceed, friction and frustration ensue. To avoid this, teams sometimes rush into a decision before they have really thought it through or gotten sufficient input. Putting a topic like that on the debate agenda forces a team to keep wrestling with it, digging up needed information, getting expert input, or just thinking more deeply.

They foster a larger culture of debate. Debate should occur constantly on a well-functioning team. Having these meetings regularly and seeking topics for them can help build the muscle and tolerance for discussion and dissension. When having a "bet the company" debate—"Should we enter a new, risky market that requires an enormous investment?"—it's important for stakeholders to participate in a number of open-ended debates. Having regular debates—arguments, even—also lowers tension because it prevents explosive fights. The principle of "self-organizing criticality"—a lot of little corrections create stability but one huge correction creates catastrophe—applies to human relationships as much as it does to markets.

THE LOGISTICS OF the "big debate" meeting should be pretty simple. After your staff meeting, the topic, owner, and participants for big debate should be sent out to the broader team (assuming you're managing managers) as well as to people on other teams who are working with your team. The only people required to participate in the debate should be those you identified in your staff meeting. But anyone should be able to attend/observe a "big debate" meeting. The debate "owner" appoints somebody to take notes and send them out to all relevant parties.

The norms of these meetings are also pretty straightforward. Make it clear that everyone must check egos at the door of this meeting. The goal of debate is to work together to come up with the best answer. There should be no "winners" or "losers." A good norm is to ask participants to switch roles halfway through each debate. This makes sure that people are listening to each other, and helps them keep focused on coming up with the best answer and letting go of egos/positions.

The sole product of the debate should be a careful summary of the facts and issues that emerged, a clearer definition of the choices going forward, and a recommendation to keep debating or to move on to a decision.

"BIG DECISION" MEETINGS

*Push decisions into the facts, pull facts into the decisions,
and keep egos at bay*

"BIG DECISION" MEETINGS typically but not always follow a big debate meeting. They serve two important roles. The first is obvious: to make important decisions. The second, though, is subtler. It can be hard to figure out when to stop debating and start deciding. I have never discovered any absolute principles to answer that question. The simple act of being explicit and

conscious about when I'm deciding versus when I'm debating is the single most helpful way to figure out when a decision really needs to be made. That's the main reason why I recommend two separate meetings.

The logistics and norms of these meetings are the same as those of the "big debate" meetings. The leader of the meeting is the "decider," whom you will have appointed in your staff meeting. The only people required to attend are those identified in your staff meeting, but anyone can attend. Notes should be taken and made available to all relevant parties. Check egos at the door. No winners or losers. The product of "big decision" meetings is a careful summary of the meeting distributed to all relevant parties. It's important that the decisions are final, otherwise they'll always be appealed and will really be debates, not decisions.

You'll need to abide by the decisions made in these meetings just like everyone else. If you know it's a topic you have strong opinions on, feel free to either attend the meeting or to let the decider know you have veto power. If you have veto power, the decider should send the decision to you to approve or disapprove before the notes go out more broadly. Use this power sparingly, though, or the meetings will become meaningless.

ALL-HANDS MEETINGS
Bring others along

IF YOU HAVE a team of ten or fewer people, you probably don't need to schedule a separate meeting to make sure everyone is persuaded that the right decisions have been made. However, as your team gets bigger, you need to start thinking about how to bring everyone along. It's shocking how fast the decisions that some people make start to seem mysterious or even nefarious to people who weren't close to the process. If your team is one hundred or more people, a regular all-hands meeting can really help to get broad buy-in on the decisions being made—and also to learn about dissent.

Silicon Valley is big on company-wide all-hands meetings. Apple's is called Town Hall, Dropbox's is Whiskey Friday, Google's is TGIF, Twitter's is Tea Time. There's something to be learned from how all-hands meetings are done in Silicon Valley, and why.

These meetings usually include two parts: presentations to persuade people that the company is making good decisions and headed in the right

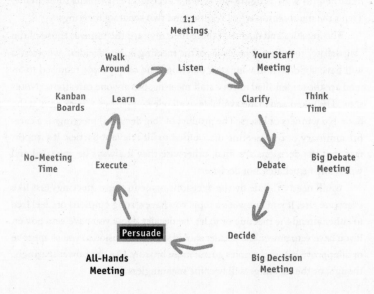

direction, and Q&As conducted so leaders can hear dissent and address it head-on. When handled well, the answers the leaders give to the questions, which are often quite challenging, are usually more persuasive than the presentations.

One of the best all-hands meetings I ever observed was the Friday after Google acquired Keyhole, the company whose technology powered Google Earth. It was fun partly because Larry and Sergey were so exuberant about the acquisition, like kids with a cool new toy. But it was also the best explanation of what they meant by "organize all the world's information." This wasn't just about Web sites and books—they meant, literally, all the world's information! The excitement in the meeting was palpable.

The presentations typically focus on one or two initiatives that are especially exciting and important. They are meant to inform everyone of broader priorities, and to get their buy-in. The presentations are generally done by the team working on the initiative. This practice at Google was important; it built the "persuade" muscle throughout the company. Also, people usually loved presenting at these meetings. "Your team wants the stage? Show them the stage!"

Q&A is usually handled by the CEO/founders and allows them to learn what people really think, and so it generally falls to them to answer these often unpleasant, challenging, or awkward questions. The way that these questions get answered is enormously important to persuading a lot of people at once that the right decisions are being made the right way.

I always admired the way Larry Page and Sergey Brin handled Q&As at Google's TGIF meetings. Larry and Sergey took on all sorts of questions, week after week, and they never used that over-prepped, over-messaged tone that CEOs sometimes fall into. Their answers were invariably spontaneous, human, and totally authentic—if occasionally sarcastic. Sometimes the answers were so surprisingly honest that Eric Schmidt would step up to the microphone and say, "Actually, I think what Sergey (or Larry) *really* is trying to say is . . ." Sergey (or Larry) would just grin and shrug. Then at the next TGIF, there they would be again to take tough, awkward questions. They weren't yet thirty at the time, but they had instinctively grasped the power of explaining important decisions and encouraging dissent.

EXECUTION TIME
Fight meeting proliferation

BY NOW, THE Get Stuff Done wheel may be starting to feel like the Meetings from Hell wheel :) If you're not careful, meeting proliferation can indeed bring to a grinding halt your ability to execute both as an individual and as a team. Being ruthless about making sure your team has time to execute is one of the most important things you can do as a boss.

One approach that many have tried is to remove chairs from conference rooms. This has the theoretical impact of shortening meetings because most people won't stand around a table for more than about an hour. There is research indicating that people are more creative when standing than when sitting. Some say sitting is the new smoking, so there may be health benefits as well. Plus, you save money on furniture. This is all appealing, but it never really works. I don't know any company that has stuck to the no-chairs-in-conference-rooms thing.

At Google, different teams tried declaring "No-Meeting Wednesday" or "No-Meeting Thursday." None was ever able to stick to it. Greg Badros, an engineering leader at Google and Facebook, set a goal of ending 25 percent of his meetings early. I loved that, but I don't think he ever hit the goal.

I have found that the most effective solution is simply to fight fire with fire. For the same reason, I blocked off think-time in calendar; I also found it necessary to block off time in my calendar to be alone and execute. I encouraged others to do the same. This helped them say "no" to more unnecessary meetings.

KANBAN BOARDS
Make activity and workflows visible

TAIICHI OHNO, AN industrial engineer at Toyota, developed Kanban, a scheduling system to make supply-chain management in manufacturing more efficient. Others have adapted the system to visualize workflows. At its simplest, you put up a board with three columns: To Do, In Progress, and Done. Then you buy a bunch of Post-its in different colors. The different colors represent different people or teams. They write their tasks on their color of Post-it and move them around from To Do, In Progress, and Done. You can quickly see who's the bottleneck. It's a great way to drive personal

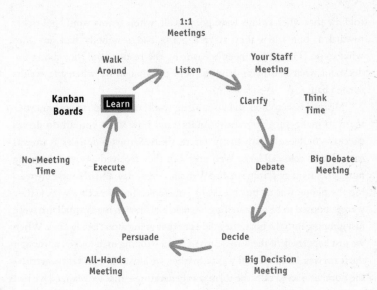

accountability but also for everyone on a team to see who needs help and to give it to them. A Kanban board is different from a dashboard because it focuses activities and work in progress. It gives your team time to identify and resolve issues *before* they hurt the results.

Making progress visible to everyone gives more, not less, autonomy to the team. When it's clear to everyone where the bottlenecks are, resources flow to the places where they are most needed, without intervention from management. If I'm on the engineering team above and I'm ahead of where I need to be, and I see that somebody else's task has fallen behind, I'm motivated to go help because I know that if that task doesn't get done all my work is for naught, or will be delayed.

Another reason why measuring activities and visualizing workflows is important is that when a business is doing really well, it's hard to tell from the results who's along for the ride and who's actually making things happen. Similarly, when the economy is tanking due to factors beyond anyone's control, if you just measure results it's hard to know who's doing a great job bailing out your boat and who's simply panicking or making the situation worse. Friends of mine who worked at Yahoo! and AOL have told me that when things were going well, whole teams would get richly rewarded; but when they started going badly, nobody had any idea what to do. They'd just been measuring the results, and they didn't understand what had been driving them or what to do when the results turned bad.

Measuring activities and visualizing workflows will push you and your team to make sure you really understand how what you all do drives success—or doesn't. Early in my tenure, the AdSense Inside Sales Team was supposed to cold-call large Web sites. But they received an overwhelming number of inquiries from smaller Web sites every day, and of course answering the phone was so much easier than cold-calling. In other words, they were supposed to be out catching big fish, but since so many small fish were just jumping into the boat, they didn't bother going after the big ones. When we just kept track of the huge sums of money rolling in, it looked as though the team was doing great. It was only when we looked at an activity metric—the number of cold calls the team was generating—that we realized we had a problem; we didn't need to pay an expensive sales force just to take orders. After we started measuring activity, revenue spiked significantly. Measuring activities also allowed us to figure out who the good salespeople were. Taking orders is a skill very different from selling.

Measuring activities will also create more respect between teams. It's always surprising how quick one team is to assume that another team sits around doing nothing, and how much resentment builds up over this. When you can see from a Kanban board what people are doing, respect tends to flow pretty naturally.

Measuring activities and displaying them publicly also tends to lead to ratings and promotions that more consistently reward the top performers and are less prone to the biases that bedevil us all. Jack Rivkin, who led equity research at Shearson Lehman Hutton, started measuring his analysts' activities as well as results. When he measured activities, it became clearer to everyone what actually drove results. As a result, Rivkin's team went from being ranked by *Institutional Investor* as number fifteen in 1987 when he took over, to number four in 1989, and number one in 1990. The objective measurement had another impact as well: fairness. Because it was so clear to everybody what drove success, bias was less likely to creep into hiring, rating, and promotion decisions when activities got measured. Rivkin's team had more women than any other in the industry.

WALK AROUND
Learn about small problems to prevent big ones

LISTENING TO THE people who report directly to you is relatively straight-forward, even if it requires time and discipline. But if you are a manager of managers, listening "deep" in your organization is much harder. You can't listen to everybody. You can't have 1:1s with hundreds or thousands of people. If you have office hours, you'll hear from the same three cranks week after week. What do you do?

I never met anyone who was better at connecting with the whole company than Dick Costolo. There were a lot of things he did to achieve this, but one of them was quite simple. He just walked around.

Try taking a page out of Dick's book. Schedule an hour a week of walking-around time. Management by walking around is a tried-and-true technique. According to historian Stephen B. Oates, Abraham Lincoln invented it by informally inspecting his troops during the American Civil War. It was part of Hewlett Packard's culture in the 1970s. It's not complicated to do.

Notice the things you don't notice when you're buried in work at your

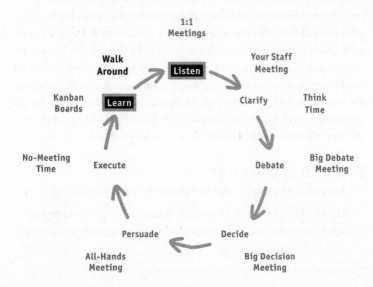

desk or racing, head down, from one meeting to the next. Ask people who catch your attention—ideally, people you haven't talked to in a while—what they're working on. Find some small problems and treat them like "the universe through a grain of sand." Awareness of these small problems can be useful in several ways.

First they'll help you find the devil in the details. Too often a boss is the last to know when something is going wrong. The reason is generally not because people are intentionally hiding problems, but because they only want to bring the important things to your attention. But a problem may be more important than they realize.

Second, being aware of small problems and maybe even rolling up your sleeves and fixing them yourself is the best way to kill the "it's not my job" or, worse, the "that's beneath me" mentality on your team. If nothing is beneath your attention, then others will pay attention to details as well.

Third, when you show that you care about the small things that contribute to customer happiness or the quality of life on your team, suddenly *everybody* cares more about them, and some of the big things start working better, too.

At one point, Dick was trying consciously to create a culture at Twitter in which people would fix small processes and annoyances rather than just complaining about them. One day during his walk-around, he passed two people complaining about the dirty dishes piled up in a micro-kitchen. Usually he would have filed that away and been annoyed by it. But this was his walk-around time, so he just took a moment to fix the problem himself. He stopped and looked around. "Do you think that would be a better place for the dishes?" he asked the two complainers, pointing to an equally convenient but less-visible spot. They nodded yes, and to their amazement, he started moving the dirty dishes there himself. Needless to say, they stopped complaining and started helping. This story got told and retold.

BE CONSCIOUS OF CULTURE

Everyone is watching you, but that doesn't mean it's all about you

"CULTURE EATS STRATEGY for lunch."* A team's culture has an enormous impact on its results, and a leader's personality has a huge impact on a team's

---

* Variously attributed to Peter Drucker, Jack Welch, and others.

culture. Who you are as a human being impacts your team's culture enormously.

Ben Silbermann, founder and CEO of Pinterest, once told me that he was worried the company's culture reflected his own personality too much. He was introverted; the company was introverted. He didn't like to argue; there wasn't as much debate at the company as he would've liked. This observation struck me, because I'd often felt the same way with my own teams but had never had the courage to articulate it. There were days when the teams I led were like a fun-house mirror, exaggerating my flaws. The culture of the team often reflected me, but not always in the way I would have chosen.

That's a scary thing. Since it's pretty much impossible to change who you are as a human being, does that mean that you can't really change your team's culture? You have a big impact; is there no way to control that impact?

Fortunately, as with all things, it's not just about you. As with your evaluations of others, focus on behavior rather than on character, on actions rather than "essentials." If you are regularly and genuinely soliciting feedback, the most egregious of these qualities will inevitably come to light. And, as I described in earlier chapters, your ability to have Radically Candid relationships with everyone on your team will move your culture toward—or away from—Radical Candor. You will influence other aspects of your culture as well, simply by moving consciously through the steps of the GSD wheel.

People are listening. Like it or not, you're under the microscope

When you become the boss, you are under the microscope. People do listen to you in an intense way you never experienced before you became a manager. They attribute meaning—sometimes accurately, sometimes not—to what you say, to the clothes you wear, to the car you drive. In some ways, becoming a boss is like getting arrested. Everything you say or do can and will be used against you.

When he led Goldman Sachs, Bob Rubin once walked the trading floor to get a feel for what was going on. He stopped and chatted with a trader who'd just completed a transaction buying gold. "I like gold," Bob said offhandedly. A few weeks later, Bob was startled to see how much gold the firm had bought recently. "Why are we so long on gold?" Bob asked. "Because you told us to. You said you liked gold!" was the response. Bob thought he was just making a friendly remark, not giving a "buy" order.

When I was at Apple, somebody told me that the bus program to shuttle employees back and forth between Cupertino and San Francisco had been delayed because Steve had to choose the leather for the interior of the busses. I happened to have lunch with the director of the bus program and asked him if the story were true. He laughed: "No." But when I then asked him how the color scheme of the busses had been chosen, he admitted that he'd gone to the parking lot and taken a look at Steve's car: silver exterior with black leather seats. So the busses? Silver exterior with black leather seats.

You don't have to be crazy successful like Bob Rubin or Steve Jobs to have a bigger impact than you intend to as the boss. Early in my career, I said to a salesman who tended to wear black shiny shirts, "I sure do like a man in a white oxford." I was chagrined to see that the very next day he showed up in a white oxford, and for every day for a week after that. Of course, I *had* been dropping a hint. But I was new to being a boss and totally unused to having people take my hints so seriously.

Often when you're the boss you might say or do something you expect to be blown off, whereas in fact you've moved way further out on the "challenge directly" axis than you had intended to.

Clarify. Be vigilant about clarifying what you are communicating

Given the level of scrutiny you're under as the boss, it's important to clarify what you're saying—even when you think you're not saying anything.

When I was at Google, I drove an orange Honda Element, pretty identifiable as mine since it was virtually alone among the herd of Priuses and other fuel-efficient cars that Google subsidized. Because my office was a couple of miles away from my boss's, I frequently drove to meetings. Parking was a disaster and my schedule was packed, so I tended to park haphazardly and in places that only vaguely resembled parking spots. Since I was pushing at work for an "ask for forgiveness not permission" culture in which people felt free to challenge the rules, this worked. But if I had been trying to create a "measure twice cut once" kind of culture, I would at least have had to offer an explanation for my parking practices, and probably would have had to reform them. I didn't park like that when I worked at Apple. . . .

Debate and decide explicitly. Don't let things that pervert your culture "just happen"

There are a number of debates and decisions that you are going to be tempted to "delegate to HR." These are often around things you'd rather not waste your brain cells on. Are you going to call it a "holiday party" or a "Christmas party"? Will there be a Christmas tree there, or not? A menorah? Will you serve alcohol at the party? How will you deal with it when you come in Monday morning to find bras and panties and a jock strap on the conference-room table? What to do about the fact that one person on your team just kicked another in the butt? True, it was just one of those friendly sideways kicks that you used to give your friends in middle school, but the recipient is outraged. Who's going to decide how to deal with it?

Believe me, it's tempting to punt on these decisions. But if you do, the decisions that do get made by HR/employment lawyers without your humanizing influence will push your culture in a "the law is an ass" direction. If nobody makes a decision, you wind up in Lord of the Flies territory. Neither is the culture you want.

Persuade. Pay attention to the small things

When I first got the job at Apple, I got a thoughtfully organized tri-fold folder with the words, "Ah, Paperwork!" written on the outside. Real thought and care had gone into making the annoyance of new-job paperwork as painless as possible. The folder was a thing of beauty—well-designed but not crazy-expensive. The choice of language made me smile. The care with which the paperwork had been assembled communicated to me even before I started what kind of work would be expected of me.

When you pay attention to seemingly small details, it can have a big impact on persuading people that your culture is worth understanding and adapting to. The office environment is part of setting a tone and culture. Silicon Valley is famous for its whimsical offices and high-end chefs. But even if you can't afford this kind of largesse, you can make sure the coffee in the kitchen is what people like to drink—and offer some green tea bags, too. One publishing company in New York responded to complaints about the coffee by having a kind of Pepsi Challenge. Coffee consumption went up dramatically and staff surveys noted real appreciation for the move.

The office environment affects culture. Do you want a Zen-like orderly, well-lit environment or a stuff-everywhere frenetic environment? The small choices you make will persuade people to act in accordance with the culture you want to build with your team.

Execute: Action should reflect your culture

It's surprising how a small action from you can impact your team's culture, even after you're no longer around.

One day I arrived at my office at Google to find that a couch had been moved to a place where it forced people to take several extra steps to walk around it. I wasn't trying to create a culture obsessed with feng shui, but that couch bugged me, and so I decided to move it. I was trying to encourage an obsession with efficiency, and those extra steps were anything but efficient. I started shoving the couch back where it belonged. A man on the team saw me and joked, "It looks like Kim's got a new job." I smiled but pushed back against his attitude: "If something's in your way, it's *always* your job to fix it!" Two years after I'd left Google, I went back to visit an old friend and saw a slogan written on the wall. "On the AdSense team, we move the couches!" Scott Sheffer, who took over my job when I left Google, said repeatedly that he felt the single most important thing I'd done to help set him up for success was to focus on the team's culture.

Learn

Shit happens. When you're the boss and shit happens, it's your responsibility to learn from it and make a change. If you don't, you create a culture that doesn't learn from its mistakes.

At Google, my team and I wanted to foster an informal culture. One of the small things we did was to turn a conference room into a "team cozy," with no tables or chairs in it, just a bunch of couches and beanbag chairs. I generally had my staff meetings there. Then one Monday morning we came in to find some men's underwear and a bra wedged in the couch cushions. Sex in the office was *not* the culture I was shooting for. Gone was the "team cozy." We were going to have to find another way to be informal.

Listen . . .

The most amazing thing about a culture is that once it's strong, it's self-replicating. Even though you've taken a number of conscious actions to impact it, you'll know you've succeeded when it truly is no longer about you.

When we built AdSense teams globally, I was nervous about what the team culture would be like in each office. I wanted to encourage all the teams to challenge authority—my authority in particular, but authority in general. I felt like I needed to go to each office in person to drive this home. However, I was trying to get pregnant and so was unable to travel. I was especially worried about the team in China. Given my understanding of Chinese culture, I thought that replicating our irreverent culture would be especially difficult there. As described in Chapter One, I talked to the leader of the team there, Roy Zhou, extensively about this. But would that really translate if I couldn't fly there myself? I was so anxious about it that if I hadn't been forty years old, I would have delayed starting a family and gone on a world tour instead.

Then somebody on the team in China had the idea that all AdSense offices around the world make a video to introduce the teams to one another. I'll confess that I wasn't expecting much. But the results blew me away; human warmth and humor were universal. The irreverence in Beijing was just as unmistakably "AdSensy" as it was in Mountain View or Dublin. And yet the nationalities were distinct. How had that happened? If I'd directed each of those videos myself as AdSense culture propaganda clips, I couldn't have been happier about how they came out. But I'd had absolutely nothing to do with any of them. How was this possible? It was because the culture was self-replicating. I'd helped to create something larger than myself. It was one of the most magical moments of my career.

GETTING STARTED

CONGRATULATIONS! YOU'VE TAKEN AN IMPORTANT step to becoming the kind of boss you want to be just by reading this book. Not that I have all the answers, but taking time out to think about how to be a better boss is a huge step.

Now it's time to start putting the suggestions in this book into practice. What should you do first? What's the "order of operations"? Explaining ideas and techniques is a very different business from operationalizing them, and I want to make sure you get started on the right foot. On the following pages is a plan to build a culture of Radical Candor on your team. And, since this book was published, I've had the opportunity to see where people struggle with this plan. So for more detailed advice on sharing your stories, soliciting criticism, giving praise, and gauging your criticism see the Afterword.

SHARE *YOUR* STORIES

EXPLAIN RADICAL CANDOR to your team so they understand what you're up to. You can also ask them to read the book, or show them videos that are on the Radical Candor website. But it's best if you explain it in your own words. What is your version of the "um" story or the "Bob" story? Tell *your* stories to your team. Show some vulnerability. Your personal stories will explain, better than any management theory, what you really mean and show why you really mean it. That's why I told all those personal stories in this book. *Your* stories will mean a lot more to your team than mine do, because they mean something to you.

PROVE YOU CAN TAKE IT BEFORE YOU
START DISHING IT OUT

START ASKING YOUR team to criticize you. Review "Soliciting Impromptu Guidance" in chapter six. And remember, don't let people off the hook when they don't say much—because they won't, at first. Embrace the discomfort to move past it. Pay close attention if you aren't getting any criticism. If you want, you can copy the Radical Candor framework in Chapter Two and track who's saying what to you there. Just because people aren't criticizing you doesn't mean they think you're perfect. If you realize that you're not getting any criticism, try Michael Dearing's "orange box" technique (see chapter six).

Soliciting guidance, especially criticism, is not something you do once and check off your list—this will now be something you do *daily*. But it'll happen in little one- to two-minute conversations, not in meetings you have to add to your calendar. It's something to be conscious of, not something to schedule. It will feel strange at first, but once you get in the habit, it'll feel weird *not* to do it. You won't ever move on from getting guidance any more than you'll ever move on from having to drink water or brush your teeth.

Now you're ready to start having career conversations. Begin "career conversations" with your team. Start with people whom you've been working with for the longest. (Review "Career Conversations" in Chapter Seven.)

Like getting criticism from your team, "career conversations" are not something you do once and check off the list. Remember, people change, and you need to change with them! That's why it's a good idea to do one round of "career conversations" a year with each of your direct reports during your 1:1 time.

In parallel: perfect your 1:1 conversations. In parallel (because it will take you at least three to six weeks to get through these three conversations with everyone on your team since you want to leave a week or two between each of the three conversations), make sure you are having meaningful 1:1 conversations with your direct reports. (Review "1:1 Conversations" in chapter eight.)

Next. After you have explained Radical Candor, asked for guidance, had career conversations, and improved your 1:1 conversations, you'll notice that you are earning your team's trust and building a better culture. Now you're ready to start improving the way you *give* impromptu praise and criticism. Remember, impromptu guidance happens best in one- to two-minute conversations. (Review "Giving Impromptu Guidance" in chapter six.) Make sure you gauge your guidance. (Review "Gauge Your Impromptu Guidance. Get a Baseline, Track Your Improvements" in chapter six.) Remember, you may think you're being Radically Candid, but one person may not have heard any criticism at all, another may have heard it as ruinously empathetic, and yet another as Obnoxious Aggression. You have to adjust for each individual. You have to be not just self-aware but relationally and culturally aware.

Take a deep breath. Assess. How's it going? What's working? What's not working? Who can you talk to? Can your boss help? Your team? A mentor outside of work? A coach? Others from the Radical Candor community? Don't try to do more new things until you feel 1) you've made good progress on the fundamental building block of management: getting and giving guidance, 2) you've gotten to know your direct reports better, and 3) you're happy with your 1:1s.

If the answer to these three questions is "yes," you're ready to perfect staff meetings, decisions, and debates for your team. You've built the foundations of trust that are central to your ability to get stuff done. Next step is to make sure your staff meetings are maximally productive. During the meeting, you are reviewing key metrics, sharing updates, and identifying your big decisions and debates. Don't let them drag on too long. Don't blow them off. (See "Staff Meetings" in chapter eight.) Now's a good time to roll out the "big decision" and "big debate" meetings. (See " 'Big Decision' Meetings" and " 'Big Debate' Meetings" in chapter eight.)

Return to guidance. Make sure you are encouraging guidance *between* people on your team. Establish a "no backstabbing" or require a "clean escalation" norm on your team. Explain that you're not going to allow one person to come and talk to you about another; you can give your team "Prevent Backstabbing" in chapter six to read, but the important thing is not their reading but your enforcement. You'll have to follow up. While this will sometimes result in extra meetings to resolve disputes getting thrown on your calendar, it will save more time than it costs because there will be fewer political situations exploding in your face.

Fight meeting proliferation. Make sure you're not getting overscheduled. Think very consciously about what you are doing that you can stop doing. Put some think time in your calendar. (See "Think Time" in Chapter Eight.) Calendar clutter is a permanent struggle for most organizations. Fight the good fight, not just for yourself but on behalf of your team!

Plan for the future of your team. Start doing a growth-management plan for each person on your team. (See "Growth Management Plans" in chapter seven.) Make sure that you are not creating a promotion-obsessed culture, and give some extra thought to how you're rewarding your rock stars (see chapter seven).

Return to guidance. Ask your team to start gauging each other's guidance. There are more of them than there are of you, so anything you can do to get them to give one another more Radically Candid praise and criticism will reinforce a Radically Candid culture and provide you with more leverage than any amount of guidance you can give or get personally. If they resist, try starting with Dan Woods's "Whoops the Monkey" technique at your next staff meeting. (See "Peer Guidance," chapter six.) This is also a good time to assess whether or not you are still doing a good job getting and giving guidance. Remember, it's hard, it's unnatural, and it's the atomic building block of management.

Walk around. You've been at this for awhile now. Do things feel different on the team? What sorts of things do you want to know but are not hearing? Put aside some time each week to walk around and have informal spontaneous chats with people. (See "Walk Around," chapter eight.) If you have a feeling that things are still not going well, and that there's a lot of skepticism on the team, go back to step one. Also, consider rolling out a "manager fix-it week." (See chapter six.) How does your culture feel? What can you do to improve it? (See "Culture," chapter eight.)

Are you a manager of managers? If so, try "skip level meetings" for everyone on your team. You'll need to do these only once a year, but it's a good idea to cluster them in a two-week period so that nobody feels singled out. (See "Speak Truth to Power," chapter eight.)

Begin to take a more Radically Candid approach to the processes that your company may have in place. Be Radically Candid when hiring, firing, promoting (see chapter seven), as well as giving formal performance reviews (see chapter six).

That's a lot of things to do, but it's not as bad as it sounds. If you take every suggestion recommended in this book, the total time required is about ten hours a week, five of which are 1:1 meetings that you're probably already holding anyway. Of course, some processes like growth-management conversations, skip-level meetings, and calibrations don't get spread out each week but will come in bursts, so some weeks you may have eight hours of work associated with your core responsibilities as a boss, others twelve others five. But that still leaves fifteen hours a week to think and execute, and another fifteen hours to deal with the various unpredictable things that you'll be asked to do.

In other words, Radically Candid management does take serious time, but it also leaves you time to pursue your own area of expertise and to deal with the unpredictable. Mostly, it requires you to be conscious, and to bring your full humanity to work with you.

This "order of operations" will help you prioritize what to do when and with whom, but I bet you still have some questions. If at any time you would like to talk to other people who are rolling out Radical Candor, or if you have follow-up questions or management dilemmas for us, we're eager to continue the conversation with you, to answer your questions, and to help you make Radical Candor a reality in your organization.

SIMPLY MAKING RESOLUTIONS or thinking that something is a good idea rarely results in real change. That is why the second half of this book is so focused on helping you implement the suggestions described here. Changing behavior is hard, but it *is* possible. In fact, you've already started: by reading this book. The best way to begin transforming your workplace is to think hard about why you want to make the change, and then to hold on to those ideals as you identify the specific things you can begin to *do* differently.

Don't get too bogged down in the details before plunging in, though, because it is the rewards of the process that will keep you energized and moving forward. Remember: *once you build Radically Candid relationships with the people who report to you, you will eliminate a terrible source of misery in the world: the bad boss.* You will achieve results you never imagined possible. You will create an environment where you and the people who report to you can love their work and working together. Perhaps most surprising, you'll find that the way you work ripples out into the rest of your life and enriches all your relationships.

Although I have focused primarily on the positive experiences I've had at work, I certainly know what it feels like to slog away in a job that is crushingly boring under a boss who sucks the joy out of everything. And the most damaging aspect of those experiences was what they did to my *personal* life. It was simply not possible to be a scintillating bundle of joy on the weekend when I'd spent the five previous days doing mind-numbing work that was being overseen by a Dementor.

It doesn't have to be that bad. You *can* take a moment to show the people you work with that you care about what they care about at a basic human level. You can warn them if they are making a mistake—not because you hold yourself superior to them, but because you care. You can help others on your team take a step in the direction of their dreams, and even teach them how to help you do the same. You can work together to achieve results that you're all proud of. And when you do these things, which are absolutely in your power to do, your Radical Candor will transform your work and your life.

AFTERWORD TO THE REVISED EDITION

Rolling Out Radical Candor

by Jason Rosoff, Amy Sandler, and Kim Scott

S INCE THIS BOOK was published, we've worked with thousands of people to make Radical Candor a reality in their organizations. We've learned a lot about areas where suggestions that seemed self-explanatory were not. Several key ideas and concepts appealed to people but felt hard to put into practice. We want to share more detailed explanations with you here so that it will be easier to make Radical Candor a reality in your work and life.

YOU

Improve using role plays and storytelling

Chapter Five of *Radical Candor* advises you to "STAY CENTERED. . . . You can't give a damn about others if you don't take care of yourself." When it comes to practicing Radical Candor, there's one common thread every time: **you**. But, what exactly should you *do* about that? Many have told us the first edition of *Radical Candor* didn't explain this point clearly enough.

For example, a venture capitalist asked Kim how to help one of his

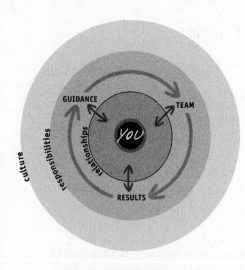

associate. Every time the associate gave feedback to entrepreneurs, they decided not to work with him anymore. Based on the description of some of these conversations, Kim had a feeling this was more than poor communication.

"Does he think he's smarter than everyone else?" Kim asked.

"Oh, yes, definitely."

"Then he doesn't have a communication problem, he has an arrogance problem. He needs to be more self-aware and more relationally aware."

The venture capitalist's shoulders slumped. "Oh, wow, this is a much harder problem than I thought."

"Yes. Only after he develops some humility and self-awareness will he be able to see the impact he has on others."

Much is written about self-awareness—the ability to recognize your own strengths and weaknesses. There's less written about relational awareness—the impact you're having on others. You may have every intention of being kind and helpful, you may be thinking and feeling all the right things, you may be fully aware of your own flaws, but despite all that, you may say something destructive in ways you couldn't have predicted or were unaware of. Or you can't bear to see it so you choose not to.

How can you learn to be more relationally aware and to use that awareness for good, not just to manipulate the other person? Relational awareness doesn't mean what you have to say is never upsetting to the other person; it does mean you need to learn how to see when you've upset someone and to show that you care even when what you have to say may be hard to hear. It means you're able and willing to see both the short-term and the long-term impact you're having on the other person, and to adjust so that impact is positive not negative.

You can improve both your self-awareness and your relational awareness. We have developed two practices, storytelling and role plays, that will help you improve both. We've tested these practices out on people in dramatically different roles and workplaces around the world and found that they worked well across different industries and cultures.

Practice: What's your story?

Storytelling is a great way to develop both self-awareness and relational awareness. There's a brief paragraph about this in the final Getting Started section, but we have been asked for more detail about how to do this and why it works. Here is an exercise we do in our workshops.

First, think of your Radical Candor story. Can you remember a time when you were screwing up, someone told you, and even though what they told you stung a bit in the moment, it helped you in the long run? If you tell your team *your* story and what it means to you, it will be a thousand times more powerful than Kim's story about when her boss told her she said "um" every third word in a presentation. When you show a little vulnerability by telling your Radical Candor story, you are doing two important things at once. One, you are demonstrating self-awareness and humility. Two, you are showing that you genuinely appreciate criticism. This will make it easier to solicit feedback—and the more feedback you solicit, the more self-aware you become.

The next three stories (your Obnoxious Aggression, Manipulative Insincerity, and Ruinous Empathy stories) will help you and your team see when you've fallen down in that goal of being kind: they will help with relational awareness.

Think about your Obnoxious Aggression story. Was there a time when you offered criticism, just trying to be helpful, but the other person experienced you as obnoxiously aggressive? Or maybe there was a time when you were offering some criticism, but you were really angry and perhaps your intentions weren't so pure. What happened? Dig deep here. What's a moment you cringe looking back on, and wonder how you could possibly have behaved so obnoxiously? Your story is by definition better than the story Kim tells about the rude "clutter sites" email she sent to her boss's boss's boss (Chapter Two) because it's *yours*. It will help you understand the impact you have on others. It will also help your team understand you and how to communicate with you so that they can help you see when you're behaving like a jerk even though you don't mean to. It will build relational awareness.

Next, think about your Ruinous Empathy story. When did you fail to give some feedback, just to be nice, only to see the person suffer as a result of failure to correct bad behavior? Don't tell Kim's Bob story from Chapter Two, tell yours. When were you trying to be nice, only to realize you'd been inadvertently cruel? The regret you feel recalling the incident and the vulnerability you show when you tell the incident will build your relational awareness.

Finally, and hardest of all, think of your Manipulative Insincerity story. When did you fail to tell a person directly about a problem, but you instead talked to others? Or was there a time when you told a person their work was good while undermining it behind their back? It's really hard to see yourself as backstabbing, passive aggressive, or political, but we are *all* guilty of these behaviors from time to time. Telling these stories can help you avoid repeating similar offenses in the future. And— you guessed it—can build that self-awareness and relational awareness muscle.

When people unpack their own stories, and share them with their teams, they start to become more aware of the gap between their intentions and the impact they're having on others. Awareness is the first step toward change. You *can* make your impact align with your intentions.

This kind of storytelling can help make you more aware of what Radical Candor means to *you* and also the impact it has on others. Every person is different, so it's important to be aware that what may feel helpful to one person may feel unbearably painful to another person. You've got to adjust how you talk so that you can be clear and kind to the other person without feeling like a chameleon. This is hard. The Feedback Triangle, our version of a role play, can help.

Practice: The Feedback Triangle

An exercise called the Feedback Triangle has been particularly useful in helping people see the impact their words have on others and to choose different words that are more kind and clear. Here's how it works:

Get together in a group of three. Describe some feedback you know you should have delivered to someone but didn't. One colleague will play the role of the intended feedback recipient. The experience is more effective if the person playing the feedback recipient hams up the defensive response. Encouraging the feedback receivers to be difficult encourages them to think of bad feedback moments they've actually experienced in their own career, so being dramatic paradoxically yields more realistic-feeling performances. It also allows the feedback givers to practice the toughest moments.

Your other colleague plays the role of observer and tracks how the conversation is going, using the Radical Candor framework. Perhaps the feedback giver starts in Radical Candor, but when the feedback receiver seems upset or even cries, they beat a hasty retreat to Ruinous Empathy. Or perhaps they start out intending to be Radically Candid, but say it so gently they wind up being ruinously empathetic. Frustrated when the feedback receiver isn't "getting it," they may become obnoxiously aggressive. Or perhaps they start out Radically Candid but the feedback receiver gets mad and responds rudely. Then the feedback giver gets angry and becomes seriously obnoxiously aggressive.

These are patterns we see all the time, conversational wipeouts that are amusing in the context of a role play, but painful in real life. Plotting them on the Radical Candor 2 x 2 framework can offer a kind of compass that leaves participants with a sense of agency. When they take a moment to see the impact they have on others, they can use that information to get the conversation back on track rather than just feeling defensive or guilty. Self-awareness doesn't have to mean self-flagellation.

The objective observer, as well as the "recipient" of the feedback, help their colleague by showing how the feedback landed: maybe too aggressive, maybe insufficiently clear. This improves relational awareness among all the participants. They get to see through the eyes of the observer and the recipient what the impact of their words was, regardless of intention. And it's fun. In an exercise where drama is encouraged and an observer is there tracking misunderstandings on the Radical Candor 2 x 2 framework, the experience is "ha-ha! a-ha!"* The humor reveals something important that had been invisible to us.

When we learn most skills—math, sales, engineering, piano, sports— we practice to improve. But when it comes to communication, we don't often get this kind of practice. That's why practicing using the Feedback Triangle or improv is a really helpful way to become more conscious of our own intention and what we need to bridge the gap between those intentions and the way others experience what we say. Practice also demonstrates how giving and receiving feedback, developing self awareness and relational awareness are skills that we can develop with practice.

SOLICIT CRITICISM FIRST

There is an important order of operations to Radical Candor:

1. solicit criticism
2. give praise
3. give criticism

4. gauge the criticism and adjust
5. encourage praise and criticism between others

The first edition describes this order of operations, but Kim's story of having Sheryl Sandberg call her on her "ums," and her story of avoiding giving Bob timely feedback and then having to fire him, were the most memorable and the most often repeated. One was about a boss giving feedback successfully. The other was about what happens when a boss fails to give feedback. The stickiness of these stories had a lot to do with the fact that nearly everyone has experienced a similar scenario from the perspective of boss, employee, or team member.

Unfortunately, the book didn't have a similarly memorable story about a boss *soliciting* feedback from an employee. As a result, many readers came away with the impression that Radical Candor is primarily about bosses

---

* The folks at The Second City, the Chicago-based comedy club and executive education group, taught *us* Radical Candor this term. It refers to what may be the evolutionary purpose of humor: insight into our own behavior—self awareness.

criticizing employees. Nothing could be further from the truth. So Kim thought she'd try to present a new story about *soliciting* feedback. Here it is:

Kim's Soliciting Feedback Story

Recently my daughter said, "Mom, I wish you weren't the Radical Candor Lady!" Of course, this was not the ideal way for my daughter to offer criticism. It wasn't exactly situation-behavior-impact. It was more like, "Gee, I wish you were a different person." Ouch! But when I was getting feedback, especially when I was in a position of authority, it was my job to listen and learn, not to teach, not to criticize the criticism, even if what she said was hard to hear.

I am prone to guilt, so I immediately assumed she meant that she felt I was neglecting her for my work. I reminded myself not to assume I understood, though, but to "listen with the intent to understand" what she meant. That meant rather than responding defensively, it was my job to ask for clarification—and perhaps to solicit even more criticism.

"Who do you wish I were?" I asked.

"I wish you were The Lady Who Minded Her Own Business!"

Her criticism was the opposite problem of what I'd at first assumed. She didn't feel neglected, she wanted me to back off!

IN ADDITION TO a story, we thought we'd offer you some research on why soliciting feedback is first in the order of operations. The goal of soliciting feedback is not only to help you be more self-aware, but also to create an atmosphere in which all employees feel sufficient psychological safety to give each other Radically Candid feedback. Harvard Business School's Amy Edmondson defines psychological safety as "a shared belief that the team is safe for interpersonal risk taking."* Her book, *The Fearless Organization: Creating Psychological Safety in the Workplace for Learning, Innovation, and Growth*, offers a great deal of research demonstrating that "In psychologically safe workplaces, people know they . . . might receive performance feedback that says they're not meeting expectations. . . . But they feel willing and able to take the inherent interpersonal risks of candor." There

---

* Psychological Safety and Learning Behavior in Work Teams, Amy Edmondson, *Administrative Science Quarterly*; Vol. 44, No. 2 (June 1999), pp. 350–383.

is nothing leaders can do that will more quickly create the conditions for psychological safety than to solicit criticism themselves, and to respond well to it.

Why is psychological safety so important at work? Over two years, a group in Google's People Operations (HR) conducted more than 200 interviews with Google employees, analyzing more than 250 attributes of 180+ active teams. What they found was that *who* was on the team—e.g., how many Navy SEALs, introverts, or Olympians with Ph.D.s—was less important than *how* they interacted together, structured their work, and viewed their contributions. They found that the five key dynamics for successful teams included: Psychological Safety, Dependability, Structure & Clarity, Meaning, and Impact. But psychological safety was by far the most important of the five dynamics, because it's the foundation of the other four.*

When leaders solicit criticism, respond constructively to it, and reward it, they begin the process of normalizing feedback as a positive force. When the CEO solicits criticism and rewards people for giving it to them it sends a signal to middle managers that they should do the same. As people at all levels of the organization realize giving honest feedback is safe and even encouraged, a virtuous cycle ensues, producing teams that function at a remarkably high level. People are more innovative when they are less afraid to take risks, and when they learn from mistakes rather than hiding and repeating them.

Seeing the boss solicit feedback once isn't enough. Fear of offending the powerful does not die easy. We can only really be sure that bosses want feedback if they make a habit of soliciting it regularly. This means finding a way to build it into a regular practice so that it happens automatically. When a boss sets aside time each week for 1:1 meetings and asks for feedback at the end of each 1:1, employees come to expect this as "normal." Establishing a regular routine signals to them that you will be asking for feedback, and makes them more generally mindful about what you might do better or change in order to make them more effective. Another great time to solicit feedback is when people are really angry with you. It's instinctive to avoid people when they are mad, but this is the moment when you're most likely to hear the unvarnished truth.

We hope a story and some research better explain why you should prove you can take it before you dish out Radical Candor. But *how* can you

---

* https://rework.withgoogle.com/blog/five-keys-to-a-successful-google-team/

solicit criticism? We'd like to go into more detail on each of the four tips for soliciting criticism offered in the book.

A GO-TO QUESTION YOU CAN ACTUALLY IMAGINE ASKING

Many workshop participants have asked us to provide more help in coming up with a "go-to" question for soliciting feedback.

As noted in the first edition, if you ask, "do you have any feedback for me?" the answer will most likely be: "Oh, no, everything is fine." To encourage a more substantive response, we need to ask for criticism in a way that is authentic and also takes into account the needs of the other person. Given the infinite permutations and combinations possible in a you + them equation, there's no one "right" question. In fact, many participants in our workshops have found it's useful to have three or four go-to questions so that they can adapt for different people on their teams and different situations. Asking the right questions can help us see into our blind spots. Here's how Jason came up with his go-to question:

Jason's Story

As I became a manager, I made most of the classic mistakes that new managers make. Perhaps the most pronounced among these was managing others like I prefer to be managed. I like to be left mostly alone with big problems. I am an introvert and for me solving challenging tasks alone is an exciting opportunity to grow. I was rarely managed in the way I liked to be, so I thought I was doing everyone a favor when I became a manager and would hand out giant mission-critical tasks and send people off with an "I know you can do this!"

A couple of years into my time as a product leader, a member of the product team, "Ann," came to me and asked if we could talk. She was clearly flustered, which was way out of the norm for her, so my antennae were twitching. We got into a quiet room, and she looked right at me and in one breath said, "I know when you gave me this project and told me you believed in me, you meant for me to feel supported, but it's super complicated and out of my wheelhouse. I feel like you're just giving me enough rope to hang myself."

I was stunned. I told her I felt terrible and asked her what I could do to help. She knew exactly what she needed: some of my time and some external resources. I thought I'd been doing her a favor by leaving her alone, and yet it had really thrown her off and made the project start much more slowly than needed. I realized I had a problem: I didn't know when to be hands-on vs. hands-off. It prompted me to start asking about exactly that: "In the last week, when would you have preferred that I be more or less involved in your work?" I learned that people not only had different default preferences, but different preferences based on the nature of the task.

Here are some attributes of good go-to questions:

- *Sincere*. People have well-tuned BS detectors. If you sound like you're parroting something you read in a book, even a great book, you're not going to sound sincere.

- *Don't ask questions that can be answered with a yes or a no*. Any parent knows that asking their kid a question like "Did you have a good day?" is likely to get little more than a "yes" or "no." Question like "tell me the best and worst parts of your day" tends to elicit more information. The same is true when soliciting feedback. In fact, several workshop participants pointed out a flaw in the question Kim recommended in the first edition. The problem with asking "Is there anything I could do or stop doing that would make it easier to work with me?" is that you give people who fear conflict an easy out: they can just say "no." These are the people for whom Radical Candor is hardest, and they need to be encouraged. Instead, ask, "*What* could I do or stop doing?" If they can't think of anything, encourage them to think a bit more. Warn them you'll ask them again next week, and don't forget to ask again.

- *Specific vs open-ended*. Some people feel safe answering an open-ended question like "What could I do or stop doing that would make it easier to work with me?" But for those who don't, a specific question might work better. For example, "I worry that sometimes I interrupt people before they've had a chance to express themselves adequately. When have you seen me do that? Will you flag it for me if you see me do it next week?" Again, there's no one-size-fits-all approach, so you have to see what elicits criticism and what elicits silence. Don't let the silence put you off. Keep trying till you get something!

- *Frequency.* If you only ask for criticism once every six months you'll get a recency bias in the replies—people will tell you about something that happened a week ago, having forgotten about a much more important thing that happened three months ago. Besides, it may be too late to fix that problem from three months ago. Asking frequently for feedback helps to increase the likelihood that the feedback is actionable. Frequency also builds feedback stamina. If you only go for a run every six months, every run will be really painful. If you do it every day, you'll miss it when you don't go.

Here are a few great questions from workshop participants. You'll see that tone varies a lot person to person.

- In the last week, when would you have preferred that I be more or less involved in your work?
- Tell me why I'm off base here.
- What's something I could have done differently this week to make your job easier?
- How could I best support your professional development right now?
- What's something I've done in the last week that made it difficult to work with me?
- What's a blind spot of mine that you have noticed?
- The most important thing you can do for both of us is to tell me when I've screwed up.
- I feel like I didn't do as well as I could have in that meeting, but I'm not sure what I did wrong. Can you help me figure it out?
- I'm really trying to do X better. I know in theory it's a problem but I'm not always aware in the moment. Can you help me by pointing it out when you see it?

Practice: Ask for a critique of your go-to questions

Brainstorm a few go-to questions. Go to a trusted peer and ask them one or two of your questions. Based on their responses, assess:

1. Did it produce useful feedback?

2. Did it sound natural, i.e., like something you'd actually say?

FAQ

Q: *Do I have to use the same go-to question each week? It's starting to feel stale.*

A: *In general, consistency (in terms of when you solicit feedback, and the question you use) tends to make people more comfortable giving you criticism—it's part of an expected routine. But it's absolutely fine to introduce some variation, particularly if your question isn't eliciting responses. Don't let the fact that you're not getting good feedback be an excuse to stop asking for it. But if what you're doing isn't working, try something new. Ask why it's not working. Say, in your own words, "I know I'm not perfect. I know there's probably a thousand things I do wrong every day. Why won't anyone tell me?"*

Q: *What if the answer I get is about something I can't fix?*

A: *First, acknowledge that you don't know how to fix it. Ask if they can help you solve the problem. If neither of you has a ready solution, challenge yourself. Is this really something you can't fix? Say that you'll need some time to think about the issue, but that you will get back to them. If you find you ultimately can't think of how to solve the problem, explain why you can't solve the problem.*

Q: *I am a new manager working with people who are a lot older than me. Will I look weak if I ask for criticism?*

A: *One of the most effective things you can do with any direct report, but especially with those who are older, is to ask them to share their wisdom and experience. It's tempting for older employees to write off younger managers as arrogant know-it-alls. Prove them wrong!*

Q: Where should I start? If I'm really being honest, I am afraid to get critical feedback.

A : That's normal! Nobody really wants to hear criticism. Focus on the fact that you can only fix the problems you know about, and that if the person cares enough to make you aware of a problem they might also help you fix it. If you have a tendency toward perfectionism, remind yourself that you're human and you're going to make mistakes; in fact, that's how you get better. Work on developing a "Not Yet" mindset, as described by Carol Dweck: "I heard about a high school in Chicago where students had to pass a certain number of courses to graduate, and if they didn't pass a course, they got the grade 'Not Yet.' And I thought that was fantastic, because if you get a failing grade, you think, I'm nothing, I'm nowhere. But if you get the grade 'Not Yet', you understand that you're on a learning curve. It gives you a path into the future."**

So, you might have made a few typos in an important presentation. Maybe you went on and on in a meeting and people felt like you took up too much air time. It doesn't mean you're a train wreck, it means you're human.

EMBRACE THE DISCOMFORT

Many participants have told us they don't really know how to put the advice to "embrace the discomfort" into action, so we'll go deeper here.

When you ask someone for criticism, you put them in an uncomfortable situation. Don't be ruinously empathetic and let them off the hook. Give them some time and space to formulate their response. Often people will be quiet after you ask. Resist the temptation to fill the silence. Silence is uncomfortable for you and for them, but your job is to endure it and even embrace it. In our workshops participants often look puzzled when we say this. But the lightbulbs really go off when we get people to practice asking the question and then sitting there silently. It sounds easy, but it takes enormous discipline.

---

* https://en.tiny.ted.com/talks/carol_dweck_the_power_of_believing_that_you_can_improve

Practice: Count to six in your head

Ask your question to a friendly colleague then count to six. Do not allow yourself to say anything no matter how awkward you feel or they look. So much of putting Radical Candor into practice is being able to move through social awkwardness. This tip can help take your mind off the discomfort. Focus on counting how many seconds your friend can endure silence before jumping in to say something? Most people won't hold out till six. They'll say *something*. It may not be profound, but it's a start.

Of course, some will remain silent. If they do, tell them you'll give them more time but that you will come back to them because you really want their feedback. And don't forget to ask again. Don't let them—or yourself—off the hook!

LISTEN WITH THE INTENT TO UNDERSTAND, NOT TO REPLY

This is another oft-tweeted line from *Radical Candor*, but many have told us it didn't really help them learn how to manage their defensiveness in the face of criticism.

Receiving criticism can trigger the fight, flight, or freeze response in us even if we have asked for it. Unjust criticism is hard, but fair criticism, particularly when it touches on something we already don't like in ourselves, is also hard.

Figure out what helps you to process what you hear without giving in to a defensive response: a breathing exercise can help; so can taking a long sip from a bottle of water. Most of all, practice with others.

Practice: Listening

Find a partner to practice with (coworker, friend, family member). One person speaks for three minutes, and then you switch roles and listen to the other person speak, uninterrupted. You can talk about whatever you want: anything you really care about, at work or outside of it.

If you're the listener, you're giving the speaker the gift of your full attention. You can nod, or say, "I see" or "I understand," but this is not the time for questions, or for you to relate their story to something *you* care about, like your favorite Hawaii vacation story, or to give the speaker that one tip that's going to forever change their life. . . . Your job is not to give advice, it's to *listen*.

What we find is that coworkers who have been on the same team for more than ten years learned more about each other in three minutes than they did in a decade working together. Listening, really listening, is incredibly efficient!

MAKE LISTENING TANGIBLE: REWARD THE CANDOR

When someone offers you criticism, they are taking a risk. It's your job to make sure they are rewarded for taking that risk, or they won't do it again. We've found the best way to reward valuable feedback is to address the problem quickly or explain clearly why you can't and seek a work-around.

Feedback can fall prey to our innate negativity bias. That means that even if you respond well to criticism nine times out of ten, it's the one time that you respond defensively that they will remember. As Rick Hanson, author of *Resilient* notes, "The brain is like Velcro for negative experiences and Teflon for positives ones." We love to focus on and tell stories about when feedback goes horribly wrong.

So make it memorable when you reward the candor. Spanx CEO Sara Blakely played the song "Oops! I Did It Again," when describing a pattern of mistakes she'd made to the whole company. Celebrate your own failures, and show how the only way you can improve is when people point them out to you. Talking publicly about the helpful feedback you've received, and how you've sought to address it, signals your view that feedback is a gift, not a kick in the shins.

Practice: Make Listening Tangible

Make a list of the three to four times colleagues have offered you some criticism recently. If you can't think of anything, it doesn't mean you're perfect. It means either you're not hearing what they're saying or they're not comfortable sharing their criticism. If you don't have anything on your list, go on a fishing expedition! And fish for criticism not praise!

At a team meeting or standup, share some feedback you received in the past week, what you learned from it, your gratitude for it, and what you plan to do about it. Ask for help from the team as you try to change your behavior or address the problem raised. Make clear that you welcome additional feedback in the given areas, and welcome it with relish if you get it.

When you take some time to show what you are doing about the feedback you've gotten, two good things happen. One, you are making your listening tangible. Often leaders work hard to address feedback but forget to share their efforts with the team. Show your work! Two, you get to learn if you've fixed the problem. Sometimes you'll learn that you have gone too far, or not far enough to address the issue raised. Maybe in aiming to avoid interrupting people, you've allowed meetings to become free-for-alls, or maybe as meetings grow long, you start to backslide. Either way, you get a chance to calibrate your response.

Practice: Reward criticism you disagree with

Think about some criticism you got recently that you basically disagreed with, but try to find some element of the criticism that you can agree with. Share the area of agreement with the person, to demonstrate you listened and that you're open to feedback. Then let the person know there are some elements of what they said that you disagree with, and ask them if they're open to a longer conversation. If they are, articulate as clearly as possible *why* you disagree, or why changing your behavior would produce worse results. Pretending to listen but silently dismissing what they're saying is the *worst* thing you can do to a relationship. That makes people feel invisible, ignored. A respectful disagreement can strengthen a relationship. Ignoring a person rarely does.

BUILD IT INTO YOUR EXISTING SCHEDULE

Now that you've practiced the four elements of soliciting criticism—coming up with a go-to question, embracing the discomfort, listening with the intent to understand, and making listening tangible by rewarding the candor—you're ready to put the four things together and make soliciting feedback a habit.

To build a new habit, it's important to minimize the effort. That means building it into your existing routines. The ideal place to solicit feedback is at the end of your regularly scheduled 1:1s with team members. It doesn't have to be a 1:1 meeting, though; different people have different approaches to these meetings. But you do need to ask for criticism frequently, so that it becomes like brushing and flossing, not an annual cleaning that you dread. It's also best to ask in private to make it less threatening to the other person and also to lower the threat to your ego and increase your chances of maintaining your composure and curiosity.

Remember, the first twenty or so times you do this it's going to feel like an unnatural act. Your job is to push through the discomfort.

Practice: add soliciting feedback to the end of your 1:1 agenda

Let your team know you plan to ask for feedback in your upcoming 1:1s. As a bonus, share the question you plan to ask. Particularly early in the process of normalizing this behavior, it's important to give them time to think about behavior that really matters to them.

PRAISE: FOCUS ON THE GOOD STUFF. REALLY.

Chapters Two and Six covered praise and criticism. Though these chapters do focus on the fact that praise is more important than criticism, most people are so anxious about criticism that they skim the praise parts. This is a big mistake. We'd like to share here the things we have done in our workshops to get people focused on practicing praise.

When you're leading a team, criticism is like your brake and praise is like your accelerator. If you want to go somewhere, you've got to use your accelerator more than your brake. If you never use your brake you crash and never get anywhere. And you'll feel safer pressing your accelerator if you know your brakes work.

When Jason was early in his career, he had a role that included inside technical sales. This meant helping clients understand some fairly complex technical things, which required a fair amount of patience and organization (two skills Jason was still working on). On one call, he was particularly disorganized and the client got confused and flustered. Jason got frustrated. He recalls:

Jason's Story

These calls were done in pairs, thank goodness, and my colleague Dave noticed what was going on and jumped in and redirected the conversation by saying, "What I think Jason meant to say was . . ." I was astounded at how much more efficiently and clearly Dave was able to say what I'd been failing to explain. As the client came around to understand what I'd been attempting clumsily to say, the conversation started to feel much better. I was super embarrassed, but also really thankful to have the fire that I started put out.

Then Dave did something that really surprised me. The client asked a question, and Dave said, "I think Jason's the best person to answer that," effectively passing the conversation ball back to me. I couldn't believe that he still trusted me to drive the call, but I wanted to live up to his faith in me. I ran the rest of the call, and everything went smoothly.

After the call, I knew I owed Dave some praise. I felt weird because I was going to have to start by admitting how badly I screwed up, but I mustered my humility and found him after lunch. As we were walking out of the kitchen I pulled him aside and said, "Dave, I was so grateful when you jumped in during our call. I think the client would have been really pissed if the conversation kept going the way it was. I was totally floundering, feeling completely incapable, and you saved me. And when you passed the ball back to me, it gave me the confidence to try again. Please feel encouraged to jump in again in the future!"

The puzzled look on his face was not what I was expecting. After a few moments he said, "I honestly had no idea that what I did was so helpful. I didn't have a plan, I just reacted. I was honestly a bit worried that you'd feel like I was stepping on your toes." I told him, "It was really skillful. I learned a lot from it." We left the conversation with him promising to flex this muscle when needed, and me hoping not to screw up so badly in the future so that he'd have to rescue me. The important thing was that Dave now knew I appreciated the way he stepped in. If I hadn't praised and thanked him, he might have continued to worry that he'd stepped on my toe and not have rescued me the next time.

SOMETIMES PEOPLE ARE reluctant to praise others because it's much easier to look "smart" when criticizing them. The goal of guidance is to help others succeed, not to prove how smart you are.

Other times people use praise as a weapon: "So-and-so is great. What's wrong with the rest of you losers?" Managers who do that basically throw the person who succeeded under a busload of peers who now feel resentful. They will not get a repetition of the success. Good praise is specific and sincere, and inspires others rather than making odious comparisons.

The focus on praise requires real discipline. After you've done the hard and painful work of soliciting criticism, it's tempting to want to give some of your own. And you've probably been holding in some criticism for a while. And very often the thing that has been bothering you has been bothering you for so long that it's all you can see or feel. You've failed to notice all the things you like about working with this person. If all you can see is the negative, you're probably not in the right mind-set for giving criticism. So focus on the good stuff. Praise first.

Also, praise helps people focus on their strengths and on doing more work that they enjoy and less of what they hate. Sometimes, you have to make sure a person gets to a level of proficiency that a flaw doesn't become fatal. But you get more bang for the buck out of focusing on strengths than weaknesses, out of maximizing the upside rather than minimizing the downside. Praise reveals what works and makes it usable, repeatable. Giving praise doesn't just make people feel good, it's practical. Praise shows how a strength can lead to success, how people can build on one success to achieve more success. Praise shows that you care personally, and it also challenges directly as it encourages people to keep doing more of what's great.

APPLY THE SAME DISCIPLINE TO PRAISE THAT YOU DO TO CRITICISM

In workshops, we ask one question (borrowed from Karen Sipprell, Kim's colleague at Apple): "How much time do you spend making sure you have the facts straight before giving a team member praise?" The answer, typically, is none at all.

When you're vague with praise, it is just as likely to leave a person feeling patronized. And either way, vague positivity has very little impact in the long term. An empty "great job!" can sound condescending and be demoralizing, exactly the opposite effect than you may have intended. *Specific* praise helps the person and the team understand what success looks like. It gives ambitious team members a model to follow. Remember, the guidelines for giving Radically Candid feedback work for both praise and criticism: do it humbly, helpfully, immediately; praise in public, criticize in private; don't give guidance about personality attributes.

Praise Practice

Pair up with a colleague and share one specific piece of praise with each other. We've found that people walk away from this exercise feeling seen, connected, and inspired. We've heard things like, "I've been doing X, Y, Z for years and didn't know anyone noticed!" leading to more engagement when they are back at the office.

It's actually not hard to find things to praise each other for, even if you just met someone in a workshop. It becomes easier for people to focus on the good stuff when you set an intention to do so, get curious, and then say something really specific. For example: "Thanks for asking that question about being late for meetings; I wasn't sure if we were going to cover it and it helped move the conversation forward," or "Thanks for listening to me when I was talking about my daughter; I really needed to talk about it."

While the primary purpose of praise is to show people what direction we're headed in/what "good" looks like, this short exercise is an effective, quick, way for people to develop a greater sense of appreciation for each other, and themselves. It's a fast, easy way to build the skill of giving voice to the things you appreciate.

GAUGE CRITICISM

"Radical Candor gets measured not at your mouth but at the other person's ear." That was another often-tweeted line from the book, but it became clear in our workshops that the sentence, while catchy, was hardly self-explanatory. How can you put that idea into practice?

People often hoped there were some magic words that would ensure their feedback would be clear but wouldn't hurt anyone's feelings. Unfortunately, there are no words that serve simultaneously as a scalpel and emotional Novocain. Sometimes Radical Candor will sting a little bit. When it does, it's your job to care personally. More often, Radical Candor won't sting because it won't have been heard. Then it's your job to challenge directly.

You can, however, use the Radical Candor framework like a compass, to gauge your criticism and guide conversations to a better place. Pay close attention to the other person's response to

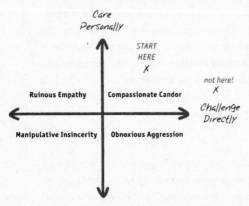

what you've said, and decide whether they need you to show you care personally, or to be more direct and clear in your challenge.

The way you listen is more important than the way you talk. When offering Compassionate Candor, start gently and then gauge the other person's response. Listen to what they say, observe their body language, look them in the eye, and ask yourself, *How do they seem to be feeling? Have they heard me?* (You cannot do this if you are on your phone or on your computer.)

If the person you're talking to seems sad, this is your cue to take a moment to show you care personally. This is hard because when confronted with someone who seems upset, it's our natural inclination to back off from what we were saying—to move in the wrong direction on the Challenge Directly dimension of Radical Candor. Instead, now is your time to show that you care.

When you draw it on a two-by-two framework, it looks so simple and easy. Unfortunately, it's actually really hard to do this. That's why it's really helpful to hire actors, who know how to cry on command, to do role plays.

I have seen many a Silicon Valley badass abandon all intentions of challenging directly in the face of tears—even though they knew these were just tears from an actor in a role play. Instead of delivering the message they are supposed to be delivering, they say things like, "Oh don't worry. It's not that big a deal." Even though it *is* a big deal and will kill the career of the character in the role play if they don't change it. Using the framework like a compass can

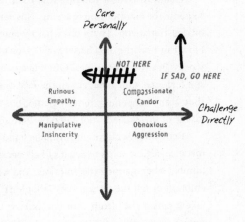

If they are sad, you need to show you care.

help keep you out of the Ruinous Empathy trap, reminding you that you *can* go in the right direction on the Care Personally dimension without going in the wrong direction on the Challenge Directly dimension.

Similarly, when you get an angry response from the person you're talking to, it's your cue to attend to the emotions in the room, to show that you care personally. This is hard because when the other person is angry, it's natural to get mad yourself. Nothing will move you down on the Care Personally axis faster than anger. In role plays I've seen even level-headed executives lose their cool when an actor playing the role of an angry employee is rude. And again, this is in the context of a role play where they know the name of the game is to care personally! When we ask people in a role play to say

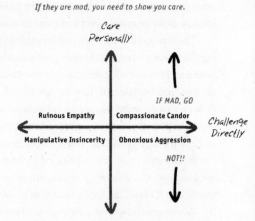

If they are mad, you need to show you care.

to the person trying to give them feedback, "The fish stinks from the head down," some participants have made incredibly obnoxious retorts, or even "fired" the actor in the role play.

One way to show you care when confronted with negative emotions is to name the emotion you're seeing. "It seems like I've upset you/pissed you off/frustrated you. That's not what I wanted to do. I'm trying to help you. How can I say this in a better way?" Don't use my phrasing, use your own words. But you get the idea. Often just naming an emotion can help a person feel seen. Our tendency in the face of negative emotions is to pretend they aren't happening. Ignoring emotions makes the other person feel invisible or invalidated—not a good way to show you care.

Remember: you might misunderstand the emotion you're seeing. For instance, if Kim starts to cry it's likely because she's furious, not sad. So be humble when naming the emotion. And whatever you do, don't judge the emotion or tell the person they "shouldn't" be feeling it. Eliminate "don't take it personally" from your vocabulary! When all else fails, a simple response to negative emotions is to ask, "How can I help?"

Other times, you'll work up the courage to give someone feedback, but then they just don't hear you. They are defensive or oblivious or hopelessly optimistic or overconfident or distracted or whatever. But you're clearly not getting through to them. What do you do then? This is your cue to move to the right on the Challenge Directly dimension of Radical Candor. Being extremely clear can feel harsh, and most people are rightly reluctant to be harsh. This is where the mantra "It's not mean, it's clear" can help.

One thing that helps in these moments is to focus on the long term. If this person is making a mistake that is going to hurt them over time, the only way for them to fix it is if they are aware of it, even if that awareness hurts a bit in the moment.

Sometimes when someone is shutting down it's because they disagree with what you're saying but don't want to say so. Your first goal is to get them to tell you if they disagree with what you're saying, and if so, why. There's a risk that when you do this, the other person will come back at you aggressively and tell you why you're a terrible person, cataloging all your flaws. If this happens, acknowledge that you are not perfect and say that you'd like to discuss these problems in a separate conversation. But right now you want to talk about the issue at hand. A useful mantra for giving criticism is listen-challenge-commit. Don't skip over giving them an opportunity to challenge you and go too quickly to asking for a commitment to change. The goal is to encourage the person to engage in the conversation, to listen, and to participate, even when that means disagreeing with your criticism (*especially* when they disagree).

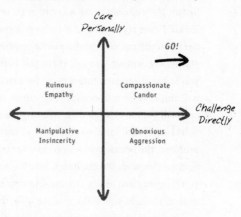

If they don't hear you, challenge more directly!

Another thing that can help when you've told someone something and they just aren't hearing you is to ask, "Just to make sure we're on the same page, can you tell me what you just heard?" Other times stating what you are feeling can help: "I don't feel like I'm being heard." Or you can try saying, "May I be much more direct with you?"

ONE MISTAKE THAT people often make is to draw attention to consequences for noncompliance with the feedback before they've given the person an opportunity to disagree with it. Many go too quickly to "your job is at risk if you don't fix this." That might be true, but if the person disagrees with the feedback, that feels like an unfair consequence. You're trying to engage the person's intrinsic desire to improve and grow in their career. Going too quickly to extrinsic punishments can harm that intrinsic motivation to do better: *If I'm already on the way out, or if I've been convicted without a trial, why should I even try to fix it?* Of course, if the problem is going to cause the person to be put on a performance-improvement plan or to be fired imminently, the sooner you tell them the better. But in an ideal world, when you're having regular impromptu feedback conversations, either the person will improve or will realize they either cannot improve or don't want to, and will look to change their role or get a job elsewhere. Unfortunately the world isn't ideal, and sometimes, no matter how clearly you point out a problem, the person takes no action. In these cases, you may have to fire the person. We wish we could tell you Radical Candor will always work and you'll never have to fire anyone, but that would be a lie. At least if it comes to that, though, you will know you give the person a fair chance.

It can also help to bring several specific examples of the problem you're trying to make the person aware of. If you get interrupted after the first one with excuses, you can say something like, "Before we go too deep on this, I want to share several other examples with you so that you see the pattern I'm seeing. After I'm done, I'll listen to your perspective, I promise. I'm open to hearing that I'm wrong. And if it turns out I'm right I am here to help you fix this." As always, use your own words, not ours.

DIVERSITY AND INCLUSION

All of us have had moments when we are so gobsmacked by something offensive someone at work says that it's hard to respond at all, let alone think about being Radically Candid. And being Compassionately Candid? When someone uses a derogatory or stereotyping term to refer to us, our first instinct is usually not to show we care personally, it's to hurl an insult back or assume a self-protective stance.

Poet Claudia Rankine puts it perfectly in her book *Citizen: An American Lyric*: "What did he just say? Did she really just say that? Did I hear what I think I heard? Did that just come out of my mouth, his mouth, your mouth? The moment stinks . . . Then the voice in your head silently tells you to take your foot off your throat because just getting along shouldn't be an ambition."

How can we handle such moments in our careers? A young woman in a workshop said that she has spaghetti dinners once a month with friends and they share these stories and practice what they could have said. The practice doesn't help with the past, but it does with the future—because unfortunately these situations repeat themselves over and over, especially around issues of diversity and inclusion.

We loved the idea of a "practice dinner," and wondered if there were a safe way to do this at work. We described the idea to Kelly Leonard, from The Second City, the improv theater where Tina Fey, Bill Murray, and many others got their start. What if we could use improv and Radical Candor to teach people to develop "diversity stamina" for these types of conversations? With the help of Second City's Anne Libera, Bina Martin, and Becca Barish, we decided to develop a workshop called Improvising Radical Candor that does just this. Watching the catharsis that people feel when practicing different responses to the infuriating things people have said to them at work is a great testament to how effective improv and Radical Candor can be to addressing issues of diversity and inclusion. The workshop was the highest-rated of twenty different trainings at the first company where we tried it. Using improv to practice playfully has really helped people put Radical Candor into practice even in the stickiest situations.

WHAT'S NEXT?

Since *Radical Candor*'s publication our programs have focused primarily on the atomic building block of management: impromptu praise and criticism conversations. Once managers are comfortable soliciting and giving guidance, they are eager to keep going and learn how to fulfill all their responsibilities as managers.

We are expanding our current offerings to cover topics like encouraging Radical Candor between team members. We explain how to create a norm of clean escalation and also how to roll out "speak truth to power" meetings. In addition, we are working on going deeper with leaders on team-building topics like having career conversations and growth management planning processes. Last but not least, we are working with leaders to help them achieve results in a Radically Candid way. We focus on understanding the "Get Stuff Done" wheel described in this book, and how to put it into practice with faster, more productive 1:1 meetings, staff meetings, debates, decision-making, all-hands meetings, and goal-setting. In addition, we help leaders figure out what meetings and processes they can eliminate so that everyone has time to execute at work instead of late at night at home.

When taken all together this content will offer a management credential. For those seeking a scalable reinforcement of these ideas, we'll also be building digital content with Second City Works to support our in-person experiences.

We'd love to invite you to work with us, and also to offer some criticism of what we are doing. As John Stuart Mill wrote, unless an idea is "vigorously and earnestly contested . . . the meaning of the doctrine will be in danger of being lost or enfeebled, and deprived of its vital effect on the character and conduct: the dogma becoming a mere formal profession, inefficacious for good, and preventing the growth of any real and heartfelt conviction."

In other words, we depend on your criticism to make these ideas realities. If you'll send us your critique of these practices and ideas, we'll promise to do our best not only to reply to you but also integrate your thoughts in subsequent editions of the book and in our executive education programs.

We can be reached online at www.RadicalCandor.com, by email at RadicalCandor@RadicalCandor.com, and on Twitter @Candor. Thank you for joining us in our mission to rid the world of bad bosses!

BONUS CHAPTER

A RADICALLY CANDID PERFORMANCE REVIEW

MANY OF THE PEOPLE we work with in our workshops ask us what kind of formal review process would best support a culture of Radical Candor. Before answering this question, I want to be really clear on one point: The biannual or annual review is performance management, which is different from developmental feedback! Radical Candor is mostly about developmental feedback, which has to occur regularly—ideally every week—in impromptu two-minute chats. You risk undermining all of your hard work spent making your culture more Radically Candid if you conflate development and performance management.

Why is it so important to keep development and performance management separate? The ratings and rewards or penalties associated with performance management trigger a threat response that makes it really hard for people to take in any kind of development suggestions. When you give someone a rating, it's natural for them to focus on how they can convince you to give them a better rating so they get a bigger bonus or a promotion, or how they can avoid getting fired. They are focused on the consequences, not on their development. Asking people to concentrate on how they can develop their skills when there's a big, honking bonus check at stake or their job is on the line just isn't realistic.

That's not a reason to eliminate performance reviews. It's a reason to *separate* development conversations and performance management. But people have often come to expect the rating and the developmental feedback will come together at one time, and only once or twice a year. So if you are trying to create a culture of Radical Candor, it's important to explain the difference between development conversations (impromptu chats that happen weekly) and a performance review (the formal annual or biannual process that tells people where they stand). You want to maximize the chances that development conversations are purely about helping each person to improve, and to allow the performance management process to focus on making compensation and promotion decisions more transparent.

Radical Candor is mostly centered on development, on the habit of soliciting and giving frequent, on-the-spot guidance. But this does not mean I don't believe in performance reviews. Indeed, I'm concerned about the trend that many companies seem to be deemphasizing them or eliminating them altogether. I predict most of these companies will have to reinstitute performance reviews. If companies decide to divert resources into teaching managers to have more frequent and meaningful development conversations before designing a new and improved performance management system, that would be a big step in the right direction. But if they eliminate performance management and don't step up their development efforts, then managers simply aren't being held accountable for managing.

Good performance management is fundamentally about results, fairness, retention, and transparency. It's about making sure that the people who have the best skills get more responsibility if they want it, so they can have a bigger impact. That improves the results of individuals and teams collectively. Plus, it would be unfair to promote incompetence or to pay the person who's doing sloppy work the same bonus as the person who is doing excellent work. It's also about retention. You want to make sure you're identifying the people achieving the best results, and doing what you can to keep them happy and productive so they don't quit. And, crucially, a good performance management system will make decisions about pay, promotions, and firing more transparent; the transparency will hold managers accountable, resulting in better, more fair decisions.

I will explore common issues related to this process below, but first I want to outline some steps for beginning the process of revamping your performance management system, if you decide that is necessary:

1. *Create a performance management team*. Performance management should be a dynamic process in which you periodically review your processes and rating categories. Crucially, it should also focus on making sure the process doesn't run away with itself—on keeping it lightweight so that it doesn't take too much of everyone's time.

2. *Multiple perspectives*. The team should include both operational leaders and HR executives. Operational leaders bring expertise on the specific proficiencies of the work; and they must be brought into it for it to have impact. HR professionals offer a broader understanding of the kinds of unintended consequences that can come from poorly designed systems. All too often what happens is that operational leaders over-delegate to HR and then refuse to participate in the system. That's not productive, to say the least.

3. *Review key elements of your existing performance review* (see below). Once you have revised it, share your proposed changes with a broader set of functional leaders, incorporate useful feedback, answer questions, and explain your design principles. Everyone will have a strong opinion, so agree to a listen-challenge-commit norm: make sure that people understand they can challenge the perf team's ideas, that they will incorporate feedback if possible, but ultimately everyone must commit to the system the performance management team comes up with. Otherwise, the process will drag on endlessly and unproductively.

4. *Communicate*: Use the new performance review process as an occasion to a) explain to employees that development has been formally decoupled from the review process, and why and b) emphasize that the goal of the new performance review process is to work toward a fairer and more transparent process, and that you will not

only encourage but expect feedback. Take occasions annually to report back to the entire team on feedback received and how it will be incorporated.

5. *Create a regular review cycle* (every three years) in which the performance management team improves the process, based on feedback from the company. Again, an important goal is minimizing the time the process demands of everyone.

Remember: arbitrariness is the enemy, fairness is the goal. The whole point of performance reviews is to demonstrate to employees that you are committed to maintaining a fair system for compensating their work, and that doing so is an integral part of achieving the company's mission. If they emerge from it with this perception, even if they don't always love the immediate feedback, you will have succeeded. If they emerge feeling that the process is unfairly punitive, random, or humiliating, or that it rewards political savvy rather than teamwork and results, you will have undermined the virtuous cycle that Radical Candor is meant to set in action.

ELEMENTS OF A FORMAL PERFORMANCE REVIEW PROCESS

As noted, every company has different needs for its performance reviews. This means I can't design a one-size-fits-all performance review, much as I might like to. What I can do is take you through the key considerations that you and your team will want to keep in mind, and reflect a bit on how Radical Candor can inform your thinking.

1. Rating or no rating

2. Categories of ratings

3. Job ladders

4. Number of ratings

5. Language matters

6. Consequence of ratings

7. Distribution of ratings

8. Forced curve or no

9. Calibration of ratings

10. Frequency

11. "360-degree" performance process or relying on a manager's unilateral assessment

12. Transparent or confidential

13. Lightweight or heavyweight

1. Rating or no rating

There is a growing school of thought that ratings are inherently flawed, and indeed there is evidence that they often reveal more about the rater than the ratee, and that they can discourage risk-taking by being overly punitive when risks taken don't pan out. Finally, and you know I agree with this critique, there's the argument that obsession with ratings gets in the way of developmental conversations.

These problems are real. But we must also look at the benefit of ratings. They can play a vital role in providing transparency into the decision-making process behind bonuses, promotions, and firings. A person may be getting regular impromptu guidance, but they don't understand the impact on their pay or career until they see the rating. Eliminating ratings can enable Ruinous Empathy to set in. Rating can force a hard conversation that ultimately helps the employee. Ratings also make calibrating managerial decisions much easier, which contributes to fairness. If there is no performance rating, individual managers' assessments can't be easily correlated with each other. In such a situation, less-effective employees whose bosses let things slide sometimes get rewarded richly, while more effective employees whose bosses are stricter may get lower bonuses or be promoted more slowly. When managers give ratings, it's much easier to see who is an "easy grader" and who is a "hard grader" and to adjust.

Communicate clearly that the goal of giving people ratings is to communicate as transparently as possible what their manager's assessment performance was like over the past few months, and the impact that performance has on their compensation. Acknowledge the limitations of ratings, and make sure people see them as a communication tool, not an absolute judgement.

2. Categories of ratings

The key question here is whether to keep it simple with a basic "overall performance" rating or to break out key performance drivers, rating each separately. It takes a bit of work to identify the key performance drivers, but doing so brings profound benefits. If you're able to identify three or four effective categories, you will simultaneously help your managers zero in with a bit more thought on areas that need work, and provide employees with a clearer sense of why they have or haven't received the compensation or promotion they deserved. One caveat: it is clear from feedback on 360s and reviews that having too many drivers becomes confusing and overly complicated. So limit yourself to three or four. Again: arbitrariness is the enemy, fairness is the goal.

So now it's time for your performance management team to choose their three or four categories. Here is where the importance of having a team of both operational leaders and HR folks kicks in. It's worth taking the time to get on the same page when it comes time to identify the categories. It's also worth the time to be thoughtful in how you express the categories. The words you choose will either convey a process that is thoughtfully aligned with your company's mission, or one that's been outsourced to a faceless bureaucrat. If people feel random bureaucracy is determining their pay and their career prospects, they're hardly inspired to do their best work.

You'll probably start with three or four generic terms that represent your key performance drivers. Don't stop there! Now think about how each word or phrase could be modified to sound less like an HR category and more like a real reflection of what your organization is trying to achieve. Is "teamwork" the right word, or maybe it's better to call this "the no asshole rule" or "collaboration." Make sure the words reflect what your company aspires to be. Getting these details right is all part of linking the process to a sense of real transparency and fairness in the service of your shared goals.

Here are four common categories expressed as "generic terms" so they'll be broadly applicable:

- *Results.* Is the person achieving their goals, doing what they are supposed to do? Do they have the skills or domain expertise necessary to be effective in their role?

- *Teamwork.* How well does the person work with others to get the

results? Do they help others succeed, or leave the proverbial trail
of dead bodies in their wake? Do they exhibit Radical Candor, both
challenging directly and caring personally?

■ *Innovation.* Does this person come up with new ideas that change
the game, or help the team do old work in a new, better way?
Innovation is not just about step-function ideas that result in, say,
the iPhone. It's also about incremental ideas. For example, the
employee who figures out that programmable keypads will allow
the team to answer routine customer-support questions more
quickly, allowing them to focus on work that is more interesting
and impactful.

■ *Efficiency.* Does this person work productively and quickly and
contribute to the team's ability to do so? For example, the
employee who can do the work asked of them a little more quickly
than others, and who shows others how they do it.

Teamwork and results are pretty obvious choices. I separated out innovation and efficiency because it's important to think about new things to do
as well as how to do existing work more efficiently. Often it requires great
innovation to figure out how to be more efficient, and the time gained by
efficiency buys you the mental space for step-function innovation. You will
want to identify the drivers that are relevant and specific to your business.

I *do* recommend using the category ratings as only the first step. But don't
insist that all managers ad here only to these categories. Before you meet
with your employee, ask yourself if there are ways in which they are adding
value that isn't covered here. Particularly for people who may be coming up
short in some areas, but whom you believe have room for growth, this reminds them that you aren't viewing them merely as four numbers on a form.
Honor the process, but don't be a mindless slave to the system!

3. Job ladders

I hate job ladders, since bad ones tend to celebrate "climbing the corporate ladder" rather than doing work that is meaningful. But they are a necessary evil. Obviously, the performance of a recently hired college graduate
should not be measured by the same standards as those of a CEO. So you
need to describe what teamwork means for an entry-level employee versus

a manager, a director, a VP, and so on. Again, the language is important here. If you get too specific, people will sometimes become too focused on checking off boxes rather than on a commonsense idea of developing skills. A job ladder shouldn't be written like a false promise you can't keep: *if you do these things, you'll get promoted.* Also if they are too specific, you'll have job ladder proliferation. Instead of having one for the major functions at a company, every subgroup will have its own ladder and then will get in a food fight with other subgroups about why theirs isn't fair. However, if they are too abstract they feel irrelevant to people's jobs and read like a list of bloviating BS. It helps to have operating executives who have done the job at every level get involved in writing the job ladder descriptions. Human Resources can then serve as editor of these descriptions.

4. Number of ratings

Many studies have been done to figure out what the optimal number of ratings are (i.e., whether each category should be rated on a scale of one to three or one to five, etc. Statisticians tell me that five to seven ratings will maximize the signal you get from people without introducing too much complexity. However, HR professionals I've talked to have suggested that is too many ratings.

Any more than four ratings gives a false sense of precision. Too many ratings make managers feel they should be able to achieve a level of granularity in their assessment of people's performance that isn't actually possible. Also, when managers have too many ratings at their disposal they tend to try to show an uptick every review to make the person "feel" like they are improving. This is not performance management, it's BS, a false sense of progress. Since performance invariably has its ups and downs, some people will have a down quarter, and if that isn't reflected in the ratings then managers are using them to measure time in a role and not performance.

If you offer only three ratings, the vast majority of people will learn nothing from their rating because the vast majority (usually about 80 percent) will be in the middle. Four ratings requires managers to divide the vast middle between those who are above average and those who are below. Many managers resist this because it results in hard conversations. But if you're in that vast middle, you really deserve to know what your manager thinks and what your team thinks.

I have settled on four ratings as generally the best ratio of simplicity to signal. But there may be good reason for you to do something different. Whatever you choose, you want a system that leads managers to make it clear to people where they stand and what the implications are for pay and future employment. Since the impromptu Radical Candor conversations focus on the intrinsic desire to improve, the extrinsic consequences of performance deserve a focused conversation.

Four ratings gives clear feedback to employees about where their performance stands, without pushing to false precision of more ratings. Separate ratings for each of the four categories you've chosen (see below) can help the performance review serve as a diagnostic for improvement (i.e., "your results are amazing, but your teamwork will hold you back"), not just a whip or a carrot in a way that a single overall rating does not. In other words, it can give you some of the benefits of more ratings without the pitfall of false precision.

A downside of four ratings is that it doesn't give you a rating for the people whose performance is truly exceptional—say, in the top 5 or even 1 percent. However, for these people you usually need to do something bespoke to keep them engaged. A process won't be sufficient.

Here's the rating grid that reflects my recommendations. Again, don't just adopt it. You'll have to figure out what works best given your situation, and with input from diverse stakeholders. And don't use such generic words as the ones I'm using.

I do not recommend using an average of the ratings for each category to produce an overall rating. The only people who could get a Great rating should have to get a Great rating in *all* categories. People who get a Not OK rating in one category get an overall Not OK rating. This will help you get to a reasonable distribution of the overall rating.

	Not OK	OK (for now)	Good	Great
Teamwork	●	○	○	○
Innovation	○	○	●	○
Efficiency	○	○	●	○
Results	○	○	○	●
Overall**		⬭ Not OK		

**If you rate Not OK in any area, your overall rating is Not OK. To get a Great, you need a Great in teamwork, results, and one of the other two. Otherwise, it's an average, rounded up.

5. Language of ratings

For the purposes of averaging, you will translate words to numbers. But when you deliver the rating, words are better than numbers. You could simply use numbers: 1, 2, 3, 4. You could use symbols, ✓−, ✓, ✓+, ✓++. However, my general feeling is that words humanize what is a potentially alienating process. Make sure the words you choose demonstrate a desire to assess each person's work in order to help them grow professionally, not to label them or judge them as human beings.

Each term should be defined clearly to everyone in the company in some very central way (e.g., a page on the company intranet), but it can also be reinforced in the review meeting. Some companies would want to be clear, for example, that a Not OK rating means "you and your manager must work together and come up with a plan to help you address the issues outlined here, because if you don't address these issues you will likely be put on a performance plan which could later lead to termination of employment."

At other companies, a Not OK rating might be less dire. The definitions should not be pages and pages long, nor should they feel like legal definitions, but two to three sentences for each ratings bucket. Each sentence should include input from the performance management team, which should always keep in mind that the goal is to be simple and clear. The result should be easy to understand and quick to read.

6. Consequences of ratings

Ratings guide variable compensation, promotions, and terminations. The ratings should make the reasoning behind these decisions more transparent to employees, lead managers to calibrate carefully, and generally make the whole process feel simple, transparent, and fair. *Something* is going to drive these decisions. Human nature suggests that when we don't make them with an intentional process, we tend to reward people because we "like" them or based on some recent experience or bias. Doing ratings and explaining their impact on these decisions will force managers to both think through and communicate the decisions more clearly and explicitly. And when management communicates clearly to the entire organization that it has put time and effort into getting the process right, it reinforces a culture of Radical Candor.

It's also important to manage the natural reaction to ratings: dwelling on the negative instead of the positive. So it's important to emphasize that the employee isn't alone, the manager will help them improve. It's also important to look for opportunities to adjust a person's role to fit their strengths (or offer them a role for which they are better suited). Of course there's a risk the person will be terminated if they can't achieve at least a basic level of proficiency in a given area.

If a person is great in every category except teamwork where they are "OK for Now" it's important to assess whether the person can be coached to work better with others. And at least for the short term, the person should be given more individual contributor work, rather than being put in management situations where they may undermine or demoralize a whole team.

Don't forget to focus on people's strengths when thinking through the consequences of a performance review. Rather than trying to push someone to improve in an area where they are OK for Now, focus on giving them more work they are Great at. Give people work that plays to their strengths, rather than killing their spirit by pushing them to do more things they are not great at doing. It's not unusual for managers to focus all their efforts on plugging weaknesses rather than helping people do more work they are great at and love. This can be highly counterproductive.

Part of what guides Radical Candor is a hope that people will excel in meaningful work. So what does this mean for people who consistently do OK for Now work in all categories but never show much improvement? Ideally, these people should be helped to find a role where they can excel. And nobody whose work is rated OK for Now should be promoted. A condition for promotion should be a majority of Great ratings consistently over time.

When a manager gives a Not OK rating, it shouldn't just hang in the air until the next performance review. The manager should work with a plan to coach the person to improve. Human Resources should assign somebody to help the manager start documenting performance issues, ensuring that the person understands what the consequences will be if their performance doesn't improve. Managers sometimes avoid giving this rating, to avoid the hassle of the next steps. HR's role here is to counsel and assist.

Rewards. Of course, promotions and compensation are at the top of most people's list of hopes after a positive review. But money isn't everything, especially when people really love their work. It's important not just to hand a person a big check, but to show them that you care personally. Take the positive moment to find out how they feel about their work, and about you as their manager. Find out what you could do to give them more of what makes them effective, and to eliminate frustrations. I watched the founder of a company that my company had bought walk away from a giant retention package because he was so frustrated that he couldn't get things done. He left with tears in his eyes, saying, "I don't feel *heard* here." This struck me because I had left a company that had given me a "forever grant"—stock options that were supposed to entice me to stay at the company "forever." It didn't work. I quit and took a job that paid me less than half as much. Why? My boss's boss refused steadfastly to listen to a single *%#! word I said. Of course, plenty of people will not be in the fortunate position of being able to walk away from the money. But people rarely do their best work with handcuffs on. And if they can afford to, they'll often walk away from a frustrating or demeaning situation, no matter how lucrative. So taking the time to *listen* to people is just as important as compensating them well.

Use your top rating to make sure you are doing everything in your power to retain the people doing the best work. Money matters, but other intangibles matter more. Remind managers to pay attention to them.

7. Distribution of ratings

There are obviously practical considerations of the distribution of ratings, not least how you divide up the compensation pie. If you are going to give big, big bonuses to people who get Great ratings, then you probably cannot afford to have 50 percent of the company in that category. In general, I would avoid having too rigid a distribution, because you may be blessed in a given year to have an exceptionally able team, or cursed with a bunch of people doing lousy work, and you don't want an expected distribution to blind you to reality. In general, the calibration process (more on that below) is what's most important.

My experience is that at any given time there are at least 5 percent of people who probably need the kind of strong wake-up call that the lowest rating delivers. But you may feel that's excessively harsh for your environment, or not harsh enough. A Great rating means you want to give people outsized rewards because you want to compensate them fairly (they accomplished more than others!) and retain them. In general, I've found that group comprises roughly (very roughly) 15 percent of a team. As stated earlier, there are usually 1 to 5 percent of a population whose work is truly exceptional, whom you want to retain at all costs. Identifying these people is an important exercise, but there is no need to create a special rating for them. That leaves about 40 percent of your population getting an OK for Now and 40 percent getting a Good rating.

I don't know enough about your organization to say whether the distributions I've described above is right for you. You'll need to decide what the consequences of each rating are and therefore what the distribution ought to be.

However, I do recommend making the distribution you expect to see transparent to the organization. If you don't, calibrations (see page 272) will become opaque and excessively frustrating.

8. Forced curve or no

There's also a lot of debate about whether to force the curve or no. That is, to tell managers they must have a rigidly defined percentage of Not OKs, a fixed percentage of Greats, and so on. This can be useful to push managers to avoid two common ways to game the system: to give every employee a trophy, or to put everyone in the middle to avoid hard conversations. However, it can result in ratings that are unfair.

One of the benefits of having the categories (teamwork, innovation, efficiency, and results) and calculating the overall rating as I outlined above, is that it takes some of the pressure off the distribution for managers. If they feel it's appropriate, they can tell every single person on their team they are great at something, and yet still be in line with the distribution guidance. The question is, does it make sense to *force* managers to hit that curve?

Volumes have been written about the evils of the forced curve. The unintended consequences and political gaming of a forced curve are terrible. I never experienced a forced curve, but I have heard crazy stories from organizations that do. There was one VP I knew who found it too difficult to identify actual low performers, so he assigned the lowest ratings Russian-roulette style. He was transparent with his team about it, and thought he was being very clever—he never had to have hard conversations with employees on his team about why they were getting low ratings or with his boss about why he didn't hit the curve. He was a lazy, unfair leader. These kinds of stories convinced me a forced curve is a bad idea.

Here is my recommendation. Don't force a curve but do put pressure on it:

- State explicitly what the expected curve is.

- Count "nonregretted attrition" (people who were fired or managed out) in the stats for the lowest rating. Track nonregretted attrition over time. Otherwise people keep their low performers around to hit a curve rather than firing them.

- Each manager's curve should be visible to peer managers; each director's ratings curve should be visible to peer directors; each VP's ratings curve should be visible to peer VPs, and so on.

- Require managers who fall outside the expected curve to provide a written explanation for why; ask a lot of questions and allow peers to ask a lot of questions. When one team's curve is notably skewed when compared to other teams, ask the question, "Did this team really contribute more/less than the other teams this rating cycle?" If the answer is no, push the manager to reassess ratings. Similarly, if one team delivered something exceptional, make sure that team's manager is reflecting this in ratings. Most managers will stick to the middle, skewing to the positive; they give out too many Goods and OKs and too few Greats and Not OKs. That's why calibration sessions are so important.

9. Calibration of ratings

A calibration is a meeting in which a group of managers get together and make sure they are all rating people in the same way—that one is not a "hard" grader while another is an "easy" grader. If you are a manager of managers, it's important to make sure all the people who work for you get together and calibrate. If you are a manager and your boss is not doing this, check in with your peers.

Calibration meetings are key for two reasons. The first is transparency fairness. They keep managers honest if they know they have to defend their ratings in front of peer managers and even higher management levels. The second is guidance for new managers. These meetings are a great way to learn about performance expectations and even cultural norms. The big downside of these meeting is they can drag on for hours. Set a hard stop and keep to it.

Calibrations are invariably painful. Say Geoff manages six people. He thinks they are all fantastic, especially Tony, whose work he thinks is "Great." Geoff's peer, Wilma, who also manages six people, does not think

Tony is so great. In fact, Wilma would probably rate Tony's work as "OK." If Wilma speaks up, Geoff might be angry or embarrassed. If she doesn't speak up, she'll resent Geoff. Their boss, Ann, *must* initiate what will be a hard conversation. If she doesn't address this, several bad things will happen. First, she won't hit the right distribution. Second, Geoff will get a reputation as an easy grader. People will still love working for Wilma, but will feel it's unfair that Geoff's team gets paid more and promoted faster because Geoff is an easy grader. This will create weird incentives. Ann could fix the problem by pulling Geoff aside, but this misses an opportunity to improve creating a shared understanding on the team of what "great" means, and it also misses the chance to get Geoff and Wilma to have Radically Candid conversations. If Ann pushes everyone on her team to challenge each other, they are far more likely to get on the same page more quickly and more deeply—and also build stronger relationships—than if Ann were to try to tweak the ratings herself. Most important, the result is more likely to be fair to both Geoff and Wilma's employees if Ann forces the conversation between Geoff and Wilma.

If Ann has several "layers" under her, the calibration meeting becomes even more important, because as companies grow, it becomes more common that a disproportionate number of the senior people get the highest ratings, and the majority of the low ratings go to the most junior employees.

When I was at Google, I asked our HR person to slice the ratings by level. Although Google worked hard to be a "flat" organization, there were eight different levels on the team I managed—level 2 to level 9. Level 2 was a customer service rep, level 9 was a Director II. Overall, our ratings distribution looked pretty good. But when we looked at the distribution of ratings for level 2 employees versus the level 7–9 employees, we found the bulk of the lowest ratings were given to the level 2s; the only top ratings went to level 8s. If I looked at how I rated the six people who worked directly for me, it was the most out of whack. This felt like self-dealing, and I knew it wasn't fair.

Before we went back through and recalibrated by level, we had a theoretical conversation. Did we really feel that there should be such a difference by level? There were some arguments in favor of a different distribution for entry-level employees. The first couple of years could be a kind of weeding-out process. Some investment banks and consulting firms generally take people right out of college into a two-year program. They invite only about 10 percent to stay, and everyone else must leave after two years. That effectively means that about 90 percent of the people leave. They don't call it missing expectations or poor performance—they just call it a two-year program and set expectations that being asked to stay longer rarely happens. The effect was like giving 90 percent of level 2 employees a bad rating. Should we do something like that? We decided we didn't want to, that we wanted our team to be a place where people got a job after college and stayed. The skills they learned in the first two years would make them more valuable. Therefore, we agreed the distribution should be the same at every level. You will have a conversation on the same topic but might come to very different conclusions.

My instinct is that it is fairer to impose the same distribution on all levels of employees. But this is an instinct not a recommendation. In some situations, there may be a good reason to vary the distribution by level. However, I do have one strong recommendation: make a conscious decision.

10. Frequency

Some companies do performance reviews every quarter, some once or twice a year, and a lot never do them. At the start-up I cofounded, I never did performance reviews and couldn't understand why they were necessary. That was a disaster, but it took me a while to see it. At Google, we did them four times a year and then twice a year. That worked pretty well, until the system got more complicated and too time-consuming.

Never doing performance reviews is a bad idea. However, doing them every quarter heavily taxes managers, and doesn't give employees much time to show improvement from the last rating cycle. So, my recommendation: do it twice a year. One can be lightweight, oral, and just between the manager and employee; the other should be written and include a light 360-degree component.

Remember, this twice-a-year recommendation is just for a rating—it's performance management, not development. Impromptu development conversations should be happening weekly, but they should be private and take two minutes and not involve a rating or a process. The move to having more frequent ratings is often a result of the confusion between performance management and development. Development is a daily/weekly thing. But if ratings happen too frequently, they get conflated with development, and conversations that ought to hook into the intrinsic desire to improve instead trigger the resistance that happens when we are judged and the judgments carry extrinsic rewards and punishments with them.

The system should remind everyone that they should be giving and soliciting two-minute feedback conversations on a daily/weekly basis. It should also remind people that if there are any surprises at all in the topics of the ratings, there hasn't been enough development happening.

11. "360-degree" performance process vs. relying on a manager's unilateral assessment

I would strongly recommend a 360-degree performance review process in which people "up," "down," and "sideways" in the organization provide input. Requiring 360 reviews is one of the most effective things any organization can do to make sure that a manager's subjective point of view does not create favoritism or allow unfair/suboptimal allocation of resources. When managers have too much unilateral decision-making it's bad for results, and it is a disaster for a boss's ability to have a Radically Candid relationship with their employees. There are few things worse for a relationship than unilateral power. Also, when your boss's boss requests you give feedback on your boss, it sends a clear "speak truth to power" message, which is also important to a culture of Radical Candor. When these reviews are transparent, 360s can also reinforce a culture of direct, caring feedback.

However, the devil is in the details here. 360s are generally more time-consuming than they need to be. During the review season at Google, I would spend about thirty to sixty minutes for every peer review I had to write, and I usually got asked to write about twenty of them. Everyone around me was in the same boat. There were benefits to having to write such extensive feedback—it did really make me think. However, I think 80 percent of the value of the reviews could have been met by simply letting people know how I thought they were doing along the four criteria. I think that 360 peer reviews in particular can be much more lightweight for the reviewers than they are at most companies. I'd recommend simply asking employees to rate their peers on each of the four criteria; no need to write anything for OK for Now or Good ratings; ask them to write no more than seventy-five words for Not OK and Great ratings. The expected distribution should be shown, and the employee's actual distribution calculated for them, so that employees can self-regulate when they see they are an "easy" or a "hard" rater.

Pushing everyone to rate on a curve helps eliminate the problem that ratings tend to say more about the rater than the ratee. It also pushes people to identify and communicate what they really think about the performance of others.

12. Transparent or confidential

FORM MANAGER USES TO FILL OUT
JOHN DOE'S PERFORMANCE REVIEW
(Quarters Y2, 20xx)

NO SURPRISES! Hopefully you're not saying anything for the first time now. You should be having regular impromptu development conversations with your peers, your employees, and you manager. If you want feedback, <u>click here</u>. If you feel you are trying and not getting any, <u>click here</u>. And if you have not said before what you're writing now, click <u>here</u> for advice on an in-person conversation before you hit submit.

	Rating				Comments
					Instructions: no need to write feedback on "OK for now" or "Good" ratings. Please write no more than 75 words explaining "Not OK" and "Great" ratings.
	Not OK	OK (for now)	Good	Great	
Teamwork	○	○	○	○	
Innovation	○	○	○	○	
Efficiency	○	○	○	○	
Results	○	○	○	○	
Overall**	[auto calculated]				**If you rate Not OK in any area, your overall rating is Not OK. To get a Great, you need a Great in teamwork, results, and one of the other two. Otherwise it's an average, rounded up.
Expected distribution	1%	30%	50%	19%	

Your distribution
(calculatd after you've finished 60% of peer reviews)

(1%) We expect to see 5% of employees get a "Not OK" rating. You only have 1%. Please review your ratings. If you cannot hit the expected distribution please explain here.
(30%) We expect to see 40% of employees get a "Not OK" rating. You only have 30%. Please review your ratings. If you cannot hit the expected distribution please explain here.
(50%) We expect to see 40% of employees get a "Not OK" rating. You only have 50%. Please review your ratings. If you cannot hit the expected distribution please explain here.
(19%) We expect to see 15% of employees get a "Not OK" rating. You only have 19%. Please review your ratings. If you cannot hit the expected distribution please explain here.

If you decide that you are going to do 360 feedback, you need to decide whether it will be transparent (what people write about their colleagues is visible to those colleagues) or confidential (what people write about their colleagues is visible only to the colleagues' managers). I strongly recommend transparent. Confidential feedback does not encourage people to Challenge Directly, and it often hurts on the Care Personally dimension of Radical Candor as well. People are often more obnoxiously aggressive when they are anonymous.

Confidential feedback does have a couple of benefits. One, it theoretically allows employees to write in shorthand—if you know that somebody is going to see what you'll write about them, you're likely to spend more time choosing your words carefully. Two, sometimes confidentiality means that people give feedback to a manager that they wouldn't otherwise give.

But, there are several huge downsides to confidential feedback. One, it doesn't force peers to have direct conversations with each other. Therefore, it is a missed opportunity to drive a culture of direct, open feedback. In the worst cases it encourages backstabbing behavior. Two, managers have to read and synthesize all the peer feedback for all employees, since it isn't transparent to them. Unfortunately, this synthesis is sometimes a value-subtracting process. Making 360 feedback transparent drives a culture of direct feedback, is more efficient for managers, and gives the employees higher-quality feedback from peers.

I strongly recommend that a 360 process involve every employee at the company. If you just do it for senior leaders, then you're giving them yet another benefit that others "lower down" in the hierarchy don't get. So do it for everyone. (Eliminate corner offices and executive parking spots while you're at it.)

Also, the sooner you start teaching people how to write good feedback, the better and more useful it will be. I'd recommend a "show, don't tell" lesson in good writing. The more abstract feedback is, the more puzzling. The more specific it is—the more you can tell a story about an incident that illustrates what you mean—the better. Teaching people how to write good performance feedback will help. But of course the best way for people to learn is to start doing it—writing it and receiving it.

And when people know that the person they are writing about will know it's them writing, they'll naturally take more care to say things in a helpful way. Of course, they'll also be tempted to say nothing at all. That's why pushing people toward a curve is so important.

I would opt for transparent peer feedback. I am not opposed to putting in a field in which people can give confidential feedback, though.

13. Lightweight or heavyweight

A heavyweight review process requires everyone who writes reviews for employees and 360 feedback "up," "down," and "sideways" to spend tremendous amounts of time doing so.

Google's process started out pretty lightweight but became more cumbersome as the company grew. By the time I left in 2010, I used to spend four hours writing the review for each of my direct reports. Even though I only had six direct reports, that was still twenty-four hours twice a year; plus, I had all my peer feedback to write—that was another twenty hours of work. It wasn't as though the demands of the business slowed down just because it was review season. That meant there were four weeks each year when everyone practically had a second job, and was in a foul mood. People stayed up too late doing reviews, and got colds. The colds spread. We all started to dread review time, to call it "perfcrastination" because other important things both at work and at home didn't get done. While I do think that forcing myself to spend this time did make me think more deeply about how I was managing the team, I am not sure that the toll this process took on the organization was in the end worth it.

Word to the wise: even if you put in place a good process, processes develop a life of their own if you don't actively manage them. A big problem at Google was that the performance review write-ups fed into the promotion process. The promotion process itself was becoming unwieldy. And the pay for seniority was dramatic. An engineering leader I knew had a recent college grad working for him who was living in his truck in the parking lot because he couldn't afford the rents in Mountain View and his college loan. Meanwhile VPs were awarded packages worth $100 million. When the stakes are that high, it's ridiculous to tell people "don't worry about a promotion." And when something you wrote two years ago in another person's peer feedback would get read in promotion committee and they wouldn't get promoted, it means you scrutinized every word you wrote with unproductive levels of attention.

Even if you're not paying your VPs insane salaries, this kind of unpredictable process creep can and does happen everywhere. Therefore, you'll need to actively monitor how long the process takes, and trim to make sure it doesn't grow beyond what you intend.

As long as you remain in control of your process, I'd recommend a lightweight review process that happens twice a year. Remember, the process will take less time and be more Radically Candid if all 360 feedback is transparent. Not having to synthesize and anonymize the 360 feedback will cut down on the amount of time managers have to spend writing feedback for each direct report. A lightweight review tool would look much like the 360 tool I described above. It would ask managers to rate their employees for each category, and ask them to input text when the employee is in the bottom or top two ratings. The overall rating would be automatically calculated, and the manager's rating distribution would be compared to the expected distribution. If the manager's distribution falls outside of what's expected, the manager must explain. The manager should be able to fill in the review form for each employee in under thirty minutes.

If the organization stresses the importance of regular, impromptu feedback, much of the need for a heavyweight review process disappears.

The manager would get a summary of the peer feedback, which they could take a look at before creating the final assessment. The report would show how many people gave which rating, and if the manager clicks on the rating, they'd see something like this:

WHAT JOHN DOE'S MANAGER SEES BEFORE FILLING OUT THE PERFORMANCE REVIEWS (Quarters y2, 20xx)

	Rating				**Comments**
	Not OK	OK (for now)	Good	Great	Instructions: no need to write feedback on "OK for now" or "Good" ratings. Please write no more than 75 words explaining "Not OK" and "Great" ratings.
Teamwork	○	②	②	⑥	
Innovation	○	○	②	⑧	
Efficiency	①	⑧	①	○	Employee: "It takes John too long to get to the point. If he wants something from me I wish he'd just ask. We've discussed this but it's not getting any better."
Results	○	②	⑧	○	
Overall*		Good			*If you rate Not OK in any area, your overall rating is Not OK. To get a Great, you need a Great in teamwork, results, and one of the other two. Otherwise, it's an average, rounded up.

Then the manager could fill out their assessment of John Doe's performance. If the manager's assessment varies dramatically from the team, the manager would be prompted to explain.

As a last step in the process, all managers who lead more than thirty people would get a message if their team's peer assessments or their own assessment of their team is out of the expected bounds.

WHAT JOHN DOE'S MANAGER SEES AFTER FILLING OUT THE PERFORMANCE REVIEW BEFORE HITTING SUBMIT

MANAGER ASSESSMENT

NO SURPRISES! Hopefully you're not saying anything for the first time now. You should be having weekly conversations with each employee <u>soliciting</u> and <u>giving</u> feedback. If you have not said before what you're writing now, click <u>here</u> for advice.

Rating

Comments

Instructions: no need to write feedback on "OK for now" or "Good" ratings. Please write no more than 75 words explaining "Not OK" and "Great" ratings.

	Not OK	OK (for now)	Good	Great	Comments
Teamwork	○	○	● !!!	○	
Innovation	○	○	○	●	
Efficiency	○	●	○	○	
Results	○	○	●	○	
Overall*		Good			

*If you rate Not OK in any area, your overall rating in Not OK. To get a Great, you need a Great in teamwork, results, and one of the other two. Otherwise, it's an average, rounded up.

You rated John's Teamwork lower than his peers did. Please make sure you explain why in your comments to John. Also Copy-paste & submit *here*.

	Not OK	OK (for now)	Good	Great	
Expected distribution	5%	40%	40%	15%	**!!! Your team is rating higher than expected.** Please ask them to get into range or explain here why your team is above the expected distribution.
Your team's distribution	2%	35%	43%	20%	Did your team really accomplish more than other teams??

CONCLUSION

I hope this bonus chapter helps you think about how the kinds of development conversations I described in *Radical Candor* can work together with a performance management system to create a culture of Radical Candor. I would love to get feedback on this, particularly from those with experience implementing performance management systems. Please send your thoughts to PerformanceReviews@RadicalCandor.com.

ACKNOWLEDGMENTS

WRITING THIS BOOK IS THE hardest thing I've ever done, and I could never have finished if it weren't for the generosity and help of many people. No book is the work of just one person, and I'm honestly not sure why we've come to insist on the myth of "the author."

The first difficulty was getting inside my own head. That required long stretches of free time, time not only to sit at my computer and write, but also to take long rambling walks to think, and to have long conversations to debate ideas. That didn't leave time for a regular job. Many thanks to my team at Dropbox, in particular Olga Navarskaya, Oliver Jay, and Johann Butting, for being so incredibly gracious about my abrupt decision to leave so that I could write this book. Thanks to Dick Costolo, Drew Houston, Adam Bain, Joanna Strober, Ryan Smith, Shannon Miller, Jack Dorsey, and

Kevin Gibbon, all of whom offer me advisory roles that gave me flexibility and time to write and also kept body and soul together.

Next came the even harder part: getting back out of my own head, once I'd gotten in. For that I depended on my editor, the kindness of friends, and the generosity of strangers.

Writing a book can feel a lot like being lost at sea. Tim Bartlett, my editor, and the boss of this book, was the life raft who rescued me from that writer's insanity. He not only saw through the madness to the good parts of the book clearly enough to buy it, he cleaned it up admirably. Writing is truly a collaboration between author and editor, and to work with Tim was to feel myself in the care of a master. He knew what to cut, what to expand, when to say, "Hello! What happened to care personally??"and when to wrest the manuscript out of my hands. Tim's clarity of thought illuminates literally every page of this book. Tim is the best of editors, and his name should certainly be on the cover along with mine.

I also want to thank Tim's wife and children, as working on this book took him away from family time and vacation time. And, as long as we are talking about interrupted vacation time, I want to thank my husband, my children, my parents, my siblings, my husband's parents, my husband's siblings, and my children for your understanding and support during those times when I abandoned you to write and then edit this book.

There is a whole team of great people at St Martin's Press who helped bring this book to life to whom I'm enormously grateful. Laura Clark's enthusiasm for the book from the moment I stepped into St. Martin's office was an enormous boost not just for the book but for me personally. I've learned a lot from her about how to market ideas. Gabi Gantz, Alice Pfeifer, Karlyn Hixson, Eric C. Meyer, Kathy Parise, and James Iacobelli were all enormously helpful, and patient with me every step of the way. There were also dozens of others whom I didn't get a chance to meet, but all of whom worked hard to get this book out and sold. Most especially Jeremy Pink, whom I've never seen, but I feel a certain intimacy with him as he improved literally every sentence in this book. The work that people in publishing do to make sure ideas see the light of day is so important to our world, and, I'm afraid, not made easier by the industry in which I've made my career. I look forward to many years of collaboration to finding out a better way forward, a better collaboration between tech and publishing.

This book would never have gotten to Tim or the team at St Martin's

Press if it hadn't been for the help of many people who helped throughout the process. My friends Adam Richman and Kim Keating were generous in their advice on how to get published. My agent Howard Yoon read a draft of this book the same day I sent it to him, and called me with an enthusiasm that reassured me I hadn't just wasted the previous three years, just when I needed to hear that most. He actually *wrote* the proposal for me when I was struggling with it. He also spent months helping me with a rewrite that was a much-needed CPR for a book that was getting crushed under its own weight. Howard is the rarest of agents, one who's as gifted with words as he is at crafting a thoughtful sales process.

And before either Howard or Tim saw the book, family and friends read draft after draft, and pounded on word after word, or dragged me away from the book on long walks, where I could regain a little perspective.

My parents, Allen and Mary Malone, probably read fifteen different drafts of the book and never seemed bored. If that is not a labor of love, I don't know what is.

My husband Andy stubbornly argued against my logic for calling this book *Cruel Empathy*, which I was determined to do for almost two years. I don't know why I argued. Andy is the soul of understanding, and when he digs his heels in, he is always right.

Several people spent enormous time editing various drafts of this book, and I am deeply indebted to each of them. Denni Cawley edited the most painful early versions of this book and helped me with research. Sierra Kephart-Clary created order out of later madness. James Buckhouse restored a sense of beauty and fun to the editing process just when I needed it most. Katya Rice saved me from getting too abstract or too specific, and was able to make a thousand small changes at the same time she was helping me focus neither too blurrily on the the forest or too minutely on any particular leaf.

Alice Traux was, during two intense round of edits, a touchstone of sanity. She is relentless in her unwillingness to accept even a hint of cliché, and always willing to hold up a mirror when what I was writing made no sense. At the same time, her concern for my morale throughout the process was a constant source of comfort. I'm deeply indebted.

Jim and Mary Ottaway edited an early version of this book, encouraged me to keep writing, and then Jim heroically did another incredibly fast and thorough edit in the final hour.

Many thanks to Catharine Burhenne-Sanderson, Steve Diamond, Maria

Gotsch, Ellen Konar, and Albert Ni, Jane Penner, and Gretchen Ruben all of whom not only read the book but also shared numerous long walks/meals /wine, pushing me to rethink whole sections of this book, and to feel a little less lonely as I wrote it. They all helped me think more clearly as I struggled to make one idea or another clear, and their compassion for me reminded me to have empathy for the reader.

Olga Navarskaya persuaded me that the Radical Candor framework I initially came up with was logically inconsistent and needed to be improved upon. It took three months of thinking to fix it and I never would have persevered if I hadn't been able to imagine her skeptical face before me.

I owe the whole second half of this book, Things You Can Do, to Daniel Rubin, who pounded it into my reluctant head over the course of several months that a management philosophy by itself wasn't going to change a damn thing or be all that helpful to anyone.

I am enormously grateful to Josh Cohen, Michael Chu, Michael Dearing, Drew Houston, Jared Smith, Russ Laraway, Elisse Lockhart, Charles Morris, Venkat Rao, Caroline Reitz, Sheryl Sandberg, Michael Schrage, Myra Strober, Richard Tedlow, Valerie Yakich, Chris Yeh, all of whom read and edited this book in great detail, each of them making numerous suggestions and comments that were essential.

Many people asked to read this book as I wrote it, and all of them helped, some of them by offering some "radical candor" that helped me see flaws in the book, others by just expressing interest and encouraging me to keep going: Dinara Abilova, Alina Adams, Matt Adams, Richard Alfonsi, Brett Berson, Gina Bianchini, Jeff Bidzos, Nick Bloom, Simon Bolger, Adam Brandenburger, Jenna Buffaloe, Matthew Carpenter, Andrew Catton, Denni Cawley, Lawrence Coburn, Betsy Cohen, Kate Connally, Jack Dorsey, Sarah Friar, Maria Giacona, Kevin Gibbon, Adam Grant, Josh Grau, Karen Grove, James Groves, Matt Hogan, Adam Hundt, Kate Jhaveri, Neeru Khosla, Elizabeth Kim, Janet Kim, Aliza Knox, Brett Kopf, Jayant Kulkarni, Christine Lee, Battle Malone, Tim Martin, Ben Matasar, Blaire Mattson, Michael Maughan, Jamie McCollough, Shannon Miller, Dobromir Montauk, Maran Nelson, Yu-Shen Ng, Andrew Peterson, Ann Poletti, Kanjun Qiu, Adam Regelmann, Robyn Reiss, Katya Rice, Louisa Ritter, Margaret Rosser, Matt Rosser, Dan Rummel, Johnny Russ, Scott Sheffer, Lindsey Semple, Lauren Sherman, Dimitar Simeonov, Mason Simon, Ryan Smith, Mollie Solon, Donna Staton, Michael Stoppelman, Jason Strober, Joanna Strober, Shea

Tate-Di, Jason Tan, Joseph Ternasky, Sophia Tsai, Casey Tunguz, Tomasz Tunguz, Dash Victor, Jackie Xu. I'm deeply grateful to each and every one of these people.

It has often been said that great artists steal. I'm not sure I'm a great artist, but I definitely stole many of the ideas in this book, many of which are simply things I've seen the people I work with do.

Three people in particular influenced this book: Shona Brown, Russ Laraway, and Sheryl Sandberg.

Shona Brown, SVP of Business Operations at Google, always prefers to remain the unsung hero, so you read fewer stories about her in this book. It was a dose of especially generous Radical Candor from Shona that launched me on my current career. Much of Google's approach to management was conceived, architected, and operationalized by Shona. She described her approach to leadership powerfully in her book, *The Edge of Chaos*, and then she proved it worked when she rolled her ideas out at Google. She was instrumental in designing the way that Google hired, reviewed, compensated, developed, and promoted people; the way that Google set and achieved goals; the way that Google made decisions; and the ongoing redesign of Google's organization to stay nimble as it grew. Her design decisions had an enormous impact on Google's trajectory.

Watching how Russ Laraway leads his teams taught and teaches me daily new lessons about what it means to be a kick-ass boss. Not only did he teach me much of what I know about management, he reminds me daily what it means to be a good human being.

Sheryl Sandberg is the best boss I ever had, and a person who totally changed the trajectory of my life. Time and again, she has pushed me to do things I never imagined I could do, and helped me take a step in the direction of my dreams.

You'll read dozens of stories about things I learned from the people whom I've worked with throughout this book. I want to thank all of them for their commitment to being great bosses, for the example they set for me in my career. I hope I did justice to their ideas as I've described them in the course of this book. There are also a number of people from whom I learned a lot about what it means to be a great boss, but who preferred to stay in the background. Much of what I've written about I learned implicitly from Tom Pickett and Scott Sheffer, who were on my team at Google, and Alan Warren, my co-founder at Juice.

Last but certainly not least, I am eternally grateful to Dan Pink for helping me see I was onto something meaningful and then giving this book its title in the space of a short elevator ride.

Everyone who helped me write this book taught me that if you're open to Radical Candor, you can find a shared humanity and sense of purpose in those moments that would otherwise be unremarkable—in that elevator ride you had to take to retrieve your bag, while walking your dog, responding in 140 characters to a remarkable Tweet from a stranger, reconnecting over a new idea with an old friend.

INDEX

THE RADICAL CANDOR FRAMEWORK:

a compass, not a personality test!

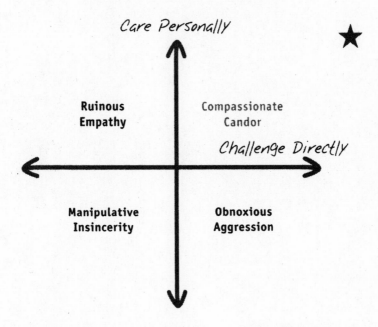

Use THE RADICAL CANDOR Framework like a compass to guide individual conversations to a better place. Please do NOT use it as a personality test to judge yourself or others. Don't write names in boxes. We all fall into each quadrant multiple times a day.

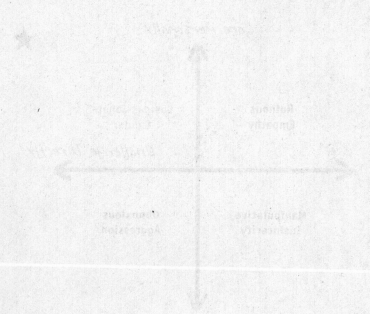